The Art of Year-Round Trail Adventuring

BOZEMAN TRAILS ILLUSTRATED

Be here n…

THREE BOOKS IN…

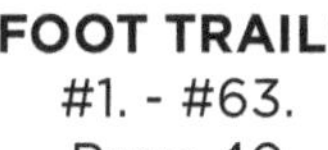

FOOT TRAILS
#1. - #63.
Page 40

BIKE TRAILS
#64. - #84.
Page 136

SKi TRAILS
#85. - #100.
Page 202

Bryan Schaeffer
Illustrator / Animator

Praise for Discover Montana Treasures

"With this multimedia Platform, Bryan created a new category of book."

-Julie Kleine
Montana Parent Magazine

Praise for The Last Best BIKE

Winner Bozeman's Choice Awards Best Local Book
& Best Local Author 2022

"May this book send you on some world class adventures!"

-Tim Hawke
Co-Author Southern Montana Single track & Architect of Copper City Trails

Praise for The Last Best SKI

"This book is for those looking to explore the winter landscape of southwestern Montana in ways as versatile as the terrain they offer. Calling all-around winter athletes. Go find your adventure."

-Andy Newell
Head Coach of Nordic Team Solutions & four-time Olympic skier

"Bryan Schaeffer uses illustration to get people outdoors. It seems like Bryan uses illustration and animation to engage his audience in a way that other mediums cannot."

- Holden Sier
Outside Bozeman Magazine

"This is my favorite type of book because it gets to the point." It's really the best of both worlds - beautifully illustrated book and you get the digital world if you want it. It's always great to have a reference guide to get you started."

-DJ Zepp
105.7 The Eagle

The Last Best Trails

"This book is filled with extremely valuable information that people normally spend tons of time researching. It is put together in a way that makes it easy and fun to read. The artwork is outstanding and the maps are super beneficial. QR codes make this even more than a book. This is THE perfect read for anyone with any interest in the outdoors."

-Cecelia Krichman
Professionally a property manager & Outdoor Enthusiast

"The perfect guidebook for tourists and locals alike. Even as someone who has lived in Southwest Montana for a few years, I will be utilizing Bryan's book as I look to discover new trails in my own backyard."

-Dani Aravich
U.S. Paralympian- Nordic Skiing & Biathlon

"Bryan has created yet another beautiful, thorough, educational and - I'd say - even inspirational guidebook for the greater Bozeman area. So much great information presented alongside his stellar hand-drawn illustrations. It'll make you want to lace up your running shoes or boots and head out the door to the closest trail or use it over time as a Bozeman bucket list of sorts."

-Justin Bigart
Musician, photographer, designer, outdoor enthusiast

"Bryan's 'Last Best' series are a blended work of art and information, providing more than enough inspiration to fill your weekends for years to come. Combining all the essential biking, skiing and hiking trails in one place is a feat of work; top that off with his illustrations that showcase the beauty of Montana, and you've got one outstanding resource."

-Christopher Kussmaul
Author Peaks & Couloirs of Southwest Montana

"This book is a guide to what I see as the true treasures of the treasure state: the joys of outdoor experience. Written by a local, helping make adventure accessible to all."

-Heidi Makoutz
National Interscolastic Mountain Biking Association - Bozeman, Head coach
Bridger Ski Foundation's Nordic Adult Programs, Head coach

"Peppered with beautifully drawn flora and fauna along with tips and history, this book is a treasure for Montana recreationalists. A one-stop shop for the best places to go hiking, biking and skiing, it's a valuable guide that is stunning enough to earn a place on the coffee table."

-Tami Asars
Outdoors-focused writer, Photographer, Author, Wilderness wanderer

ACKNOWLEDGEMENTS

This book wouldn't be possible without the input of the dozens of people and organizations I interviewed for the books.

I recorded the first few interviews to reference back to later on in case I had missed something. After listening to the recording of my interview with four-time Olympic Skier Andy Newell, I realized these discussions were interesting enough to become Podcast episodes.

Each section is high-level, with a link to the Podcast as an opportunity to dig in deeper and learn more about the subject, place or history, etc.

Thank you to all the Podcast interviewees (over 50 now)!

Special thanks to the land organizations that make these human-powered trail activities possible.

Thank you to the Custer Gallatin Forest Service, Mariah Leuschen, for organizing Podcast interviews and topics.

Thanks to the vibrant local ski organizations. Jenny White at the Bridger Ski Foundation, Jen Adams at Crosscut, Christine Baker at Big Sky, and Dan Lakatos at the Yellowstone Club.

Thanks to the avid mountain bike groups. David Tucker at SWMMBA, Heidi Makoutz leading the way with the fantastic NICA program, Molly Bowman for her commitment to Youth Cycling in Bozeman, and Tim Hawke for being persistent as #=$!! to realize his vision of building Copper City Trails.

I appreciate the insights and lessons learned by talking to other guidebook authors. John Zilly, Bryce Stevens, Craig Romano, Tami Asars, Ben Werner, and Chris Kussmaul, thank you for being an inspiration and sharing your enthusiasm about year-round trail adventuring.

Thank you to Dr. Shane Doyle for helping me to solidify my historical research and providing invaluable insights into the lives of first nations people here long before European westward expansion. There are many lessons we can learn from the old ways.

Thanks to my production team of designers, animators, and editors for consistently being game to continue creating new maps and animation composites, reading, and providing expertise where I fall short.

Thanks to my family.

My parents for instilling their insatiable wanderlust. Thanks for dragging me out of bed when I didn't want to go up into the mountains. Now I'm eternally hooked.

My wife Anne, daughters Kiersten, Meghan, and Torrey, and ever-ready-to-go golden doodle Loki. Thank you for visiting these and hundreds of other trailheads in all weather and conditions.

And finally, thank you for taking a chance and purchasing this book. This new format is non-traditional and different from what you would expect from a guidebook. Thanks for investing your interest in this project.

I hope it pays back dividends as a place for imagining your adventures and making lifelong memories with your friends and families.

Every Last Best Trails Book is packed with digital content

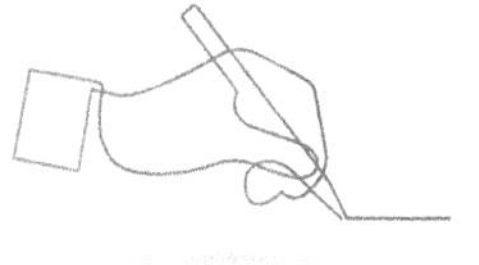

ILLUSTRATIONS

Hundreds of hand-drawn illustrations & hand-crafted maps in each book

ADDITIONAL RESOURCES

QR code smart links play Podcast interviews with local experts for each section

VIDEOS

QR code smart links play animated films & educational video content created by studio SINTR®

TAP & GO

Trailhead GPS coordinates for each trail
Regional trail maps show the lay of the land

THE LAST BEST TRAILS MONTANA

Bozeman TRAILS Illustrated - Montana: An illustrated/animated celebration of human-powered trail adventures in the Bozeman Montana area.

www.thelastbestTRAILS.com

For more information about Bryan or his publication, please contact the publisher at thelastbestbike.com

Illustrations were hand drawn on paper and edited digitally in Adobe Illustrator and Photoshop.

ISBN: 978-1-7347066-6-6
V1.0

Thank you to The Last Best TRAILS Contributors:
Alex van Gelder - Cartographer, Animator
Kelsey Dzintars - The Last Best SKI logo design
Kevin Hilton - Animator
Tom McGurk - Composer
Claudia & Meghan Schaeffer - Copy Editing & Proofing
Tim Hawke, Bob Allen, Stacie Mesuda & Anne Schaeffer - Content Feedback
Dani Aravich - Marketing
Ella Kunze - Marketing & Sales
ella@thelastbesttrails.com
Cecelia Krichman - Sales & Distribution
info@thelastbesttrails.com

Many thanks to Anne Schaeffer, Kiersten, Meghan, Torrey and Loki for sharing countless days on the trails from dipping toes in streams to scaling mountain summits in the research for this book. Thank you to my parents for getting me stoked about year-round trail adventuring literally pulling me out of bed at ungodly hours. Now I'm hooked.

NOTICE OF RISK

Disclaimer: Trail sports can be dangerous.
You can fall, and things can fall on you. You could suffer from hypothermia, frostbite, heat stroke, or get sunburned. You could get lost in the backcountry. You could get run into by another hiker, biker, skier or animal. Getting proper guidance on technique, gear and evaluating terrain and conditions are all important in order to have fun and be safe. This book is designed to help with that, but all of those variables are subject to change. Do your research and keep up your fitness and safety chops. That will make the experience more fun and rewarding.

The Last Best TRAILS is an introduction to foot trails, mountain biking and skiing in the greater Bozeman area. It is not a replacement for proper technique and safety instruction. The user should assume all risks.

Printed in the United States of America

Front cover - Kiersten and Meghan Schaeffer descend the Bridger Mountains in to the valley of flowers during the golden hour - illustration by Bryan Schaeffer

A huge thanks to our Podcast interviewees!

Foot Trails:
Gallatin Valley Sherrif Search And Rescue - Scott Secor
Co-Founder Trails.com - Bryce Stevens
Mountaineers Books - Tami Asars
Mountaineers Books - Craig Romano
Indigenous Plant Foraging - Jacob Zimmerer
Custer Gallatin National Forest Supervisor- Mary Erickson
Custer Gallatin National Forest District Ranger - Corey Lewellen

Mountain Biking:
National Interscholastic Cycling Association - Heidi Makoutz
Southwest Montana Mountain Biking Association - David Tucker
Crosscut Mountain Sports Center - Scott Schmidt
Copper City Trails Architect - Tim Hawke
Bozeman Youth Cycling - Molly Bowman
Bozeman Pedal Project - Mel Cronin
Gallatin Valley Land Trust - EJ Porth
Excel Physical Therapy - Jason Lunden
Big Sky Community Organization - Adam Johnson
The Big Sky Biggie - Natalie Osborne
Big Sky Resort - Christine Baker
Bob Allen Photography - Bob Allen
The Bike Kitchen - Hailey Renner
Bangtail Bikes - Rob Funderburk
Owenhouse Cycling - Jason Donald

Nordic Skiing - Cross Country:
Nordic Team Solutions - Andy Newell
North Face Endurance Athlete - Erika Flowers
Lone Mountain Ranch - - Laurie Spence
Crosscut Mountain Sports Center - Cliff Montagne
Bridger Ski Foundation - Heidi Makoutz
Crosscut Mountain Sports Center - Fay Johnson
Crosscut Mountain Sports Center - Seth Hubbard
Crosscut Mountain Sports Center - Nick Michaud

Backcountry - Touring:
The Bozeman and Big Sky Backcountry Ski Guide - Ben Werner
Peaks & Couloirs of Southwest Montana Guide - Chris Kussmaul
Ski Mountaineering Racing (Skimo) - Justin Bigart
Excel Physical Therapy - Jason Lunden
Ski Touring Yellowstone National Park - Jim & Claudia Schaeffer
Outside Bozeman Magazine - Simon Peterson
Gallatin National Forest Avalanche Center - Doug Chabot -
National Avalanche Center - Karl Birkeland

Alpine - Downhill:
Bob Allen Images - Bob Allen
Montana's Sweet 16 - Cory Birkenbuel
Yellowstone Club - Dan Lakatos
Big Sky Resort - Christine Baker
Bridger Bowl - Shannon Griffin
Protect Our Winters - Graham Zimmerman

The author backpacking with daughters

TABLE OF CONTENTS
THE LAST BEST TRAILS

THE LAST BEST TRAILS

Intro

Kiersten Schaeffer high centered on a log backpacking in the Beartooths

PREFACE

Trails are the passageways that connect us to outdoor adventures.

Hundreds of people move to Bozeman every year and thousands travel to the area for its world-famous skiing and outdoor recreation. The greater Bozeman/Big Sky area "The Bozone" encompasses an area from the headwaters of the Missouri to the West to the Absoroka Beartooth Mountain Ranges to the East and Yellowstone National Park to the South. The Bridger Mountain range just outside of town encloses the Bozone to the North. This is the area of focus of this trails book.

With so many trails and year-round adventures to be had in this greater Yellowstone region, the goal of this book is to be the virtual trailhead. The Last Best Trails is a starting point base camp for your trail adventures scheming. Whether it is a morning stroll around town trails with family members of all ages, or an epic mountain traverse, this book will give you the lay of the land and resources to dig in deeper.

The second purpose of this book is to advocate for public lands.

The access to year-round trails is part of what makes Bozeman such a desirable community. There is a connection with the health and wellness of the people here and the restorative connective powers to commune with nature that this provides.

When we spend time together outdoors together breathing the mountain air, experiencing wildlife, getting the blood flowing, we deepen the connections between each other and the natural world that we are a part of.

This book was developed with the input of dozens of local trail experts, athletes, and land management organizations. We encourage you to listen to the Podcasts and learn more about how these public lands are cared for. With careful planning and representation, we have a better chance of preserving these sacred places for future generations.

The Last Best TRAILS is about year-round real life human-powered trail sports in the greater Bozeman and Big Sky area. The book has literally been "drawn" from the past 6 years of exploring "The Last Best Place" on foot, bike, and ski.

Exploration and adventures shouldn't be limited to the ultra-elite athletes.

We invite all ages and experience levels to experience getting out year-round in SW Montana.

The Norwegian term "friluftsliv," means open-air living.

The practice of open-air living encourages outdoor adventures for all ages in all types of weather.

In this day and age of remote work, virtual reality, and artificial intelligence, meaningful experiences with real people in nature are more critical than ever.

This book's mission is to start the stoke about our true treasures in this region of the treasure state and give a starting point of how to get the most enjoyment out of each activity safely.

The author in the field sketching one of hundreds of scenes for the book and animated shorts

HOW TO USE THIS BOOK

Thank you for purchasing Best of the NW's The Last Best TRAILS Montana.

This is not your average coffee table book; it is a secret passageway to the world of human-powered trail recreation in SW Montana Yellowstone Country.

I've always thought the best way to learn about something is to ask the most knowledgeable person about a subject directly. This book is the result of over fifty interviews with local athletes, program directors and land management organizations.

You will find QR code links to the interviews on the Podcast where you can listen and learn more. These are some of the local organizations that build the outdoor communities within Bozeman and Big Sky.

Filled with hand-drawn illustrations of local trails, interviews with local experts and custom maps for each sport, this book is just as comfortable on the coffee table as it is in your day pack out on the trails.

Look for bonus content QR codes that can be scanned via camera in your mobile phone or device (no app required).

Open the camera on your mobile device and hold it over the square so the target lines up (don't snap a photo).

Once the link is recognized, a button will pop up to activate the link. Tap the button to load content on your phone. Video playback works best on WiFi or 5G.

See the scenes come to life in full-color animated scenes and videos.

The regional GPS map can be used as a reference point and to get directions to the trail head. Look for QR codes for bonus audio/video content.

Links to Online Content

Follow on Instagram **@bryanschaeffer** for content updates.

Scan QR Codes for exclusive digital content

STATE PLANTS & ANIMALS

Montana State Motto

Oro Y Plata (Gold and Silver)
The Treasure State

The state's previous capital, Bannock, is just a short distance from where I grew up. During pioneering times, it had been a booming gold town, but now the gold is long gone, and all that remains of this once bustling city is some well-preserved structures. Montana's history is filled with many boom and bust cycles like this. However, what persists is the flowing creeks, spring snow melts that give rise to flowers, and the never-ending parade of wildlife passing through.

Now the latest gold rush is the land itself. World-class recreation abounds for outdoor enthusiasts and sportsmen alike.

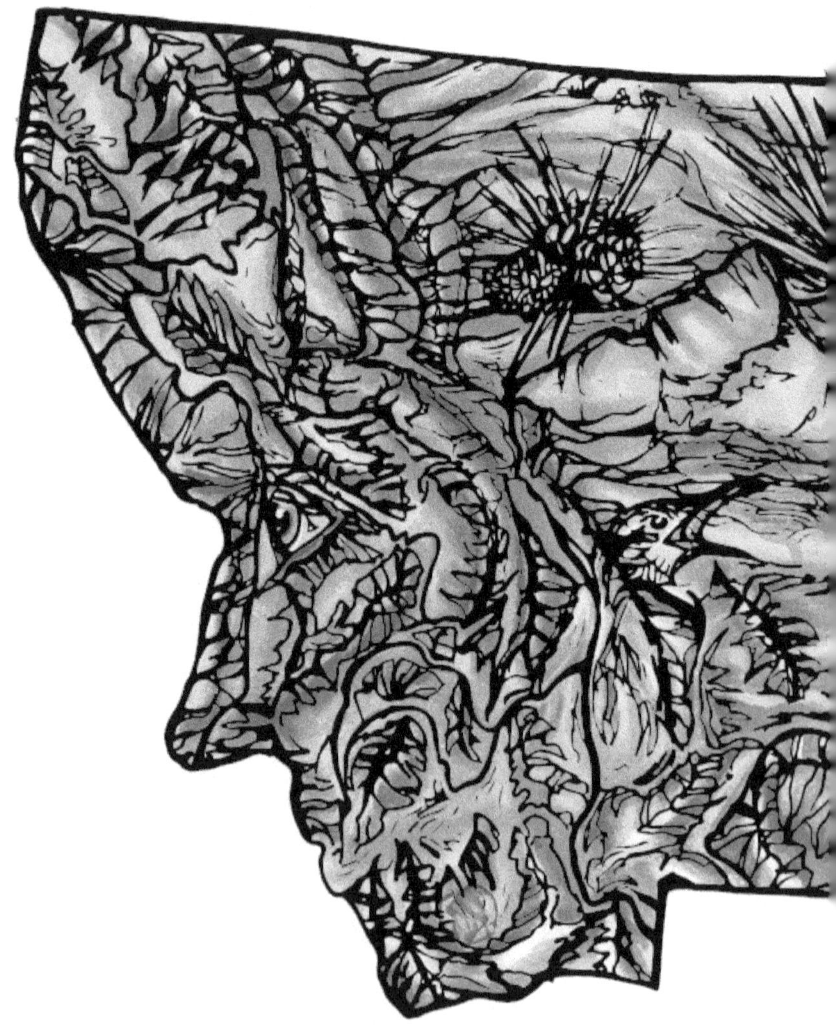

Montana "Treasure Map"

Studies show being active in the natural world is necessary for physical and mental health. We must actively participate in legislation that protects our public lands for future generations.

This book will give you some ideas of where a few of these treasures are so you can "discover" them for yourselves.

MONTANA TREASURE MAP
WATCH
DISCOVER MT TREASURES
THE LAST BEST
TRAILS

MT Map Animation

State Flower: Bitterroot
State Bird: Western Meadowlark
State Tree: Ponderosa Pine
State Grass: Bluebunch wheatgrass
State Fish: Cutthroat Trout

State Animal: Grizzly Bear
State Insect: Mourning Cloak Butterfly
State Gem: Sapphire
State Dinosaur: Mayasaurus
State Motto: Oro y Plata (Gold & Silver)

DEDICATION

This book is dedicated to my twin daughters, Kiersten and Meghan Schaeffer, who leave for college in the fall of 2023 to start their next adventures.

Raising a family - it is said "the days are long and the years are short." We do things to make memories of the time spent together. For our family, spending time on the trails is where we have memorable quality time. Sanctuary is found under the pines, on ridge lines, and in mountain lakes. We like to explore, so we don't always visit the same places but look to new fresh places to discover throughout the year.

It isn't always easy motivating the family to get outdoors every weekend.

While we can't help you pack lunches, load the car, or drive to the trailhead, we can we can provide information on where and when you can have the best experiences year-round on the trails in SW Montana, focusing on locations within a few hours' drive of Bozeman.

Conditions change and weather shifts, so don't procrastinate.
Seize the day!
You mat not get another chance.

Be here now.

Kiersten & Meghan Schaeffer enjoying the golden hour while backpacking in Glacier National Park

ILLUSTRATION INSPIRATION

Art Technique Video

In February 2013, my wife and I traveled to Sweden to race in the World Masters Cup. W arrived in Stockholm with winter in full swing. The races were cold slow, and harsh. My 15-kilometer race was one degree away from being canceled due to cold temperatures. While my skis weren't too fast on the highly crystallized snow, I completed the race without frostbite. A photo of my rhyme encrusted Ice beard printed in the American Cross Country Skiers annual was my claim to fame (not my racing time).

Despite the cold darkness of winter in Sweden, there was warmth in the Nordic communities.

During our trip we visited the home of famed artist Carl Larsen. The country home along a large forested lake was reminiscent of Montana's Flathead lake. His descendants have preserved his home since the 1830s letting the public view it as a cultural museum during certain times. It closes to the public in the evenings for family dinners. This tradition has carried on since the 1890s. We toured the rooms where his children were painted playing dress-up. The family picnic and sledding areas outdoors look just as they did over 100 years ago.

Carl Larsen was a famous artist of the time in his homeland Sweden and beyond. His detailed line-work combined with vibrant colors and realism capturing folk scenes and family life made him the Norman Rockwell of Sweden.

Inspired by Japanese printmaking Carl Larsen's line work took a life of its own. He was a prolific artist, admired and respected within his lifetime.

A devoted father and husband Larsen's character, work ethic, and accomplishments are aspirational. His realistic scenes punctuated with the black line reinforcement inspired my technique of drawing natural scenes, starting with the lines first.

ILLUSTRATION TECHNIQUE

This book and the animated films accompanying it utilize an illustration technique developed and refined over the past few years and 600+ drawings.

Each illustration is hand-drawn on paper with Blackwing pencils (the brand of choice by Walt Disney and other animators).

Micron pens are used to draw over the soft pencil lines reinforcing the definition of shapes and contrast. The finished pen drawing is digitally scanned and converted into vector artwork. Colors are painted digitally.

The finished artwork is prepared for the printed book and composited for use in animation.

I hope to recreate scenes of happy family life in the outdoors in a way akin to how Carl Larsen made everyday life a work of art reflecting his time and place.

The author drawing at his desk while recovering from Achilles tendon rupture repair surgery

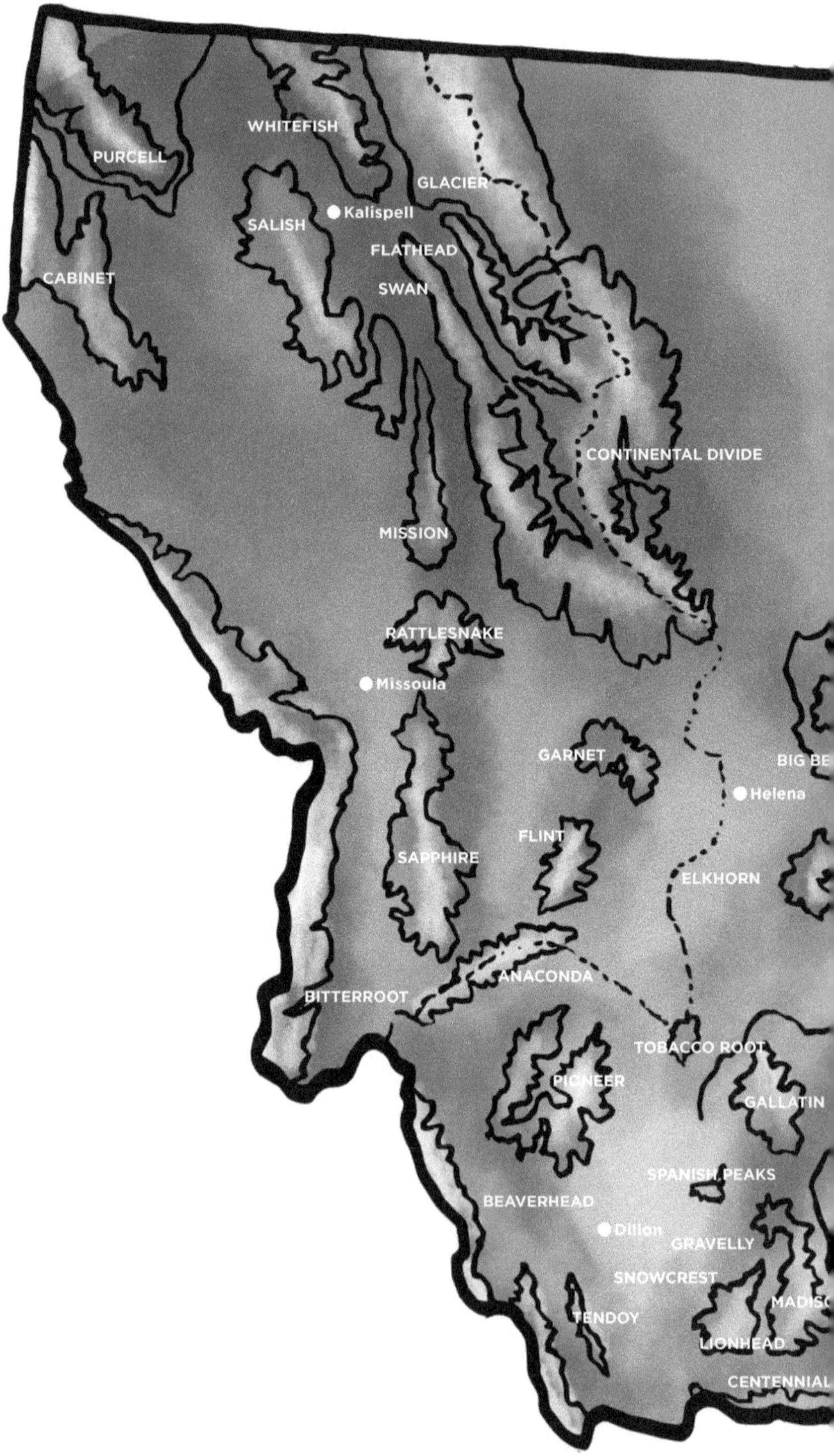

WHITEFISH
PURCELL
GLACIER
Kalispell
SALISH
FLATHEAD
CABINET
SWAN
CONTINENTAL DIVIDE
MISSION
RATTLESNAKE
Missoula
GARNET
FLINT
SAPPHIRE
ELKHORN
ANACONDA
BITTERROOT
TOBACCO ROOT
PIONEER
GALLATIN
SPANISH PEAKS
BEAVERHEAD
Dillon
GRAVELLY
SNOWCREST
TENDOY
LIONHEAD
CENTENNIAL

Montana's Mountains

There are mountain ranges all over the place in this state named for mountains.

The Absaroka-Beartooth Range - The Roof of Montana, home to Montana's highest peak - Granite. See video link of climbing the peak in The Last Best Ski GPS map (page 225).

Yellowstone NW Ranges - Madison, Gallatin and Gravelly

SW Montana Isolated Ranges - Pioneer, Anaconda-Pintler, Highland, Tobacco Root, Ruby, Snowcrest and Flint Creek

Western Boundary Ranges - Bitterroot, Centennial and Beaverhead

NW Montana Ranges - Purcell, Cabinet, Whitefish and Salish

Northern Divide Ranges - Bob Marshall, Scapegoat and Great Bear

Swan & Clark Fork Ranges - Swan, Mission, Garnet and Rattlesnake

Broad Valley Ranges - Bridger, Crazy, Big & Little Belt, Elkhorn, Castle, Highwood and Big Snowy

Glacier National Park Mountains

HIGHWOOD

LITTLE BELT

BIG SNOWY

PRYOR

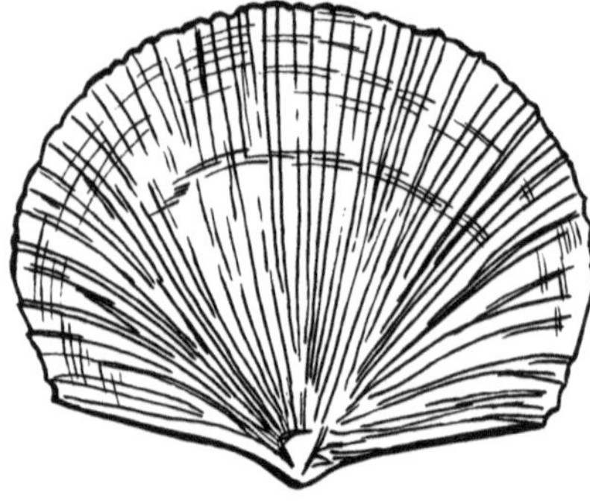

ANCIENT HISTORY

The earliest living inhabitants in what is now Montana were brachiopods, conodonts, crinoids, fish, mollusks, and sponges. The Late Devonian shallow sea covered most of North America. Some of the oldest rocks in the world can be found on mountain ridges and peaks of the Bridgers and Gallatin Mountains. Pre-Ravalli rocks date back 3.8 to 2.5 billion years. If you look closely, you can see rocks that resemble rippled seafloor on these mountain peaks.

They were, in fact, uplifted from deep below the earth along the continental divide fault. The pressure forced deep rock beds to the surface and far above the surrounding lands forming these mountain ranges.

Dinosaurs roamed these lands and left their fossilized bones as clues to how they lived in this place but in a much different landscape. The famed paleontologist Jack Horner who was the expert consultant for the Jurassic Park movie series, also contributed to the success of the Museum of the Rockies dinosaur programs and exhibits.

The ice age 12,000 years ago covered the landscape with super glaciers. As they receded, they carved U-shaped valleys, leaving glacial cirques at the base of granite peaks. Freeze and thaw cycles fractured massive rock gendarmes into boulders fields, grinding rocks with snow and ice and tumbling them over time into round river rocks.

These scattered rocks across mountain drainages, valley floors, and riverbeds.

Humans have lived here for at least 12,600 years (see a brief history section). Adapting and contributing to the ecology of the land along with the elk and bison herds that proliferated valleys and foothills of SW Montana. At the end of the ice age, leafy plants became more scarce as prairie grasses became prevalent.

Thus came the end of the age of the woolly mammoths and the rise of the great American bison herds. Cloved hooves dug spreading diverse grass seeds throughout the migrations of the massive herds. First Nations people lived in abundance. Bison numbers grew to the tens of millions. Cleverly adapting to the nuances and opportunities of each season, migrating with the animals and indigenous plants like the bitterroot, camas, biscuit root, chokecherries, medicinal barks, and berries.

Plant life and ecosystems emerged around this new climate as the glaciers receded. Annual snowpack filled rivers in the spring, and sequential blooming of plant life attracted foraging animals to migrate where the harvests were in season.

Living in Montana year-round can be like living in four different places.

The landscape changes dramatically each season. Hot and dry summers burst out into forest fires. Mountain trails cleared of snow, offering cooler temperatures as relief from the heat and access to otherwise difficult-to-reach alpine lakes, meadows, and peaks.

Colder temperatures bring in the fall. Deciduous trees drop their colorful leaves as migrating animals start for their wintering areas. Hunters test their skills in navigating wild spaces to fill their tags and freezers with wild game.

Obsidian speartip quarried from Obsidian Cliff in Yellowstone National Park

When winter comes in earnest, the Gallatin valley is covered in layers of snow, building up the snowpack.

Hiking boots are replaced by skis that glide across winter landscapes, breaking trails, following a skin track, or sliding across groomed surfaces. Deep cold smoke powder face shots are followed by a dip in a local hot spring or après ski by a crackling fire.

Big Mike Animation

Springtime is a process of freeze-thaw and repeat, giving glimpses of warm summer days fleetingly replaced by snow showers or cold rain. Eventually, the snow melts, for good and the brown, dead colors show signs of life. Grasses turn green, trees bud and leaf out. Hillsides and meadows become carpeted with wildflowers. The trails melt out and dry.

People visit the places they remember, areas where a discovery is made, a friendship cast, or the quiet solitude of nature is found, cementing a memory of our being alive in this place and a glimpse of time in this dynamic, ever-changing world.

Big Mike coming to life at The Museum of the Rockies | Bozeman, MT

LAND ACKNOWLEDGEMENT STATEMENT

Lands in this book were traditional seasonal hunting grounds for the Shoshone, Bannock, Crow, Nez Pierce, Assiniboine, Kootenai, Blackfeet, and many other First Nations People.

Remains of a young boy found in Wilsall, Montana, prove that Native Americans have been here for at least 12,600 years. Archeological finds at the Madison Buffalo Jump show a sustained period of bison harvesting in that area spanning 2,000 years. A tumultuous time in the 1800's during westward expansion depleted the bison from the area and displaced native people to reservations outside the greater Yellowstone ecosystem.

There are no reservations in Gallatin County, although 25 tribes historically used the Greater Yellowstone ecosystem.

The Blackfeet, whose reservation is in northern Montana near Glacier Park, the Crow, whose reservation is in southwestern Montana, and the Shoshone, with reservations in both Montana and Idaho, may have spent the most time in the area hunting and gathering plants and roots.

Humans have been drawn to the Bozeman area for thousands of years.

They traveled routes that have been in existence since the first people migrated to the area via the Old North Trail, a route that crossed what is now the Bering Strait on a landmass called Beringia.

First Nations, pioneers, mountain men, stagecoaches, railways, and roads all follow travel routes that have been in existence for thousands of years.
Where did these passageways for human migrations come from, and why?

Let us peek back through history.

The first people migrated on The Old North Trail across what is now the Bering Strait in a landmass called Beringia on foot. Likely following animal migrations, early migrations crossed northern Asia as the ice sheets opened across Canada, then moved south along the edge of the Rocky Mountains.
These early migrants expanded their explorations and settlements throughout the Americas and to the tip of South America in Patagonia. The Clovis people who likely migrated following the woolly mammoth left traces of their stone spear tips along the way.

Wooly mammoths foraged on leafy plants, but as the climate changed and these plants became increasingly rare, grasses became more prevalent, this lead to the mammoth's demise and rise of the North American Bison. Wild grasses give off a specific scent as they mature and become ripe for foraging. The bison are attracted to ripening plants in certain areas, similar to how salmon return to their birthplace. The fragrance is connected with the blossoming of the grass. With the arrival of spring moisture and the sun's warmth, plants follow the increasing warmth of the sun and, as the snow melts, a wave of green covers lowland prairies, across foothills and fills in mountain valleys.

Just as the plants take their cue from increasing warmth from the sun in the springtime, grazing animals follow the plants as they grow, guided by the winds that carry the scents of the blossoming grasses. Nomadic tribes, then, followed the bison as they migrated to places where the grasses were ripe for grazing. The nomadic people migrated through the Gallatin Valley, following the bison, in a cycle of the seasons that centered on hunting and gathering, camping in places that also provided the necessities of shelter and access to water.

Winter campsites were along rivers and in valleys that provided windbreaks and some protection from winter storms. As animals - deer, elk, and bison - came to the water to drink, they were harvested. Again, with the spring break-up and rivers rising, the people moved on to the ripening grasses in the foothills where the bison grazed, harvesting the indigenous plants as well as the buffalo.

Traveling to find food, however, was not the only reason for the tribes' seasonal migrations. Trade with other bands and tribes, as well as the social interactions that accompanied these gatherings, provided opportunities for sharing knowledge and culture. A sign language used throughout the region is evidence of inter-tribal relations. Many tribes - Sioux, Blackfeet, Crow, Hidatsa, Shoshone, Lakota, Dakota, Nez Perce, Bannock Arapaho, Salish, Cheyenne, Gros Ventre, Cree, and Assiniboine - used the area along the Old North Trail near the three forks of the Missouri as seasonal hunting grounds. The Madison Buffalo Jump, west of Bozeman, had been used for two thousand years and as recently as 200 years ago to harvest bison, the "lifeblood" of the Plains Indians.

Montana is Medicine Wheel Country

The Medicine Wheel represented the seasonal circle moving of camps.

Winter campsites along rivers with windbreaks gave access to running water in the wintertime, and as animals came down to drink they could be harvested. The circle maps guided hunter-gathers in an annual cycle, harvesting food at nature's pace.

It was time to move on during the spring break-up. Rivers rise, grizzly bears awake from their slumber and essential roots, and indigenous plants begin to ripen in the foothills. Traveling to find food was not the only reason for the seasonal migrations.

Trade relations and social interactions were significant. Annual meetups of different groups passed the sharing of knowledge. A universal sign language used throughout the region is evidence of inter-tribal relations. This dynamic land of extremes was not well suited for stationary camps. The Crow migrating from the mid-west were traditionally agricultural people. They brought seeds with them to plant in Montana. This practice was abandoned when the harsh climate did not cooperate.

Indigenous plants were harvested seasonally instead.

The Sioux, Blackfeet, Crow, Hidatsa, Shoshone, Lakota, Dakota, Nex Pierce, Bannock Arapaho, Salish, Cheyanne, Gros Ventre, Cree, and Assiniboine all use an area along The Old North Trail near Three Forks as a seasonal hunting grounds.

Before horses were introduced to the Americas by the Spanish, Indian camps were moved by travois dragged by dogs. These two pole framed units were laterally braced to carry food, lodges and supplies prior to the invention of the wheel.

Because natural resources were abundant, possessions were kept to a minimum with the nomadic lifestyle. Great significance was placed on ceremony and tradition and the movement patterns of animals, plant growth and seasonal weather changes - all contributing to the essential tribal knowledge necessary to living on the Great Plains. Family groups dispersed in bands of about 20 persons, which reduced overcrowding and conflict over the use of natural resources. The annual harvest at the "pishkin," (translated

Bison Hunt Animated

as "deep blood kettle") or buffalo jump was a place where tribal nations gathered to refresh their supply of bison meat for winter use.

When the timing was right - a large herd of bison grazing near a known pishkun - the people skillfully corralled the herd within cairn-marked drive lines. When the herd was in a crucial position, the animals would be spooked by "runners" disguised as wolves, antelope or buffalo calves who ran alongside the herd, waving the pelts and luring the buffalo to the edge of the cliff. The runners then leaped to safety onto ledges just below the cliff 's edge as the buffalo stampeded over the cliff. These brave runners fulfilled a vital role in the harvesting of the bison and, along with the collective power of the entire community who participated in the harvest, helped to ensure the survival of the tribe.

Every part of the bison was used for shelter, food and supplies. A ceremony was given to thank Tatonka (Boishoen -Shoshone, Biishe - Crow) for making this sacrifice for the people. This was the way of life for many generations.

Before the mass extermination of the North American Bison by white settlers in the late 1800s for their pelts. Bison were said to be so plentiful during the annual rut massive herds would form filling the entire landscape thick with bison. It is estimated as many as 30 million bison were roaming North America as the time of Lewis and Clark's expedition.

This was the way of life for the tribes of the Great Plains before the near extermination of the North American Bison by white hunters in the late 1800's. It is estimated that 30 million bison roamed North America at the time of the Lewis and Clark Expedition (1804-1806).

Madison Buffalo Jump 1750

Lewis and Clark Expedition - 1806 Return Route Through the Gallatin Valley

One of Jefferson's primary goals for the Corps of Discovery was to discover a water route between the Missouri and Columbia Rivers with a minimal Rocky Mountain portage. This hadn't been achieved on the westward journey to the Pacific.

On the return trip from the Pacific, Lewis and Cark split the expedition at Three Forks. On July 3, 1806, Lewis traveled north on the Missouri River to explore the extent of the Marias River while Clark, guided by Sacajawea (carrying baby Pomp) led a group of ten men and 49 horses into the Gallatin Valley.

Clark mapped the journey, re-uniting with Lewis and the rest of the Corps of Discovery at the junction of the Yellowstone and Missouri Rivers in eastern Montana on August 11, 1806. The overland section of the journey between the three forks of the Missouri and the Yellowstone River passed through the Gallatin Valley.

Navigating east along the Gallatin River and following the snow-capped Bridger mountains, Clark spent the first night camped along "the butifull navigable Stream,"," which is east of the town of Logan, at a current landfill site.

By comparing many of the challenging stretches of the expedition, this stretch was fairly "uneventful," historians proclaimed, "Clark's interlude of pure enjoyment as the most comfortable of the entire expedition." The river was named by Clark as the Gallatin after Albert Gallatin, the U.S. Treasury Secretary. The Native American name for the river was the Cherry River, known for its abundance of chokecherries.

Because the swampy ground and beaver-impacted terrain along the river made travel by horse difficult, Sacagawea guided the Corps along the well-known paths of the indigenous people which followed the ancient migration route of the bison. This route took the Corps through the area where the towns of Manhattan and Belgrade are now located. They traveled this route with little complaint, other than what Clark referred to as a "nuisance" for horse travel.

They moved south around the East Gallatin River to avoid more beaver construction near the present-day fairgrounds, the Corps crossed over Sourdough Creek along Kagy Boulevard, where Montana State University and the stadium sit, making a second campsite in the valley in a meadow along Kelly Canyon road. They traveled from Kelly Creek to Jackson Creek by Green Mountain northeast of Chestnut and to Billman Creek before connecting to the Yellowstone River and then eastward. This section is slightly north of north of Bozeman Pass.

Sacagawea advised the group to cross the gap farther to the south of the Bridgers to exit the valley. They found trees large enough to carve two dugout canoes near present-day Livingston and completed the next stretch on the Yellowstone River.

Ancient Pathways Today in Gallatin Valley

Many footpaths in the Gallatin Valley that began as migration routes and used by bison became stagecoach routes, followed by the railroad in the late 1800's and eventually, the highways that we travel today. Much of these historic routes is now Interstate 90 .

The Gallatin Valley was known as the "Valley of Flowers" by indigenous people was communal hunting ground for many tribes, and a place of peace and abundance. The Treaty of Laramie in 1851 that was signed by Red Cloud with the United States marked a large area of south-central Montana as "common hunting grounds" for the tribes that historically used the area. The Flathead and Blackfeet Treaties signed with the US government in 1855 reinforced this concept.

It is incredible to think these migration routes are the same paths created by ancient migrating animal bison herds!

Colter's Run - 1808, Three Forks of the Missouri

The story of John Colter's legendary run to escape Blackfeet Indians has inspired books, films, and an annual trail run.

Colter's fitness and survival skills were developed as a guide on the Kentucky frontier. His ranger skills so impressed Lewis and Clark that he was hired to be a member of the Corps of Discovery where he served as a navigator, hunter and negotiator between the various tribes along the Pacific Ocean and the return to St. Louis.

Eager to return to the lands rich in beaver, Colter was honorably discharged from St. Louis so he could join a group of trappers headed back up river to the Three Forks area. The trapping venture disbanded, but Colter was determined to explore what is now the Greater Yellowstone area. Making a 500-mile loop through what is now Yellowstone National Park and Teton National Park, he became the first white person to witness mud pots, geysers and steaming waters. Upon returning to Fort Raymond (located at the mouth of the Big Horn River) after his long winter journey, Colter was ridiculed when he told about the sights he had seen; the area he had explored was mockingly called "Colter's Hell."

Undeterred by previous hostile encounters with the Blackfeet, Coulter led a group of Crow and Shoshone back to the Three Forks area to negotiate trade.

On the journey back to Fort Raymond, the 800 Crow and Shoshone were attacked by 1,500 Blackfoot warriors.

Colter and his allies eventually were able to fend off the Blackfeet and he returned to Fort Raymond to recover from a wound in his leg that he sustained in the battle. When his leg was healed, Colter returned to Three Forks with his partner John Potts. They were in a canoe on the Jefferson River when they encountered several hundred Blackfeet Indians on the riverbank. They motioned for Colter and Potts to come ashore. Colter complied and was promptly disarmed and stripped naked.

Potts refused to comply. He shot and killed a Blackfoot man on the shore. He was immediately riddled with bullets and arrows, then dragged to shore and chopped into pieces, a practice that was to ensure that he would not come back to cause harm in the afterlife.

A council was held to decide what to do with Colter. He was able to convince the Indians that he was a slow runner, but he was told to run for his life. Some historians think that the Blackfeet, who considered the beaver to be a sacred animal and did not want the trappers to decimate the beaver populations, meant to give Colter a scare and, if he survived the ordeal, would have a harrowing story to share with other potential trappers upon his return.

As Colter took off running, many warriors began to chase him across the grasslands along the river. He ran for his life and after a few miles of sprinting barefoot and naked, exhausted and bleeding from the nose, he had separated from most of the men, with one brave trailing only a few dozen yards behind. Worried about being speared in the back, Colter suddenly stopped and turned abruptly to face the brave with his arms outstretched. Stunned by Colter's stunning appearance, the brave tripped while attempting to launch his spear, thrusting the tip into the ground and breaking off the head. Colter overcame the brave and used the spearhead against him. Taking the fallen brave's blanket, he resumed fleeing. After running about five miles from the starting point, he found a beaver lodge in the river where he hid himself until nightfall when the pursuers gave up looking for him. Colter then walked 250 miles in eleven days to the trading post on the Big Horn River, surviving on roots and berries that he found along the route.

To the Gold Rush -1864-68
The Bozeman Trail

By the mid-1800's, The Oregon Trail was bustling with pioneers, many of whom had decided to take a journey north into the gold fields of Montana upon the discovery of gold in Bannack, Virginia City, and Alder Gulch.

John Bozeman born in Georgia in 1835 headed west in 1860 to join the gold rush. Leaving Bannack and returning East just at the time of the rich gold discovery in Alder Creek, Bozeman vowed to return in haste and make a shortcut back to the gold lands. To forge a shortcut from St. Louis to Montana's gold rush lands, John Bozeman helped establish the Bozeman Trail through Wyoming Territory into the gold fields. As a short cut to the gold fields, Bozeman's route veered off from the Oregon Trail, traveling northward along the east side of the Bighorn Mountains of present-day Wyoming. He ignored the request of the Sioux, who had won the hunting rights to the Powder River Basin and north, he continued to take wagons on this more direct but dangerous route through Sioux territory.

The famous mountain man Jim Bridger, in the meantime, was guiding covered wagons along the west side of the Bighorn Mountains, which was a safer route to the Montana gold fields. Bozeman's trail rejoined the Bridger route westward near what is now the current I-90 route through Livingston. Bridger's route then followed the valley to the northwest crossing over the Bridger

Mountains into current day Bozeman, while Bozeman's route crossed more directly west over Bozeman Pass and into the Gallatin Valley.

John Bozeman's route became known as the Bozeman Trail; however, it was short-lived despite the establishment of military outposts along the route to protect the wagon trains from Indian attacks. After several years of conflict and battles, Red Cloud won a treaty securing the greater Powder River Basin and lands along the Yellowstone as grounds as long as there was a viable livelihood to be made from hunting of elk and bison. In 1868 Red Cloud signed a treaty with the U.S. Government that guaranteed the closure of the forts along the Bozeman trail, including Fort Ellis outside of Bozeman. The forts were promptly burned by the Sioux, ending the Bozeman Trail.

However, by the late 1880's the buffalo had been hunted to near extinction, ending the nomadic way of life for the Plains Indians, and Indian reservations were established. (Fortunately, the dwindling population of bison in the newly formed Yellowstone Park were protected as poachers were caught and tried.) Finally, the connecting of the Northern Pacific railroad from the east reached Bozeman in the 1880's, tunneling through the mountains of Bozeman Pass and meeting the western tracks in Gold Creek, MT, with the driving of the last spike in 1883. The Gallatin Valley and the Greater Yellowstone area was now set to see pioneers, ranchers and farmers, and entrepreneurs coming into the area that would dramatically change the landscape and bring great changes, socially, politically, and economically in the 20th century.

MODERN-DAY GOLD RUSH

Montana's history in the 19th and 20th is one of boom-and-bust cycles in mining, logging, farming grains like wheat and barley, and cattle ranching. Prior to the westward expansion, Native Americans

who roamed the land for thousands of years were able to survive and thrive in the inhospitable environment because of their relationship with the migrating bison and with the land itself. The trappers and mountain men who found solace in the immense wilderness gave way to miners coming from the East seeking instant wealth.

Settlers followed and the vast plains were turned into expansive wheat fields and cattle ranches, with towns and cities being built to provide the many services that the growing population required. Over the span of a couple centuries the land and its resources have been the draw for the thousands of people who ventured westward seeking new opportunities for themselves and their families.

The modern "gold rush" is the land itself.

World class recreation abounds in Montana which draws outdoor enthusiasts and sports people alike. With tourism surpassing agriculture dollars brought into the state, today people are drawn to this area to recreate and to live. Just as with past migrations of people to the state, Montana continues to beckon individuals with adventurous spirits who are inspired by those who came before - for their grit as they faced challenges inherent in the character of the land and for their determination to survive and make a living out on the plains, along the rivers and in the mountains of Montana.

As you have your own experiences on the trails of SW Montana while hiking, biking or skiing, remember its rich heritage and the people who came before.

We can learn from the past

Thanks to Dr. Shane Doyle, Crow (Apsáalooke), for providing insights about ancient life in Montana. A special thanks to Rachel Phillips from the Bozeman History Museum for helping to locate articles, news clippings and books for the research of this article.

Montana migrations - traversing Big Sky Country through the millennia

POTTY TALK

Somebody's gotta say it...

Edited by Outside Bozeman Editors Corey Hockett & Mike England

Have you been to a place where the most pristine alpine-lake views were spoiled by toilet paper strewn across the landscape? Have you seen and smelled half-dug holes overflowing with human excrement? Have you been to local trails lined with colorful poop-filled bags sitting on the side of the trail? This is a surefire way to ruin the aesthetic of a wildly beautiful place, not to mention a health hazard by contaminating water sources.

I don't think people trash places intentionally. $#!+ happens. But when nature calls, we all need to be prepared. There are rules of engagement that keep forests pristine, clean, safe, and attractive. Follow them.

PLAN FOR POTTY TIME

When there is the luxury of a trailhead outhouse, use it.

These generally exist in high-traffic areas and places that have the budget to permit and build an outhouse. Be prepared for the toilet-paper stocking situation to be variable. Packing your own TP is a good backup plan.

In locations where there are limited facilities or long morning lines to the privy, please train your bowels to release quickly on command. Forcing lines of agonizing people to wait for what seems like an eternity should be avoided.

Training your bowels to operate like a Swiss watch is another conversation, but some tips include eating plenty of roughage and timing your coffee intake to operate as a laxative. I have a friend that took a morning dip (tobacco) that got things moving, although I wouldn't necessarily recommend that.

PACK IT OUT

Bags aren't just for dogs.

Always bring along extra bags, be they zip-locks, small doggie bags, or larger produce bags. They can be used to pack, and double-seal, all manner of waste, particularly used toilet paper.

When I was a kid, the local park was strewn with dog feces. At some point, city ordinances across the country decided it would benefit everyone to require cleaning up after your pup. Now, it is commonplace to find dog-waste stations equipped with small plastic bags and disposal receptacles.

If you simply hate carrying your dog's waste out, make Fido pack it out himself. Dog packs are great for leashes, snacks, and packing out doggy waste. Anything is better than leaving the bag on the side of the trail. Many trailheads have receptacles for dog waste where they can be deposited.

Other places to keep in mind are zones where waste doesn't biodegrade fast, like high-altitude areas. Using blue bags is common practice in harsh alpine conditions. You'll notice they're required on popular mountains like Mount Rainier. These bags are similar to the green bags that you find at any dog park, except they come with zip ties and a translucent outer bag. The double bagging helps to contain the odor. Big-wall climbers use a similar technique with an inner plastic bag packed into a carabiner compatible "poop tube."

My wife and I typically used dog-waste bags for our toddlers, who didn't always feel like taking care of business until we were miles down the trail.

Always pack out other biohazards (don't bury) such as feminine-hygiene products.

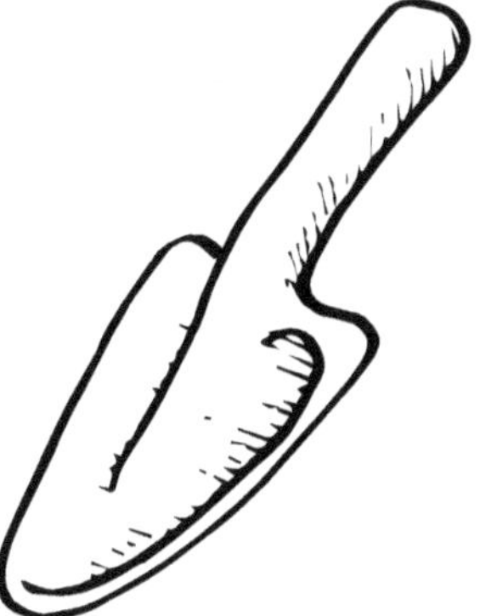

BURY IT

The trowel never touches...

In lower elevations where biomatter exists, soil bacteria and organisms break down the waste and reabsorb it into the environment. Boy Scout rule, if I remember right, is to dig a latrine trench or cat hole at least 6" deep and far from visual or olfactory proximity. Latrines should be at least 200 feet (or 75 steps) from any water source. Bury the waste with soil and cover with needles or topping of your choice that matches local decor. Make sure you are a good distance away from any trails as well. See if you can be a bathroom ninja and "leave no trace." Use sticks, rocks, or a fancy digging trowel. Remember, the trowel never touches...

Keep in mind that a shallow poop grave may be exhumed by foraging critters. Nasty, yes, but the best way to deal with this eventuality is to bury your human waste and pack out the toilet paper. It's a less-gross package for you to carry and a less-gross sight for everyone else who comes behind you.

IN SUMMARY

1. Use the facilities (if they exist).
2. Bury it or pack it out—either way, no one should ever be able to tell you "went there."

EXTRA TIPS

Wet-wipes can double as cleansing for messy parts. On longer days, keeping things clean and chafe-free can save you from getting chapped. You know what I mean if you have experienced miles of this agony. If you're without TP, try smooth rocks (not too abrasive), leaves (not poison ivy or stinging nettles), or my personal favorite, snow. Bring a small container of hand sanitizer (or an extra wet-wipe) for afterward.

With the right preparation, taking care of business can become an enjoyable part of your outdoor experience, instead of something to dread. Not to mention, our forests (and the people out in them) will thank you for it.

10 ESSENTIALS

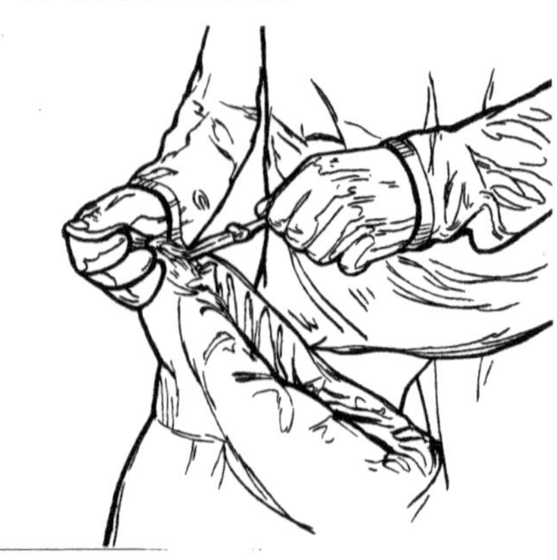

Using remote trails out in the elements requires packing more safety and preparation equipment than you would on town trails. I like to pack water, insulation and nutrition, even on local training days.

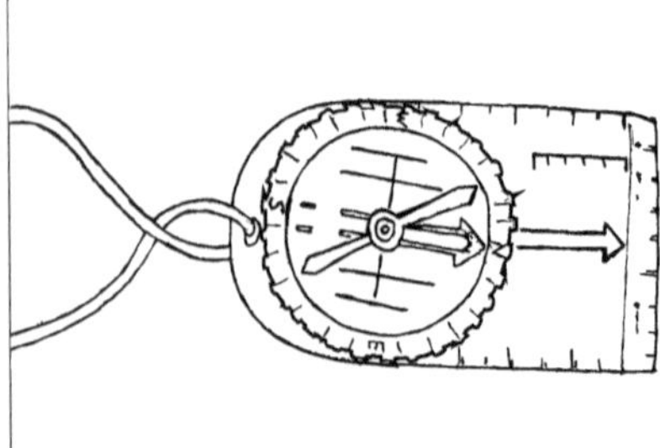

1 Navigation

- A map & compass, GPS, or a mobile device with a photo of the map can save some packing space. Be aware that mobile phone reception will be limited or non-existent in most of these locations.

The combination of a physical trail map, topographical map and phone app (like onXmaps) will help you determine your location via GPS even while off line. Physical maps make it easier to read larger areas to get the lay of the land, and they never run out of batteries.

There is a place for traditional 5:1 Topo printed maps and GPS devices/ phone apps. There is no replacement for a printed map to get the lay of the land for trip planning and navigating in the field. The large-scale fold out maps give a broader context that you just can't get on a tiny GPS or digital phone screen.

A 5:1 topo map used with a compass can help you navigate the topography, give a better sense of parallel drainages, contours features and obstacles. These are crucial in navigating high-country above market trails through talus, snowfields and alpine terrain.

A printed map can be supplemented with a GPS device when unfolding a large map in inclement weather or when darkness makes finding your position difficult or impossible. Being able to turn on a device and mark your exact location helps to pinpoint the location on the printed map.

Traveling off-trail in alpine or bushwhacks can be much slower than hiking on an established trail and makes it much easier to get lost or turned around. Checking your position frequently in these circumstances can help make more informed navigation and safety decisions.

Save battery life by putting your phone on airplane mode. GPS still works off the cellular grid and you will save battery life with the phone not constantly searching for a signal. For extra battery life, bring a solar charging battery pack. Most can be positioned on the top of your pack during the day for recharging the battery, then plug into your phone at night to recharge the phone from the battery pack. Make sure to keep the phone warm at night (keep insulated) as cold temps will zap the battery.

These are some of the useful navigation and trail apps

- Topo Maps - Downloading detailed 5:1 topo maps for use offline is an accurate way to check your position and navigate, in conjunction with a printed topo map.
- All Trails app - provides mapping and recommendations, lets you give ratings and read trip reports of recent trips.
- OnXmaps - A land ownership database, it helps you to see who owns/manages every parcel of land in Montana. Great for off-trail or hunting use.
- TrailForks - Designed with mountain biking in mind.
- Strava - Chart your activities and see what routes others are doing (and how fast they are doing them).
- Google Maps - use The Last Best Trails GPS map (page 51 for Hike trailhead links) to get driving directions to the trailheads and see where hike, bike and ski routes are, along with extended options.
- Shows services, restaurants, gas stations and lodging etc.
- Gallatin National Forest Travel Plan, current edition, for the "big picture" of public and private lands and up-dated information about access to public lands.

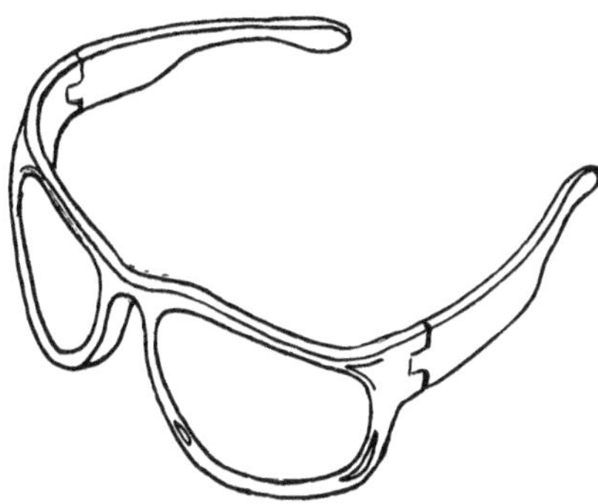

2 Sun Protection

- Sunglasses with polarized lenses for mountain travel and sunscreen are crucial. Face stick or Dermatone will work well for exposed areas such as your nose, cheeks and ears. For exposed higher-elevation excursions above the tree line, I recommend a sun hoodie. With SPF 50+ and highly breathable material. A hoodie will prevent your head, arms and torso from getting nuked on high elevation snow fields.

3 Insulation

- A key factor I pay close attention to is exertion levels. In the winter, wearing layers of skintight wicking fibers (tights or long johns with insulation and shell layers on top) allows for comfortable movement in different states of exertion.

A little to a lot of heat is produced from movement (especially at high-intensity and up hill). At lower exertion levels a layer of insulation will keep you warm. When you stop hiking, during breaks or at camp it is important to have a thicker insulation layer to keep you warm.

On a cool early morning ride, starting a bit cold can save stopping later to remove layers. Once warmed up you will be producing a lot of body heat.

Having dry, warm layers to put on when resting or changing pace (ie. a lightweight down puffy or long sleeve sun shirt in the summer) is a good way to stay warm when expending less energy.

In the shoulder seasons an insulated polypro t-shirt with removable arm sleeves is a great way to have layering flexibility without bringing more garments than what you will end up using. Knowing what is most comfortable to move in during different seasons and conditions takes some practice.

It is a good idea when emptying your pack after a trip to take inventory of what clothing you used and didn't use. Factor your learning into the next trip. Keeping a gear closet with your favorite garments on hand will give you more time on the trips and fewer items in the gear bin.

In this cold, dry climate, wool performs exceptionally well. New wool-blend base and insulation layers are warm, lightweight and less itchy than they used to be. A Bozeman company, Duckworth, sources its premium wool from sheep raised near Dillon, MT.

DRESS FOR SUCCESS

There is an old Norwegian saying that there is no such thing as bad weather, just bad clothing. The standard way to dress for outdoor activities is using the layer system. This consists of three layers, 1. Base Layer next to the skin 2. Insulation Layer sandwiched in-between the base layer and 3. The shell provides protection from the elements similar to the roof and siding on a house.

The most important layer for hiking, running and backpacking is the base layer. This layer next to your skin works as a second skin and functions to provide some insulation while wicking moisture away from your skin where it can evaporate and keep you dry. This is a major

consideration in preventing hypothermia. Synthetics and wool are superior to Cotton, as cotton will absorb water and hold it in the fibers next to the skin instead of wicking away. These performance materials use your body heat to push the moisture on to fibers that pull the moisture away from the body and to the exterior surfaces where it evaporates.

Exercise with a polypropylene layer and keep a change of clean cotton clothes in the car to make the trips back from the trailhead more comfortable.

Endurance athletes may prefer more form-fitting base layers that enhance movement with some compression. Leisure hikers might find a more relaxed fit to be more comfortable for long days on the trail. Full-length tops and bottoms also known as "long johns" work like a second layer of skin, offering micro-insulation, moisture wicking and sun protection. Sun shirts, sun hoodies and other garments are designed with sun protection in mind and have a high UPF protection similar to sunscreen and are a good option to protect from sun exposure, especially in places where reflection from the sun is amplified, as on snow fields, at altitude and on the water.

THAT'S A WRAP

The shell or outermost insulation layer is the third layer of the system. Shells, like the other layers come in a variety of weights, and also waterproofness. Shells are designed to keep out the elements - wind, rain, and snow. Shells can have a semi-permeable membrane to keep out the moisture and wind while allowing your system to "breathe." A mesh of tiny holes sandwiched between an outer layer and inner liner or fused into the fabric itself, lets tiny vapor molecules escape while preventing the larger water droplets from entering. Many shells are also treated with a DWR coating on the outside to enhance the waterproofness (think of water rolling off a ducks back). The coating does, however, eventually wear out. If you find your shell is "wetting out" - water soaking through the membrane - the DWR can be reapplied in the wash with products like Nikwax, restoring the waterproofness of the layer. Some shells have heavier, more weather proof hoods and shoulders with "soft shell" lower backs and under arms or zipper ventilation "pit zips."

In colder weather accessorize with hats, gloves and neck gaiters which can be worn as a face mask, beanie hat, balaclava (head and neck) or be used as a bandage in a pinch.

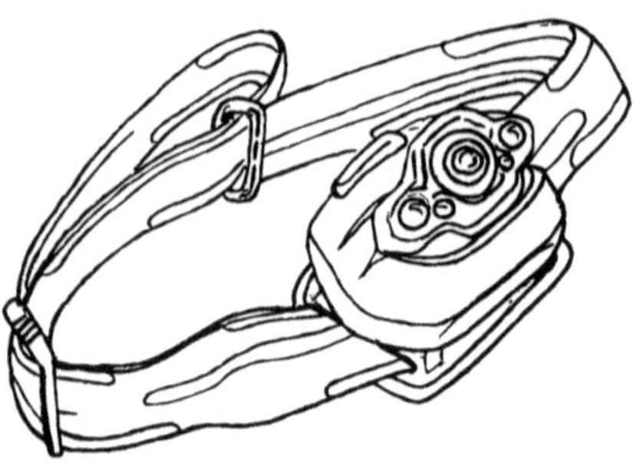

4 Illumination

- Most headlamps now weigh ounces and provide many hours of illumination, so there is no reason to leave home without one and risk "benighting" yourself or getting lost in the dark. Bring a light whether you think you need it or not.

Pack extra batteries with charger for longer trips. With new technology small lights are so minimal that a head lamp becomes a small LED USB powered light in your pack. That way you will never have to worry about hiking out in the dark without a light. Pack spare batteries and check your charge occasionally.

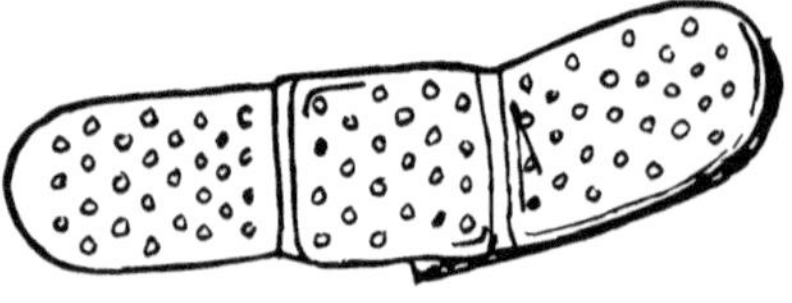

5 First Aid Supplies

- It is impossible to be prepared for everything, and there are countless ways to prepare a first-aid kid. I recommend bringing items that have multiple uses to avoid redundancy and extra pack weight. A standard kit of bandages, medication, splints, and a cutting utensil is good to have in the car. On a light and fast trip I always bring ibuprofen, Benadryl, a Swiss Army knife, some twine and a roll of athletic tape. Clothing like a handkerchief can serve as sun protection and can be used with the tape/twine for emergency bandages, making for an efficient minimal first-aid kit. Ski poles can double as a splint as long as you have some twine/ tape to fit them. Wearing protective pads can prevent many scrapes and bruises, especially on elbows and knees.

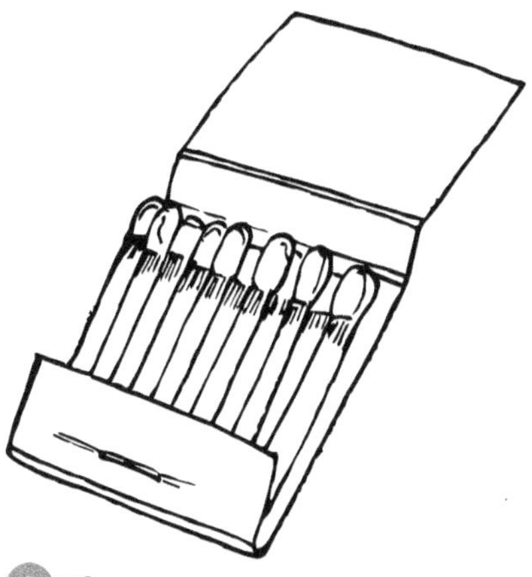

6 Fire

- Waterproof matches and lighters are a good choice for your pack. Flint and magnesium, steel wool, and laundry lint are a few other options (a bow and lathe if you are in the 1% that can actually start a fire this way).

7 Repair Kit and Tools

- Athletic tape, twine and the Swiss Army knife that are already in the first-aid kit will go a long way in making repairs. Along with duct tape, some extra batteries for your headlamp are also a good idea. Pack a mountain biking multi-tool as well. This should have a series of Allen wrenches as well as a chain tool.

8 Nutrition

- Eat lots of carbohydrates, whole grains, fruits, and vegetables. Endurance Mountain Bikers should eat 7-9 fruits and vegetables a day to replace and restore micro-nutrients. Long before your peak race or extended backcountry trip, you should test energy drinks and water combinations to make sure you know what works for your energy needs and your gut, especially during higher exertion levels. At the end of your biking day, during your glycogen window (the 20-30 minutes following exercise), refill with carbohydrates and proteins to maximize recovery.

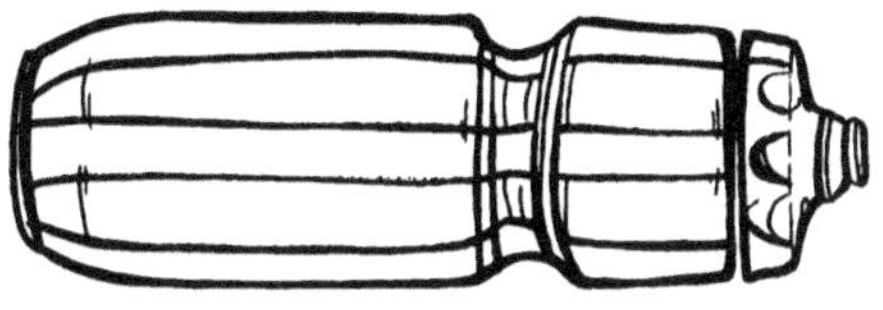

9 Hydration

- Hydration is crucial for maintaining performance and function of our bodies.

Since there aren't any drinking fountains on these trails you will need to pack a canteen, Nalgene, water bottle, or hydration pack. These all work as long as they don't leak. I like to bring multiple hydration vessels on a longer trip in case one leaks, breaks or gets broken or contaminated.

Heat, exertion and time on the trail will determine how much water you will bring. It is a good rule of thumb to have the carrying capacity of at least two liters and pack more water than you think you will need.

Many of these hikes are near water with the exception of ridge lines and summits.

There are opportunities to refill your

water hiking along streams and mountain lakes. Always filter your water. It isn't worth risking getting the dreaded "beaver fever" - giardia.

Options for Hydration:

- Pump - bulky but durable, long-lasting and reliable.
- UV - Ultraviolet light like what is used to kill bacteria and parasites in many municipal water systems, but in a mini form. Strain water first, works best in a water bottle or container with even distribution of light. As batteries can die, bring backups. Learn how to read the light system to determine if the water is finished being treated.
- Gravity Filtration - Systems with filter and nozzle either hanging bags or squeeze bags to move the water through the filter. These systems have modular components and different size water bladders from small trail-side squeeze bottles to 3-liter bags for hanging at camp. Filters can get clogged, need to be cleaned occasionally.
- Chemical - Iodine or other less nasty-tasting chemicals mixed into your water kills bacteria and parasites.

Water absorption can be aided by adding electrolyte mixtures and salt tablets to the filters water.

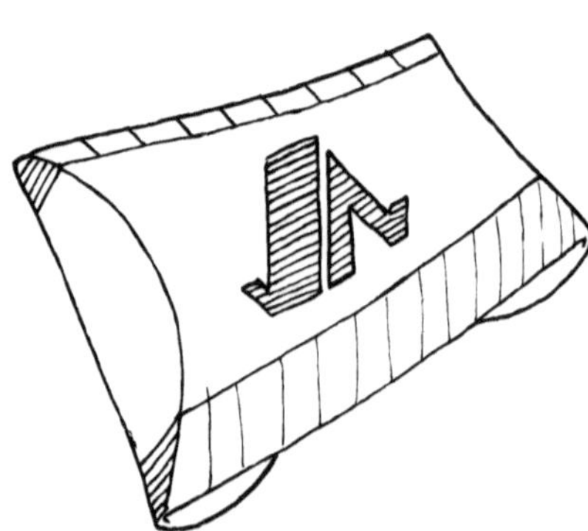

10 Emergency Shelter

The base of Maslov's hierarchy of needs is safety and shelter.

If we are going to achieve well being or even enlightenment from outdoor pursuits we need the basics covered first.

Any amount of time overnight away from our home shelter requires us to pack a temporary shelter. When packing for an overnight trip, the shelter component can take up a significant amount of space within the pack.

There are a few main categories for portable shelters most of them being packable backpacking tents.

Two wall tents are best suited for the most extreme environments and conditions. Tie downs reinforce the structure and are able to hold up to strong winds and heavy snows, giving the tent even more stability. They should be pulled tight so the tent surfaces are taut like a drum. The vestibule space in front of the entry door can be dug deeper into the snow to serve as a place to put on boots and shelter packs.

Two walled expedition style tents have more poles, heavy duty zippers and typically more durable fabrics which makes them heavier than the other types of tents.

Family-style camping tents in the geodesic dome style for car camping and backpacking tend to be larger, bulkier and heavier but offer more space for the weight.

Ultra-light backpacking tents or three season tents are ideal when weight is a concern. These tents tend to have more mesh for ventilation and protection from bugs. They are better as seasonal shelters when backpacking at mountain lakes or under protected tree canopy in less windy and exposed areas. Some weigh as little as a few pounds.

If you are going out for a long day in the mountains, overambitious objectives or foul weather can lead to an unplanned night out in the backcountry. When weight reduction for speed of travel is important, emergency shelters like traditional space blankets can be used. However, they can be a challenge for keeping the wind out, they are noisy and crinkly and are nearly impossible to repack.

Most survival blankets that don't enclose on three sides do not keep heat in and wind out successfully.

A lighter sack for trail running or to use as an emergency shelter is the Owl bag, Sealed on three sides, light and stretchy, it will keep the heat in and wind out. Pull it up over your shoulders, but don't put your head in the bag.

These are a few options for temporary shelters in emergency situations.

SAFETY

Hiking, Trail Running, Peak Bagging, Backpacking, and Mountain Biking can be dangerous.

You can fall, things can fall on you. You could get hypothermia, frostbite, heatstroke or get sunburned. You could get lost or collide with a car, bike, animal, rock, trail or tree.

Using the right technique, wearing the correct gear and properly evaluating terrain and conditions are all important to have fun and be safe on and off the trail.

While it is impossible to remove all risk from trail adventuring, which would also remove the fun, safety should always be the priority.

Make the experience more fun and rewarding. Do your research. Get proper skills training (we will talk about progression of skills later), develop fitness and, if you are mountain biking, know how your bike works.

By their nature, mountain trails have obstacles like roots, rocks, loose soil, steep side-hills and deadfall.

Every trail should first be ridden with a cautious pre-ride and re-ride before embarking on a free-ride.

Packing the hike-specific ten essentials can help you get out of a jam. Make sure to take the time to read the section of this book.

The more advanced trails have obstacles that are "higher consequence." Wearing protective gear like knee pads, elbow pads, shoulder pads, shin guards, back braces provide extra protection. Some riders opt to do the climbing sections of a trail with just a helmet and donning protective gear at the top before beginning a fast and technical descent.

Mountain bikes optimized for trail performance often remove street-friendly reflectors and safety gear. If you are riding to the trailhead on city streets and highways make sure to wear reflective clothing and use flashing front and back lights. This is especially important in the early morning and evening when visibility is reduced. When transporting your bikes to and from the trailhead, make sure they are securely fastened and locks are set. Know the safety features of your rack. A bike falling off your vehicle in the parking lot or, worse yet, off the road, is a bad deal for the bike and for other drivers.

The most common injuries sustained while biking are road rash due to sliding, impacts to knees, elbow and shoulders and head injuries due to the impact of ejection over the handle bars.

Always wear a helmet.

New technologies make helmets safer (and cooler looking) and come within a variety of price ranges. Buy a helmet that is ANSI certified. You can check this by looking at the tag inside the helmet.

Make sure your helmet is fitted correctly according to manufacturer's recommendations. This typically means that the strap is snug but not choking tight. You shouldn't be able to pull the helmet over the top of your head exposing your forehead. This is an area where many injuries occur due to the trajectory forces of an "endo" and the weight/velocity of your melon ejecting over the bars.

Make sure your forehead is covered.

Traveling in remote areas also requires first aid awareness and preparation for changing weather conditions.

Have a plan for worst-case scenarios. Know basic first aid and learn where the nearest medical centers are.

Wear clothes in layers. Pack warmer insulation for stopping or in case of equipment failures.

PROGRESSION OF SPORT

Start small with short distances and moderate elevation gain on smooth surfaces to get a feel for navigating. You can use the first trips of the season to brush off the cobwebs, transitioning from winter to spring and as a benchmark for fitness. Introductory outings will give you a better idea of what to expect in regards to distance, elevation gain profile and the character (surfaces) of the trails, whether it is hiking or biking. With subsequent trips, you should note progress in your endurance, strength, and skills.

Your equipment and overall preparedness will develop and improve as a result of ramping up throughout the season.

BEAR COUNTRY

Recreating in any area displayed in this book has the potential of hazardous animal encounters. Cattle grazing on the Highland Glenn trails, rattlesnakes hiding between the rocks at Copper City or bears in the bushes of Bear Canyon are all real possibilities.

Perhaps the most significant mountain biking/wildlife risk in Montana is startling a grizzly bear.

Much of the riding (especially in the Big Sky area) is in grizzly bear country. Special considerations should be taken when biking in grizzly country. Take the time to learn about proper bear safety practices.

Grizzly bears are the top of the food chain in the Rocky Mountains. Adult males can weigh in at over 400 pounds and smaller mother bears protecting their cubs can aggressively fend off a male bear. This apex predator has a chase response like a dog. So a bike passing by at high speed can trigger this response or engage a mother's protective response. Either scenario is problematic for a hiker or a biker.

Every year this region experiences human deaths due to bear mauling.

Victims of grizzly bear attacks are often solo. Traveling in groups of four people is a good practice. All members should carry bear spray. A few companies make bear bells that can be attached to your bike. These can be useful to alert potential wildlife on or near the trail for the lead biker of the group. Don't attempt to outrun or outride a grizzly bear. If you encounter one speak softly, avoid eye contact and step sideways away from the animal.

Have bear spray drawn and ready to use. Pay attention to wind direction. If you come across a bear on a trail and are startled, the reaction time to respond with bear spray will most likely be impacted. That is why it is important to travel in groups of people carrying bear spray. The second, third or fourth person can act as back up to deter the bear from charging or can use the spray.

Trails are often used as game trails for deer, elk and bears, especially in the early mornings and evenings, so be especially cautious during those times.

Traveling into these wild places on a bike is a privilege and the local animals should be respected. Try to avoid undue stress to them while on their turf.

A black bear scratching his back in Yellowstone National Park

Close Encounter

The author's close encounter with a grizzly bear on the Gunsight Pass trail

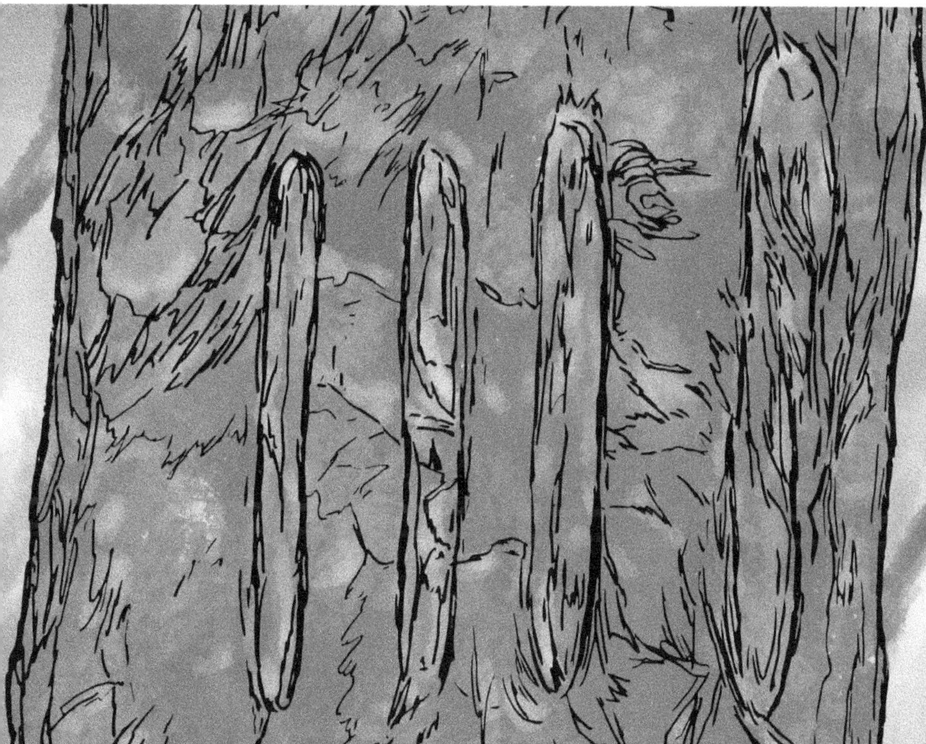

Grizzly bear territory scratch marks on a Douglas fir tree - Teton National Park

WILDLIFE WATCHING

The abundant wildlife in the greater Yellowstone ecosystem is a large part of what makes this region so spectacular. The animals that live here are able to thrive when their habitat is intact. The best time to see wildlife is in the dawn and evening hours when animals are most active. Yellowstone National Park is a destination for roadside wildlife watching. Sighting scopes with the added stability of a tripod enable close viewing of animals without disturbing them.

Large lenses are ideal for capturing quality images of wildlife while not disturbing the animals.

Give 25 yards of space for bison, moose, coyotes, and elk.

Bears and wolves (and other predators) should be observed from a distance of 100 yards or more.

Papa with a high-powered sighting scope watching a grizzly bear interact with a coyote in Yellowstone

Wildlife Safety

PHOTOGRAPHING WILDLIFE

DSLR or mirrorless cameras with large sensors and the ability to e-mount long lenses - 200-600 or even larger lenses like 1200mm Super Telephoto lenses - braced by a tripod or monopole will give the best quality photos, while maintaining a safe, non-disruptive distance from the animals.

Lenses can be rented for day or weekend use at Bozeman Camera. There are rental shops in Gardiner and West Yellowstone for renting sighting scopes. Or just politely ask one of the observers in the park for a look through their scope.

Grizzly bear and coyote playing cat and mouse - Yellowstone National Park

FOUR STEPS TO SOLITUDE

Alpine lakes with sandy beaches, riverside fir forests, and flower-filled alpine meadows are only a few of the places we search for solitude in SW Montana.

With increasing population density (more are getting out on the trails than ever before) rather than complaining about the crowded trails or attempting to travel back in time, there are more common-sense options for finding solitude in the great Montana outdoors.

While drive-up access to waterfront and campgrounds provides mass access to outdoor spots, they also draw the largest crowds, especially in the summer. Getting on the trail and hiking even a little distance opens the doors to exploring beyond the crowds.

Here are four tips for finding solitude in the outdoors.

To find uncrowded places let's look at conditions that draw the largest crowds in the first place.

1. PROXIMITY TO URBAN AREAS

The trails that are closest with easy access to urban centers get the most traffic. We won't name names, but if you have been here for a summer, you know where they are. Well known and publicized, easily accessible trails draw more people, especially when the weather is good. Scenery, ease of access and word of mouth make popular trails even crowded. While the usual suspects are popular for a reason, they aren't the only trails of similar characters, distance etc. Solitude seekers need to dig a little deeper in researching their trail adventures.

2. WEATHER

If you wait for the sun to come out, the crowds will come out, as well.

People in the Bozone come out of their shells when the sun shines. Those in search of solitude aren't deterred by the cold, wet and dark. Check out the forecast on the NOAA web site which can track elevation as well as GPS for more precise forecasting.

I have been on many typically popular trails with few or no people.

Find solitude by going early, in light rain, and further than the masses venture.

Getting up early and traveling long distances in dark, wet conditions isn't for everyone, but that is why it works.

As the Norwegians say, there is no such thing as bad weather - just bad clothing. So, gear up. (There are plenty of fantastic shops in town to get you outfitted with quick-drying base layers, insulation, and weatherproof shells.) Consider that winter storms can dump snow, making certain roads impassable. And that shoulder season rains can leave some approach roads (ie. sticky gumbo) impassable. If the weather is very severe, choose routes that are first to be plowed and save the deeper mountain adventures for when the roads will be dry and passable.

Anne Schaeffer enjoying a moment of silence away from the crowds - Yellowstone National Park

3. DISTANCE

If you go to any given popular trailhead on a sunny summer afternoon, you will see throngs of people walking the trails right off the parking lot or from any of the easiest accessible trailheads. If the parking lot is packed, the first stretch of the trail will likely be packed, as well, but venture a few miles down the trail and the number drops. A couple miles further and the number drops exponentially. One of the best ways to find solitude, even on weekends in the nicest weather, is to go further.

Expect crowds on the first few miles of the top 10 most popular Bozeman trails

Going further does require a higher level of fitness, confidence, and experience than does going with the masses, but the rewards can be well worth it. Trying to find a campground in the summer on a whim can be a daunting, if not impossible, task, but if you drive a bit farther out of town and hike more than a few miles up the crowds will disperse.

Another way to ditch the crowds is to go farther by going faster.

I fell into trail running by trying to do longer hikes but not having the time to hike them. Jogging the flat and downhills or just not stopping movement to take breaks for water and food - have both accessible in your pack while continuing to walk - allows you to cover more miles, if you are used to trail running, and you can soon be beyond the crowds.

4. TIMING

It is frustrating to spend the week planning your weekend hike, get the whole family packed up in the car, only to arrive at a trailhead with a full parking lot. The popularity of a hike isn't always reflected in the size of the parking lot. Some trailheads have an unproportionate ratio of parking to popularity of the trails. You can't change the size of the parking lot or the popularity of the trail, but you can choose when to go there.

If you want to do one of the most popular (ie. crowded) hikes in the Bozone and don't want to be in a cattle line on the way up the trail, it is crucial to start early. Climbers call this an "alpine start" and it mandatory for any serious climbing endeavor.

Giving an itinerary to friends and or family is important when venturing out on the trail. Use GPS devices for sending a message if you are running late or if you need to notify search and rescue in an emergency. In addition, having appropriate extra clothing along is helpful. A dry set of clothes (preferably cotton) for the ride back in the car or for après hike and extra water in the car are helpful after finishing a hot, sweaty hike or biking trip.

Isn't pushing comfort zones for discovery part of the adventure?

So, yes, there is a way to find solitude in the increasingly crowded Bozeman outdoors, but it comes at a price. Sleeping in, getting a late start, going on the best weather days to the most popular trailheads is a guaranteed way to be sharing the trail with the most people possible.

If your goal is solitude, you need to do the opposite.

Showing up at the trailhead under these conditions and complaining about the overcrowding is futile. Expect popular trails to be busy on sunny days in peak hours. Displaying patience and common courtesy to your fellow hikers, bikers, or skiers makes the experience better for all of us.

Trumpeter Swan foraging for aquatic plants - Yellowstone National Park

FAST OR SLOW SAVOR THE JOURNEY

If you have a goal in mind - to summit a peak, reach a waterfall, lake, beach, or viewpoint- you will find trails in this book to satisfy your need to check a destination off a list.

The other approach is journey-focused.

Time and pace are more relaxed.

Keener observations can be made when we slow down and take time to look around us, observing details in the nature (ie. water droplets forming on a leaf, the folds of the underbelly of a mushroom).

With a camera along, we look at the world in a different way. Bird watching, plant identification, and observing wildlife are other ways to be a part of the natural world that we are venturing through.

Having children along is one of the best ways to slow down and enjoy the journey; they are naturally curious.

Fast or slow, journey or destination - the choice is yours. Savor moving through the natural world.

Sebastian Petzing takes a moment to stop and smell the Beargrass, photo reference - Sebastian Petzing

The Trails Await!

The next two steps are up to you.

Discover Montana Treasures

Each of us has a path.

If we are fortunate we share a long adventurous stretch with family and friends along the way.

The journey is filled with challenge, delight, discovery, and doubt. Rainbows follow rain just as light emerges from the darkest cold of night.

This cycle is experienced again and again like the seasons. The path forces us to grow stronger, more resilient, more connected to the soil, rocks, roots, moss, the animals and each other.

The trail forks and ways part.

Memories of these shared journeys converge into stories.

Stories with real people, in real places, creating unique experiences.

These are The Last Best Trails.

For updates, more info and links go to:
www.thelastbesthike.com

1. Pete's Hill
2. Cherry River Fishing Access
3. Chestnut Mountain
4. Bear Canyon
5. Sourdough (Bozeman Creek)
6. Painted Hills Connector Trail
7. Triple Tree Trail
8. Kirk Hill Trails
9. Leverich Canyon
10. South Cottonwood Creek
11. College "M" Trail
12. Mount Baldy
13. Drinking Horse
14. Sypes Canyon
15. Middle Cottonwood Trail 586
16. Corbly Gulch
17. Crosscut Mountain Sports Ctr
18. Ross Peak
19. Fairly Lake
20. Sacagawea Peak
21. Frazier Lake
22. Grassy Mountain
23. Stone Creek
24. Langhor Accessible Loop
25. Lick Creek Loop
26. History Rock
27. Crescent Lake Loop
28. Blackmore Lake
29. Mount Blackmore
30. Hyalite Lake
31. Hyalite Peak
32. Emerald Lake
33. Heather Lake
34. Palisade Falls
35. Storm Castle Peak
36. Gallatin Riverside Trail
37. Garnet Lookout
38. Lava Lake
39. Swan Creek
40. Fairy Lake
41. Golden Trout Lakes
42. Windy Pass
43. Pioneer Falls
44. Hell Roaring
45. Ousel Falls
46. Beehive Basin
47. Porcupine Creek
48. Buffalo Horn Loop
49. Tepee Creek
50. Fawn Pass
51. Pine Creek Falls
52. Pine Creek Lake
53. Black Mountain
54. Passage Falls
55. Elbow Lake
56. Mount Cowen
57. Emigrant Peak
58. Bear Trap Canyon
59. Madison Buffalo Jump
60. Lewis and Clark Caverns
61. Missouri Headwaters State Park
62. The Beaten Path (East Rosebud)
63. Granite Peak (West Rosebud)

WINTER BOOT PACKED TRAILS

Pete's Hill, College "M" trail, South Cottonwood, Palisade Falls, Grotto Falls (Ice climbing approaches)

BEGINNER TRAILS

Pete's Hill, Cherry River Interpretive Trail, Snowfill Dog Park, Sourdough, Ousel Falls, Fairly Lake, Grotto Falls, Swan Creek, Hell Roaring, Porcupine Creek, Langhor Loop, Bear Trap Canyon

MODERATE TRAILS

College "M" Trail, Drinking Horse, Corbly Gulch, Sypes Canyon, Lava Lake, Hidden Lakes, Windy Pass, Pioneer Falls, Middle Cottonwood, Golden Trout Lakes

STRENUOUS TRAILS

Beehive Basin, Elbow Lake, Pine Creek Lake, The Beaten Path

ADVANCED TRAILS

See Peak Bagging page #133

I LIKE to HIKE

Meghan Schaeffer hitting the trails

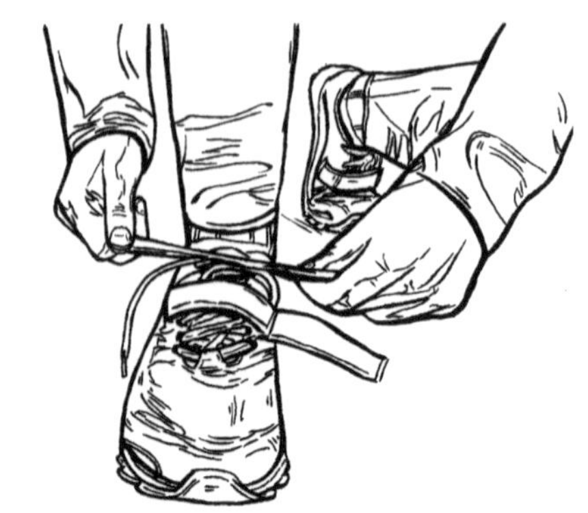

TRAIL FOOTWEAR

Fortunately hiking can be one of the most minimal outdoor activities. The most important equipment that you will need is good footwear. Depending on how you intend to approach these foot trails - from barefoot trail running to backpacking/mountaineering with heavy packs loaded with winter gear, there are many options for footwear.

MINIMAL

- Barefoot, Vibram 5 Fingers, Barefoot Sandals

The best-selling book "Born to Run" brought to our attention the history of human adaptation to traveling many miles in search of food, prey and shelter, and the connection between our physical endurance development and mental focus and growth.

Vibram 5 Fingers

RUNNING FLATS

- Minimalist trail running shoes with enclosed toes

The major consideration for selecting footwear for trails is how far and how fast you plan on going - hiking or running, short and fast, long and slow, or long and fast - all factor into shoe selection. Determine if weight or support/weather proofness will be the most important for your adventure.

Minimalist Trail Running Shoes

TRAIL RUNNING SHOES

- Heavily cushioned to zero drop

Shoe styles and trends ping pong back and forth from ultra-minimal barefoot shoes to ultra-padded elevated platform shoes (see illustrations). Illustration 5-fingers, racing flats, Altras, Hokas here...

The popularity of trail running has spawned many styles of footwear, spanning the gamut from sprint performance to endurance comfort.

Cushioned Trail Running Shoes

SHOES

GoreTex TRAIL SHOES
- Heavily cushioned to zero drop

You might want to try out a variety of footwear on short sections of trail to determine their comfort, fit and appropriateness for overall use. Heavier waterproof boots require more of a break in period and may benefit from the use of custom foot beds for additional arch support. Lighter weight shoes don't offer as much support, but they give you a better ground feel while strengthening your feet.

GoreTex Hiking Shoes

HIKE

Gear

HIKING BOOTS
- Traditionally sturdy sole leather high tops covering the ankle

Standard hiking boots have lug soles, high top leather uppers with durable heel and toe bumpers and come with resilient laces that hold up to a lot of punishment. Some lighter high top versions of trail running shoes look like a mix between trail running shoes and Nordic ski boots. Equipped with lightweight lug soles, some are even embedded with micro spikes for traction on ice and hard snow.

Hiking Boots with Traction Soles

MOUNTAINEERING BOOTS
- Heavy-duty boots for off-trail or packing heavy loads on rough surfaces, talus and snow provide support and protection

Traditional mountaineering boots were built by skilled cobblers, often in Italy and in the mountainous parts of Europe. Durable calf skin uppers were treated with wax and other coatings to maintain waterproofness. The heavy-duty boots made it easy to kick steps in the hard snow. They did require a breaking-in period, just like a baseball glove, to get the right fit. The rigidness of the boots enables the fitting of metal crampons with straps.

Modern-day mountaineering boots have a similar cut and shape but use lighter modern materials and vibram soles. While these may be more nimble, they aren't as durable as the old-school classics.

Mountaineering Boot

WHAT MAKES A GREAT HIKING TRAIL

There are many hiking trails in this region. We continue to explore and dog-ear guidebook pages when we complete a hike. Instead of listing every trail in the region we are curating what we think are the best foot trails for family hiking, adventure hiking, trail running, and backpacking. This gives shorter options and recommendations for trails that are great for the whole family. Extend the adventures for more ambitious hiking or trail running. Make longer loops for backpacking, peak bagging and more. Montana is a big state. Big Sky country is expansive and there are many classic hikes here. While we focus on the greater Bozeman, Big Sky/Yellowstone corridor, in this book for information about other Montana hikes, refer to Douglas Loraine's "100 Classic Hikes - Montana."

You can craft your own adventure from these recommendations.

All of the trails in this book are featured because they are area classics or at least high-quality experiences. There are recommendations for other trails with similar character that you can reference for additional exploration beyond the most common ones. These are well-known trails in the Bozeman, Big Sky area.

Even though hiking is all about the journey, having a prime destination that can't be reached easily any other way is a key ingredient of what makes a great hike.

While we may be satisfied to skin up and ski down a random ridge, or bike laps in the forest on a bike, foot travel is more motivated by what we will see and experience. This hiking package includes interesting trail contours with varied plant life and ecosystems, dramatic viewpoints, ridge lines, or summits. These are all things that can make a great hike.

While there are hundreds of trails in this area, this book is biased towards the foot trails that offer these benefits as opposed to other trails that may lend themselves better to biking or skiing. So our recommended routes in this book have something unique and tend to be some of the most popular in the area due to the dramatic scenery or attractions.

These trails are accessible to all ages. We designed this book with entire families in mind. In the progression of sport, we will give recommendations to extend your route (where applicable). Loop options add challenges with fun trail running routes, peak bagging and shuttles. There is something for everyone in this book regardless of experience.

It is our goal to encourage you to get out there. Do some forest bathing. Experience our public lands (responsibly) and share these experiences with your friends and family.

PROGRESSION OF SPORT

Start small with short distances and moderate elevation gain on smooth surfaces to get a feel for navigating. You can use the first trips of the season to brush off the cobwebs transitioning from winter to spring and as a benchmark for fitness. On subsequent trips you can go further, higher and faster. Intro outings will give you a better idea of what you might expect on other trips when you have an idea of distance, elevation gain profile or the character (surfaces) of a trail.

Your equipment and overall preparedness on the trails will develop as a result.

We have rated these trails as easy, moderate and challenging. The markers of standard distance, cumulative elevation gain and trail character (smooth, flat, steep, rocky, rooty) will round out the difficulty level. All of these trails are class 1 with the exception of some scrambles (class 2,3 and up) on the area's peaks.

PLANNING YOUR OBJECTIVES

This book is designed to give you ideas about where to hike and what you need to pack. Supplement this book with a map of your destination from Beartooth publishing.

READY TO HIKE

Now that you have an idea of how to start preparing, let's take a look at the lay of the land.

Types of hikes. These are the standard classics in the area. Popular places have higher impact on the land. We can all have a better experience if we are considerate to other people on the trails.

NORDIC WALKING

Just like its winter sibling, Nordic skiing, Nordic walking utilizes poles to provide stability and supplement leg power. Hiking or running with poles reduces strain on the knees, especially descending, and provides more power for climbing.

TREKKING POLES

Designed for hiking, trekking poles are different from winter ski poles. They are height adjustable either by telescoping articulation with clamp locks to secure the appropriate height or by using collapsible sections (Z poles). They are sized for hiking, similar to alpine skiing poles, and are adjusted to be slightly higher than the top of the hips. The poles can be lengthened for descents, shortened for climbing, or gripped at different heights for side hill travel. Constructed of steel, aluminum, or carbon fiber, each has its own merits.

Steel poles are more durable, especially from side impacts, than Carbon. I like to "clank" my poles together when hiking in bear country, but don't do this with carbon poles. Aluminum is lighter and the best choice for most uses. Carbon is the lightest and most rigid, providing the best power transfer in higher-intensity activities like sky running.

In most models of trekking poles the bottom tips, or ferrules, can be changed to metal or rubber to give you optimal grip on the surfaces you will be traveling.

Trekking poles can significantly reduce stress on the knees and provide more stability and balance while shouldering heavy loads.

FOOTWEAR

It will take some experimenting to find a winning footwear and sock combo for your trail activities. Good fitting footwear will allow your toes to wiggle but won't allow your foot and heel to slide from the back of the shoe. Mid foot high ankle footwear should lock down to prevent your heel from sliding up when rising on your toes. Test footwear by walking down at an incline to make sure your toes aren't hitting the front of the shoes (a surefire way to lose toenails). Try out different brands and makes with more than just the shoe size to consider. Look at widths, flex and rise to find a pair that will perform well for you on the trail.

GAITERS

The word guêtre was borrowed from the French to describe the leather covering of the ankle used in "pleasant dress."

There are now gaiters for all types of hiking boots and trail running shoes. The full length comes up to just below the knees and are designed primarily for mountaineering to keep out snow and rock debris. They have a mid-foot strap that secures in front of the heel shank.

Shorter, above-the-ankle gaiters, also known as talus gaiters, aren't as waterproof, but if sized to the shoes and it they fit well, they will keep out rocks, dirt and offer some water repellency. Size correctly and adjust to keep them from riding up. Some mountain running shoe models offer Velcro on the heel to help keep the custom-made gaiters in place.

SOCKS

Good fitting and performing socks will reduce your chance of getting blisters.

Cotton socks should be avoided for trail use as they absorb water instead of wicking moisture away from the skin like wool and synthetic fibers do.

Some blister sufferers swear by toe socks (Injinji) that prevent toes from rubbing together. These literally fit like a glove but are more difficult to put on. Ankle-height socks can fit under talus gaiters to keep out debris. Calf socks provide compression and are popular with some ultra-runners. Wool socks are the choice for colder temps. With a variety of thicknesses, wool socks can be a good, durable choice for summer hiking as well.

FOREWORD

by Erika Flowers

Former pro-Nordic skier & North Face Endurance Athlete

The sun was just peaking over the horizon as we fired up our camp stove and flipped our first, golden brown pancake on the top of the Bridger Ridge. I was 15 years old and my friend and I had agreed the night before that pancakes must certainly taste better on top of the mountain. We decided to test it. We woke up at 3am, jogging and hiking with the faint glow of headlamps bobbing up and down along the Sypes Canyon trail, with the ridge in our sights and maple syrup in our packs.

I spent my summers growing up in Bozeman, bounding around Triple Tree trail, getting lost trying to connect Sourdough and Kirk Hill and snacking on Mott's fruit snacks while hiking up Saddle Peak with my dad and sister. I thought I knew my way around Bozeman's trails.

When I returned to my hometown as an adult, I realized I'd barely scratched the surface and began to discover the seemingly endless possibilities for adventure on foot in the mountains of southwest Montana. Blackmore was the backdrop for convincing my Vermont boyfriend that Montana might be a place he could live one day as my husband. Hyalite played host to the start of a three-day run from Bozeman to Mammoth Hot Springs. Pete's Hill now serves as my pre-work power loop and the M has

become my go-to for early morning miles with friends. The network of trails that crisscross southwest Montana drew me back to the state for their perfect mix of easy access paired with the possibility of rugged adventure.

For some the trails are a place to train, to push their bodies against the pull of gravity and loose rock on the way to the summit of Baldy or Sacajawea Peak. For others, the trails are a place to connect, catching up on life with friends while slowing down to marvel at the arrow leaf balsamroot that line the Bridger Foothills trail every June. For all, the trails provide a home for our feet to explore and revel in the wild and natural beauty of Montana.

The trails that connect Main Street to the mountains also connect a community, stitching together a shared love of the land. May this book serve as a colorful guide to explore the area's vast network of hiking trails, the wild places and natural landscapes they unlock, and the communities they connect.

Erika and husband Andy running through "The Valley of the Flowers"

HIKE

Scan to watch animated film

Kerplink, kerplunk - Torrey doing her best "Blueberries for Sal" impression - huckleberry picking in the Beartooths

THE LAY OF THE LAND

Greater Yellowstone Trails Bozeman - Big Sky and Beyond

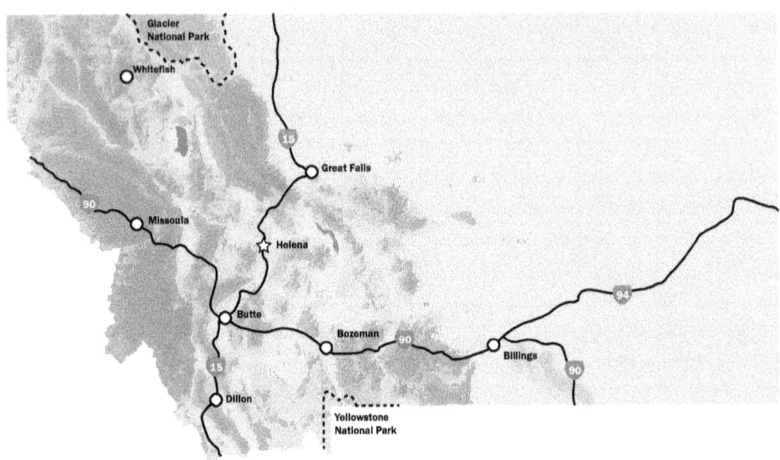

Now that you have an idea of preparation for the trails, let's take a look at the lay of the land.

The Bozeman area has long been used by native peoples as a seasonal hunting ground and travel route. Fondly referred to as "The Valley of the Flowers," hikers in June will see hills covered with Arrowleaf Balsamroot, Sticky Geranium, Fire Weed and many other perennials carpeting the hillsides and valleys. The Bridger Range runs south to north and butts up to the north edge of Bozeman. The recognizable white "M" marks the southern edge and the entrance to the east side of the Bridgers and the Bangtails.

Chestnut Mountain lies in the I-90 corridor heading east towards Livingston and the Paradise Valley, which is one of the two Montana entrances to Yellowstone Park .

Bear Canyon is southwest of Chestnut Mountain, separating it from Mount Ellis.

Mystic Lake sits 10 miles in from the Sourdough/Bozeman Creek trailhead south of Bozeman. This is the center piece of some of the longer trail routes that are featured in The Last Best BIKE.

Foothills of the Bridgers taper abruptly to the southwest of town in the Leverich and Kirk Hill trails. These areas are five miles south of town and, due to their proximity, are popular for mountain biking and trail running. However, this area pales in scenery compared to the state's most popular US Forest Service recreation area, Hyalite Canyon.

Hyalite Reservoir is the center of outdoor activities within the area. This focal point gathers its water from Hyalite creek - the best hike in the canyon.

Hyalite Creek trail ascends along Hyalite Creek and past a dozen waterfalls to the alpine Hyalite Lake and Hyalite Peak at 10,300 feet. From here, the Gallatin crest travels further 20+ miles to the southeast.

Before entering Gallatin Canyon, is the entrance to the Spanish Peaks. The road that accesses the Spanish Peaks passes through Ted Turner's ranch, with fields of grazing bison, and is the dramatic entrance to a backpacking alpine paradise. The Spanish Peaks has abundant mountain lakes, peaks, and wildlife. Mountains in this range include the highest mountain in the area - Gallatin Peak at 11,015 feet, Beehive Peak - as well as Beehive Peak and "the blaze," a well-known destination for back country skiers and rock climbers.

A series of drainages on both sides of the Gallatin River offer hiking trails and climbing access at the mouth of the canyon to old-school rock routes on the Gallatin Tower, Skyline Buttress, Spare Rib and other formations that are visible from the highway.

Lava Lake captures more than its fair share of moisture and is lush with vegetation along "Cascade Creek", a nod to the Pacific Northwest.

Heading south through Gallatin Canyon, the view eventually opens up to Big Sky and the first dramatic view of Lone

Discover Montana Treasures Bozeman, Big Sky & Beyond

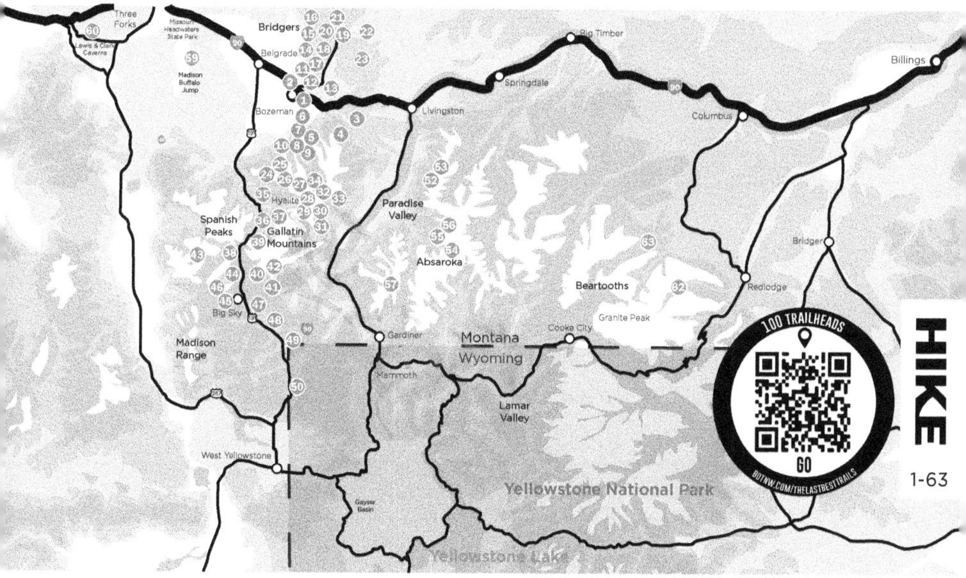

HIKE

1-63

Mountain, the home of Big Sky Resort (the largest ski area in North America).

Big Sky's town trails and easy access include Ousel Falls, a community favorite..

Up the road just past Big Sky Resort on the way to Moonlight Basin is the classic trail to Beehive Basin. At 8,500 feet an unnamed lake sits in the alpine basin in front of a rock outcropping and a steppingstone to Beehive Peak, properly bordering the southern edge of the Spanish Peaks.

Heading south from Big Sky, the highway continues to follow the Gallatin River and enters the western edge of Yellowstone National Park. There are many trailheads along the highway going towards West Yellowstone, Montana's western entrance to the Park.

Western Meadowlark
(Sturnella neglecta)
This bird with its distinctive springtime song is about the size of a robin and is often seen on fence posts in prairie settings.

Western Meadowlark - The distinctive black "V" shape on its chest and a bright yellow body help to identify this bird. The Western Meadowlark is the state bird of Montana, as well as several other states.

Montana state bird, the Western Meadowlark

BOZEMAN FOOT TRAILS
Bozeman Town Trails

The Bozeman area has long been used by indigenous peoples as a shared seasonal hunting ground and travel route. Fondly referred to as "Valley of the Flowers," hikers in June will see Arrowleaf Balsamroot, Sticky Geranium, Lupine, and other perennials carpeting hillsides and valleys.

Black-capped Chickadee

(Poecile atricapillus)
The Black-capped Chickadee is ever-present in the Bozeman area year-round.

This small North American bird with a distinctive "black cap" can be found in many Bozeman backyards or parks. It is a passerine bird in the tit family, the Paridae. The chica-dee-dee-dee song is only one of the 16 vocalizations the small songbirds make.

Chickadee along Bozeman town trails

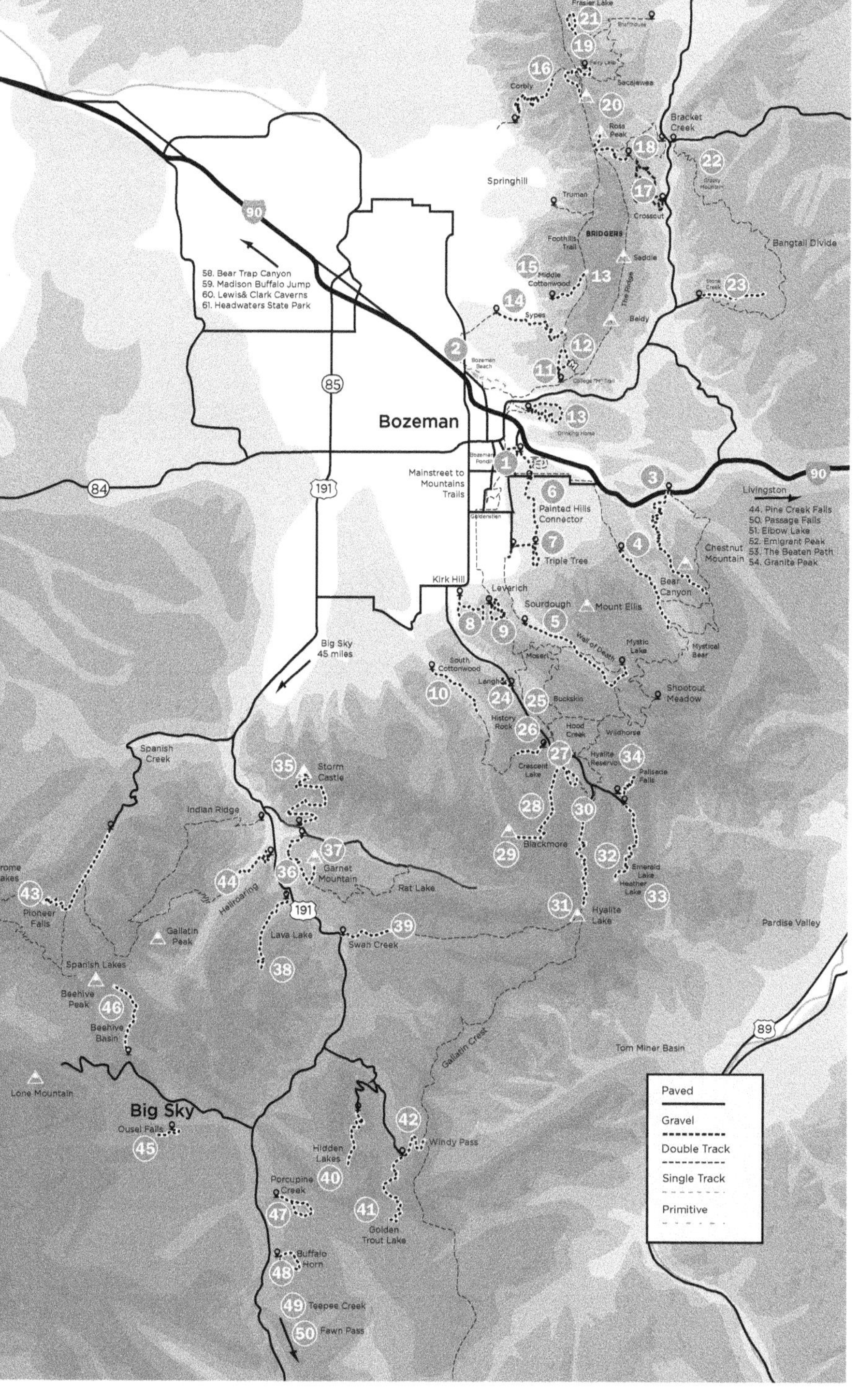

HIKE 1-50

Bozeman Town Trails, City of Bozeman, Gallatin Valley Land Trust, Custer Gallatin National Forest

BOZEMAN ON FOOT

01. Town Trails - Pete's Hill

Loop: 4.4 miles to several miles
Elevation gain/loss -100 + 100 feet
Top Elevation 4,960 feet
Difficulty: Beginner
Land: GVLT - *Off leash Dog Park*

The trail on Pete's Hill is officially named **The Chris Boyd Highland Ridge Trail**, but most locals go with the name Pete's Hill. The wide gravel path cresting the hill is often a parade of dog walkers (one of the few off-leash dog parks in Bozeman), moms with rugged strollers and elderly hikers from the nearby retirement community.

Single track trails along the hill's edge offer multiple bench-filled overlooks with unobstructed views across Bozeman and the valley.

Adjacent to Lindley Park and Sunset Hills, the trail connects to GVLT trails on all sides. The paved and graveled **Galligator trail** splits diagonally across town, serving as the main trail connector between downtown Bozeman, the library, MSU and the Museum of the Rockies. Highland Glen trails extend to the east and are groomed in the winter by The Bridger Ski Foundation for Nordic Skiing.

Main street to Mountains Trails are connected north to south along the edge of downtown Bozeman to the University and Museum of the Rockies via the Galligator Trail. This diagonal stretch of trail is mostly a shaded, wide gravel path with offshoots along the adjacent stream and other connection points to Pete's Hill Bogart Park, The Langhor Community Gardens and The Museum of the Rockies.

The southern Bozeman trailhead of **Tuckerman Park** has a mix of grasslands, tree-covered aspen groves and thickets along Sourdough Creek and crosses Riley's Bridge through the Sundance Springs Neighborhood.

One direction of the Main street to Mountains Trails goes north to Kagy Boulevard where the trail travels past the golf course by another community garden. Another direction goes southwest along a second stream connecting both Sacajawea Middle School and Morning Star Elementary School to the MSU Arena and the Museum of the Rockies.

With some road travel along 3rd Avenue, it is a short distance to the southern **Painted Hills Connector** Trailhead, **Triple Tree Trail**, then Sourdough Canyon (Bozeman Creek), Leverich Canyon, Kirk Hill, South Cottonwood and the entrance to Hyalite Canyon just south of town. Further east at four corners is the junction to the Gallatin, Big Sky and Yellowstone National Park, all south of Bozeman.

Taking in the views from a Pete's Hill bench

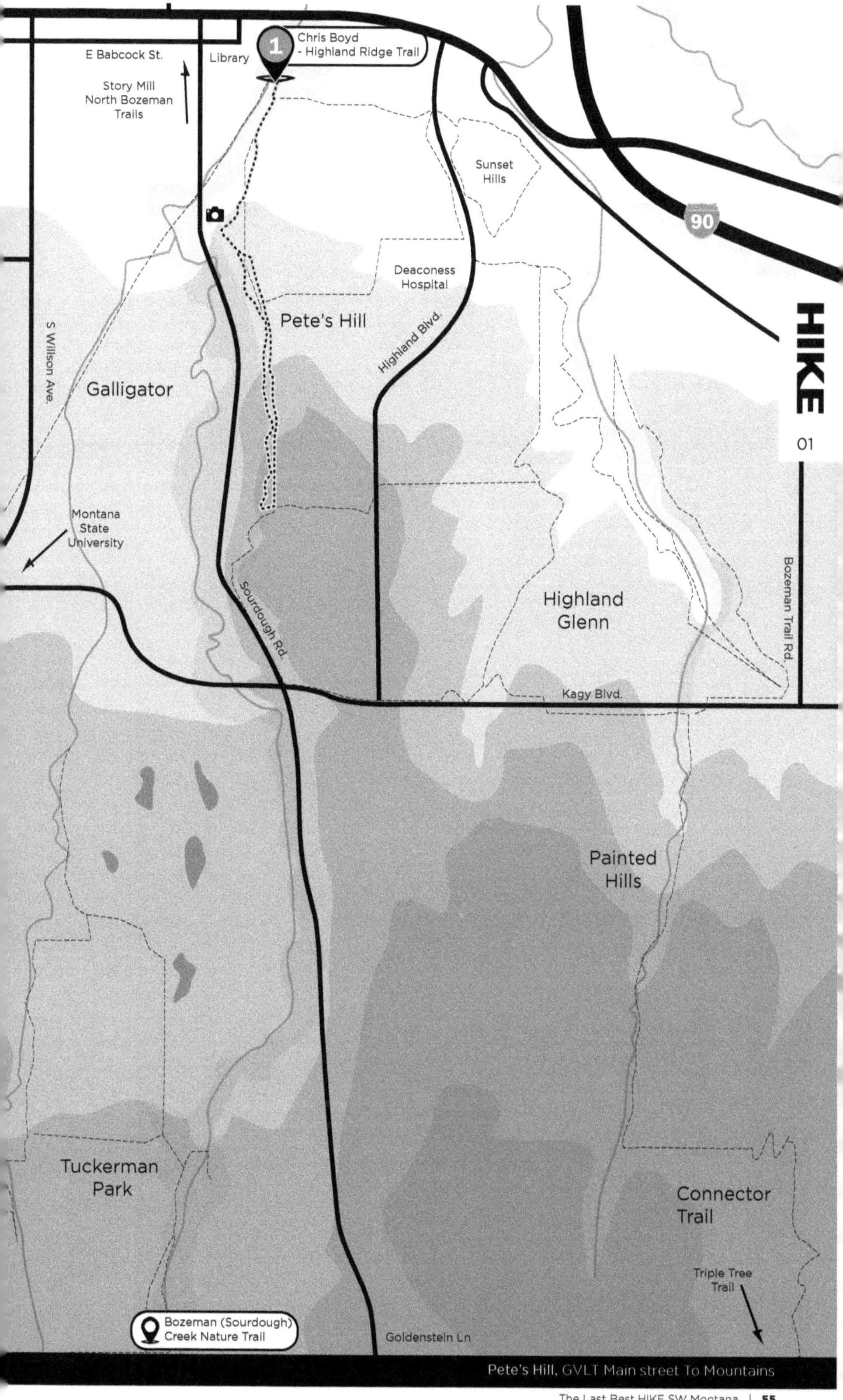
1
Chris Boyd
- Highland Ridge Trail
E Babcock St.
Library
Story Mill
North Bozeman
Trails
Sunset
Hills
90
Deaconess
Hospital
Pete's Hill
Highland Blvd.
HIKE
01
S Willson Ave.
Galligator
Montana
State
University
Highland
Glenn
Sourdough Rd.
Bozeman Trail Rd.
Kagy Blvd.
Painted
Hills
Tuckerman
Park
Connector
Trail
Triple Tree
Trail
Bozeman (Sourdough)
Creek Nature Trail
Goldenstein Ln

Pete's Hill, GVLT Main street To Mountains

BOZEMAN ON FOOT

02. Cherry River Loop

Loop: .8 miles to several miles
Elevation gain/loss -5 + 5 feet
Top Elevation 5,246 feet
Difficulty: Beginner
Land: GVLT - *Dogs allowed on leash*

In contrast to the current names of rivers, assigned by Lewis and Clark after certain government officials, the indigenous names of each river were given by their special attributes. The Gallatin River was originally known as The Cherry River due to the abundance of Choke Cherries within the area.

At the time of Lewis and Clark, Bozeman was filled with marshes and bogs created by prolific beaver dams. This made travel through the area on horses "a nuisance." Marshes were eventually drained to make farmland and buildable land and the beaver population diminished. Cherry River fishing access gives a sense of what the land used to be like ages ago.

A short interpretive loop on a wide gravel path wraps around wetlands with Bridger Mountain views.

The Cherry River trail is a perfect mellow spot to get some fresh air. Everyone from little tykes to grandparents will enjoy mountain views over quiet ponds.

Search Cherry River Fishing access
Bozeman, MT
Trailhead (45.71171,-111.05082)

This family-friendly trail has a wider loop option and can be connected to Glen Lake, otherwise known around the area as "Bozeman Beach." Equipped with a swimming area and a sandy beach, volleyball nets and climbing rock, this is a popular spot on summer days. Other trail options are also provided past the parking lot into grasslands in the East Gallatin Recreation area.

To the north, the Snowfill dog Recreation Area is an off-leash dog park with a 1.25 mile gradually hilly loop hike. This is not connected to the main system and has a separate trailhead that can be reached by Mcilhatten Road next to the Bridger Creek Golf Course.

Story Mill trails off the Storymill playground offer wide gravel paths with bridges that cross oxbow waterways through forested nooks and open grasslands.

All of these trails provide short treks and longer loops by connecting them via the East Gallatin Connector to the Bridger Creek trail through Legends Neighborhood on the way to the paved M Trail to the east. Or go south on the Storymill spur, past the Cannery District on city streets to downtown.

Female Mountain Bluebird, Cherry River slough, Bridger Mountains in the background

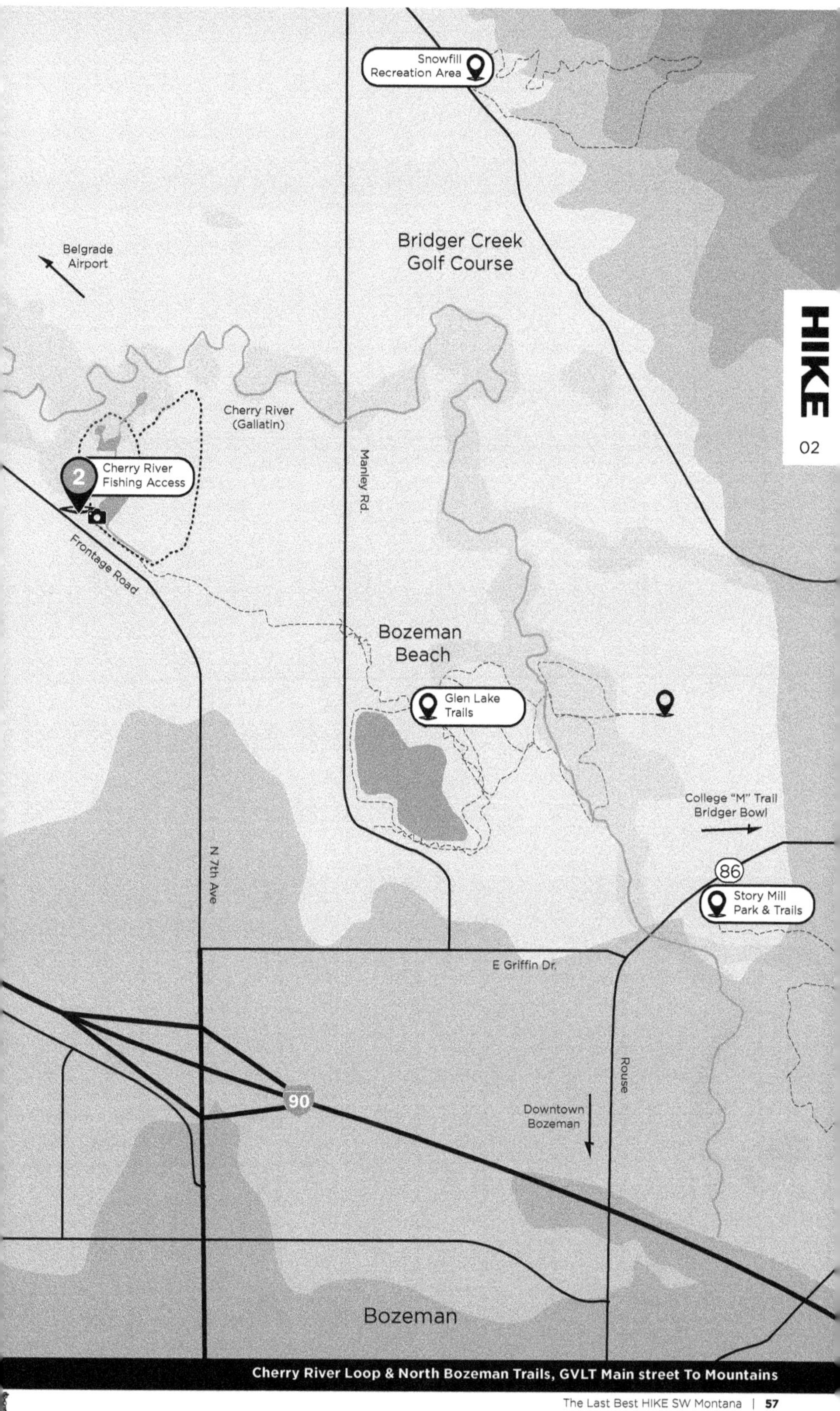

Cherry River Loop & North Bozeman Trails, GVLT Main street To Mountains

03. Chestnut Mountain

Out-and-Back: 13.8
Elevation gain: 2,519 feet
Top Elevation: 7,481 feet
Difficulty: Hard
Land: Custer Gallatin National Forest

The Chestnut Mountain trail crosses Rocky Creek at the trailhead bridge. Climbing switchbacks to the right, views open along the western ridge facing Bozeman. A right-pronged climber's trail leads to sport routes on the steep limestone crags of Frog Rock. This aptly named feature resembles a tree frog climbing the mountain ridge when viewed from Bozeman. The Chestnut Mountain trail continues steeply upwards, gaining upper meadows and, finally, the rolling rocky summit with views across Bozeman, the Bridgers, Paradise Valley and Mount Ellis to the south over Bear Canyon.

Return on the route or shuttle back to Bear Canyon Trailhead. There is also a fantastic mountain bike loop known as the Goosenut. See Mountain Bike trail #68 on page 169.

Search Chestnut Mountain To Frog Rock Trail, Custer Gallatin National Forest Trailhead (45.64502,-110.88089)

04. Bear Canyon

Out-and-Back: 8.2 miles or less
Elevation gain: 1,463 feet
Top Elevation 6,792feet
Difficulty: Moderate to Easy
Land: Custer Gallatin National Forest

This trail follows the stream past some trailside rocky outcroppings that kids use as play forts. Cross a bridge, taking a left on the wide gravel path to switchbacks that climb up the hillside to the north of the creek. Hike through cattle guard and over bridge to further trail junctions. Make a short lollipop loop along the stream, or continue left to a historic cabin and connect with Chestnut Mountain Trail. A right turn leads up double tracks (often shared with ATVs) to the Bear Lakes. Dirt bikes, four wheelers and mountain bikes use these trails to loop and access deeper trails within the area. (See mountain biking trail #67 on page 168. for the Bear Canyon Sourdough Loop option.) The New World Gulch Trail is better on foot than wheel as muddy, loose and rocky areas punctuate this section that isn't as well maintained as the other Bear Canyon trails.

Search Bear Canyon Trail Custer Gallatin National Forest Trailhead (45.60696,-110.92147)

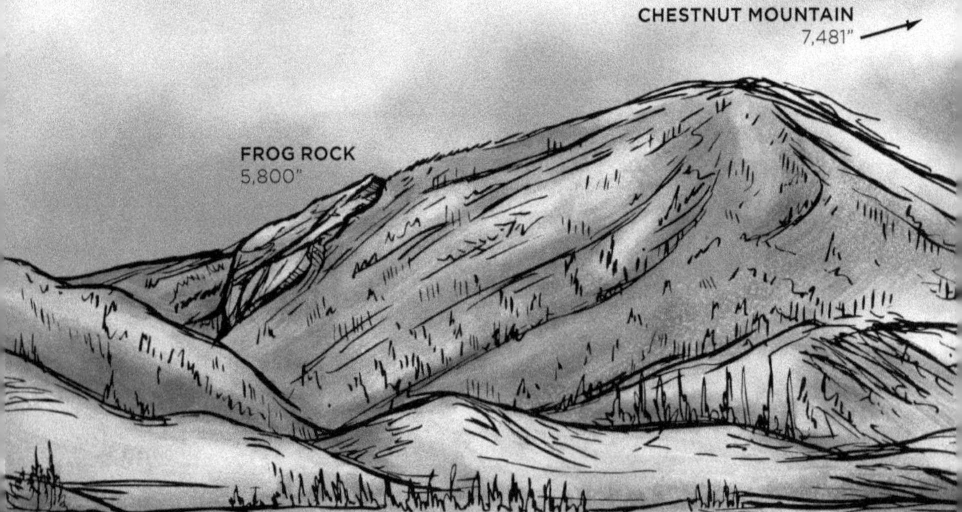

CHESTNUT MOUNTAIN
7,481"

FROG ROCK
5,800"

Frog Rock on the side of Chestnut Mountain

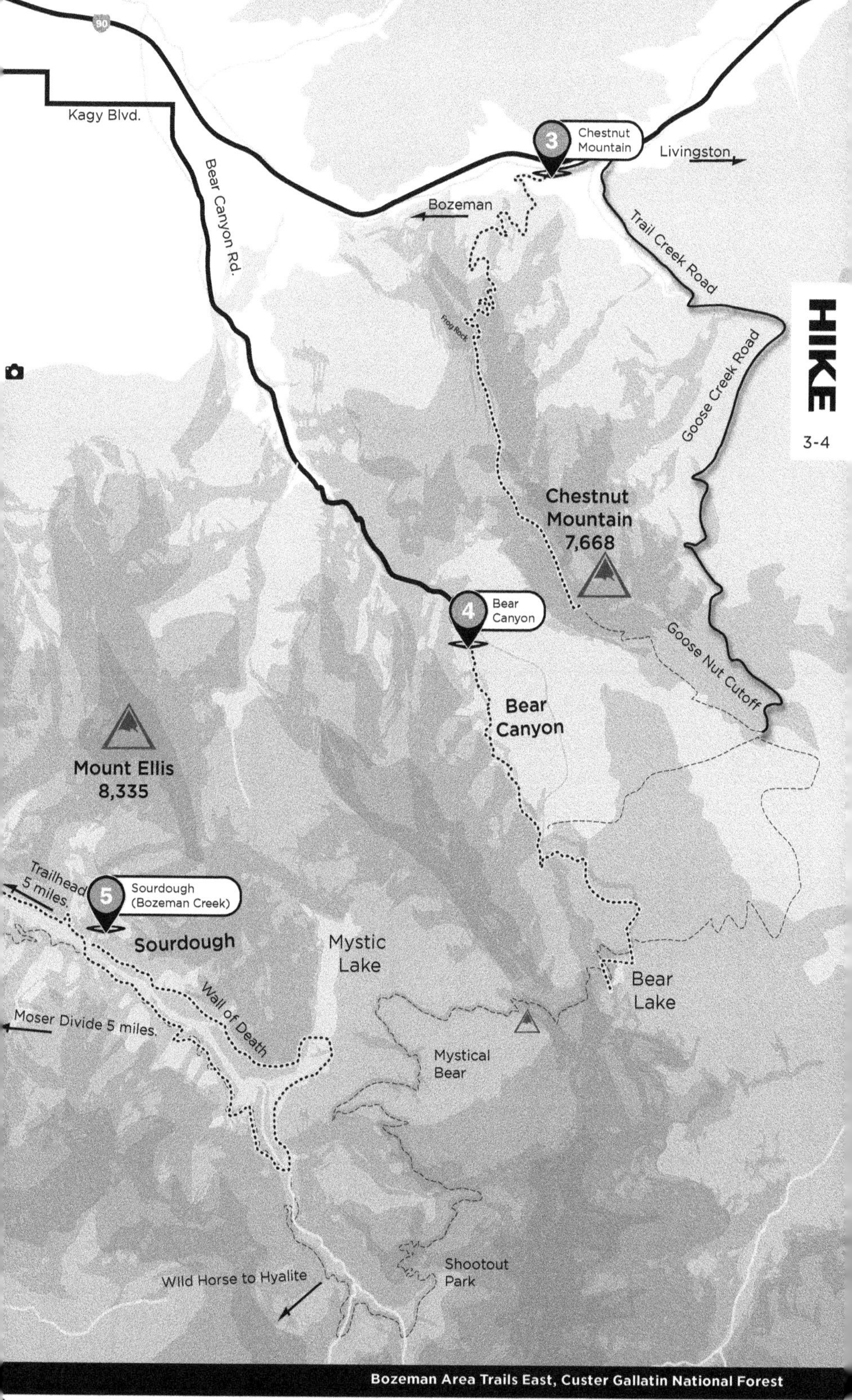

Bozeman Area Trails East, Custer Gallatin National Forest

05. Sourdough (Bozeman Creek)

Loop: .8 miles to several miles
Elevation gain/loss -5 + 5 feet
Top Elevation 5,246 feet
Difficulty: Beginner
Land: GVLT - *Dogs allowed on leash*

The Sourdough trail alongside Bozeman Creek is one of the primary water sources for the city of Bozeman. This converted gravel road is the most popular south-end Bozeman trail. Go as far as you choose. Popular turnaround spots are the resting area bench at 1 mile, poop house at three miles and the bridge at nearly five miles. From the bridge, the road continues up to Mystic Lake at ten miles with an alternate return route down "The Wall of Death" trail (see mountain bike p.170).

Or take a right at the junction up the hill from the bridge to Moser junction. Similar elevation gain and distance as Mystic Lake, this divide connects to Hyalite or Leverich/Kirk Hill. Groomed in the winter by the Bridger Ski Foundation, this trail sees a lot of foot and dog traffic in the first few miles, thinning out the farther you get from the trailhead. Extended loops to Bear Canyon are possible, more often traveled by Mountain bike than on foot due to the distance and elevation gain. It is an off-leash area for dogs, with a waste deposit area provided at the trailhead. Please don't leave poop bags along the trail, pick up dog waste and remember that Bozeman Creek is one of the city's primary sources for drinking water.

Search Mystic Lake - Bozeman Creek Trail, Custer Gallatin National Forest Trailhead (45.59215,-111.02654)

Torrey and Loki heading up the Sourdough trail along Bozeman Creek

Wild Turkey

(Meleagris gallopavo)
Wild Turkeys are native to North America.

This large ground bird can grow up to four feet tall and roosts in trees at night as protection from predators. Gathering in woodsy habitats with open spaces and leaf cover, groups are called rafters, gaggles or flocks.

Wild turkey in full display; flocks of turkeys can commonly be seen on the southern edge of town

BOZEMAN ON FOOT

06. Painted Hills Connector

Out-and-Back: 8 miles
Elevation gain: 810 feet
Top Elevation: 5,282 feet
Difficulty: Moderate
Land: GVLT - *Dogs allowed on leash*

Thanks to continued efforts by GVLT and local landowners, this last remaining connection section was finished in the fall of 2018, connecting Highland Glen trails to Triple Tree via the Painted Hills. This four-mile stretch of trail climbs more heading south from town. Moderate grades are great for trail running and biking. Some steeper sections like "Switchback City" link these otherwise flowing hillside trails. It includes nice Bridger views right from town to the Triple Tree loop through residential neighborhoods with some acreage.

Search Painted Hills to Triple Tree Trail
Bozeman, MT
Trailhead (45.65586,-111.00637)

07. Triple Tree Trail

Loop: 5.4 miles Lollipop Loop
Elevation gain: 958 feet
Top Elevation 5,906 feet
Difficulty: Moderate
Land: Custer Gallatin National Forest

This popular trail can be accessed from the main parking lot off 3rd Avenue South or the informal trailhead road crossing Painted Hills Connector trail junction south end. The trail climbs an open grassy field then descends through a tree canopy and stream crossing, climbing again to the junction. Switchbacks then lead down to a boardwalk stream crossing. This shady spot is popular with kids and dogs on hot summer days.

Take a right at the aspen-filled fork to make a clockwise loop. Sustained switchbacks climb a well-graded path used by hikers, runners, and mountain bikers alike. Arrowleaf Balsamroot flowers fill the open hillside in the springtime, where a well-placed bench is a welcome place for a break and view of the valley.

Watch for runners and bikers on the descent. A leg to the right climbs directly up to the "True Triple Tree" where you can see the namesake trees at the crest of the hill. Keep dogs on leash and give the right of way to other trail users when in doubt. Keep your eyes open for an occasional bear frequenting the area.

Search Triple Tree Trail
Bozeman, MT
Trailhead (45.61302,-111.02165)

Hay baled for harvest along the Painted Hills connector trail

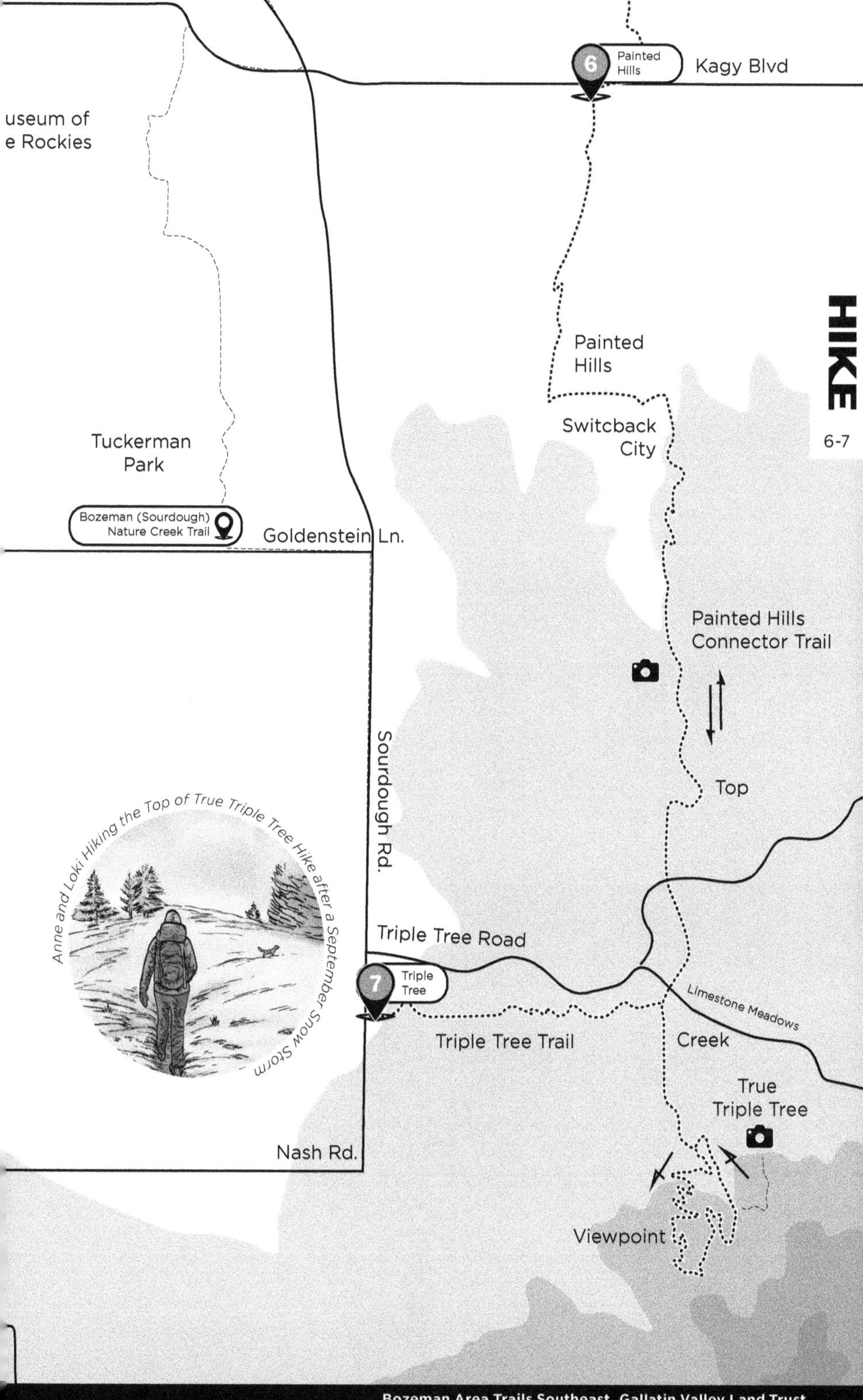

Bozeman Area Trails Southeast, Gallatin Valley Land Trust

BOZEMAN ON FOOT

08. Kirk Hill Trails

Loop: 1.6 miles
Elevation gain: 649 feet
Top Elevation 6,004 feet
Difficulty: Moderate
Land: Custer Gallatin National Forest

Heading south from Bozeman on 19th street as the road turns abruptly west is the trailhead to Kirk Hill trails.

This trail is a series of short, steep connecting loops that traverse and climb the wooded hillside, topping out at the Moser road and connecting to the upper Leverich trail. These trails are foot travel only, unlike the ultra-popular (for mountain bikes) Leverich loop. Great alternative to the busy "M" Trail for hill intervals as a close-to-town option.

Search Kirk Hills Trails
Custer Gallatin National Forest
Trailhead (45.59121,-111.06346)

09. Leverich Canyon Trail

Loop: 5 miles
Elevation gain: 1,269 feet
Top Elevation: 6,924 feet
Difficulty: Moderate
Land: Custer Gallatin National Forest

This lollipop loop's recommended travel is clockwise. Take a left at the junction a quarter mile up the trail from the parking lot. Long switchbacks right from the junction waste no time ascending the forested hillside. The right ones seem longer and harder. A few peek-a-boo views in between rocky flower-filled ridges lead to more switchbacks through the rocky and rooty trail. A makeshift bench at the top of the climb signals the beginning of the epic buffed-out MTB descent (see bike trail#71 on page 171). There are fewer bikes in the winter and springtime as the aspects tend to hold on to snow, so hiking might be a better option. Be aware of mountain bikes traveling the descent at high speeds. A bridge crossing signals that you are almost back to the junction by the trailhead.

Search Leverich Canyon Trail
Custer Gallatin National Forest
Trailhead (45.58403,-111.04066)

Breaking trail after a spring storm dumps two feet of fresh powder on Leverich

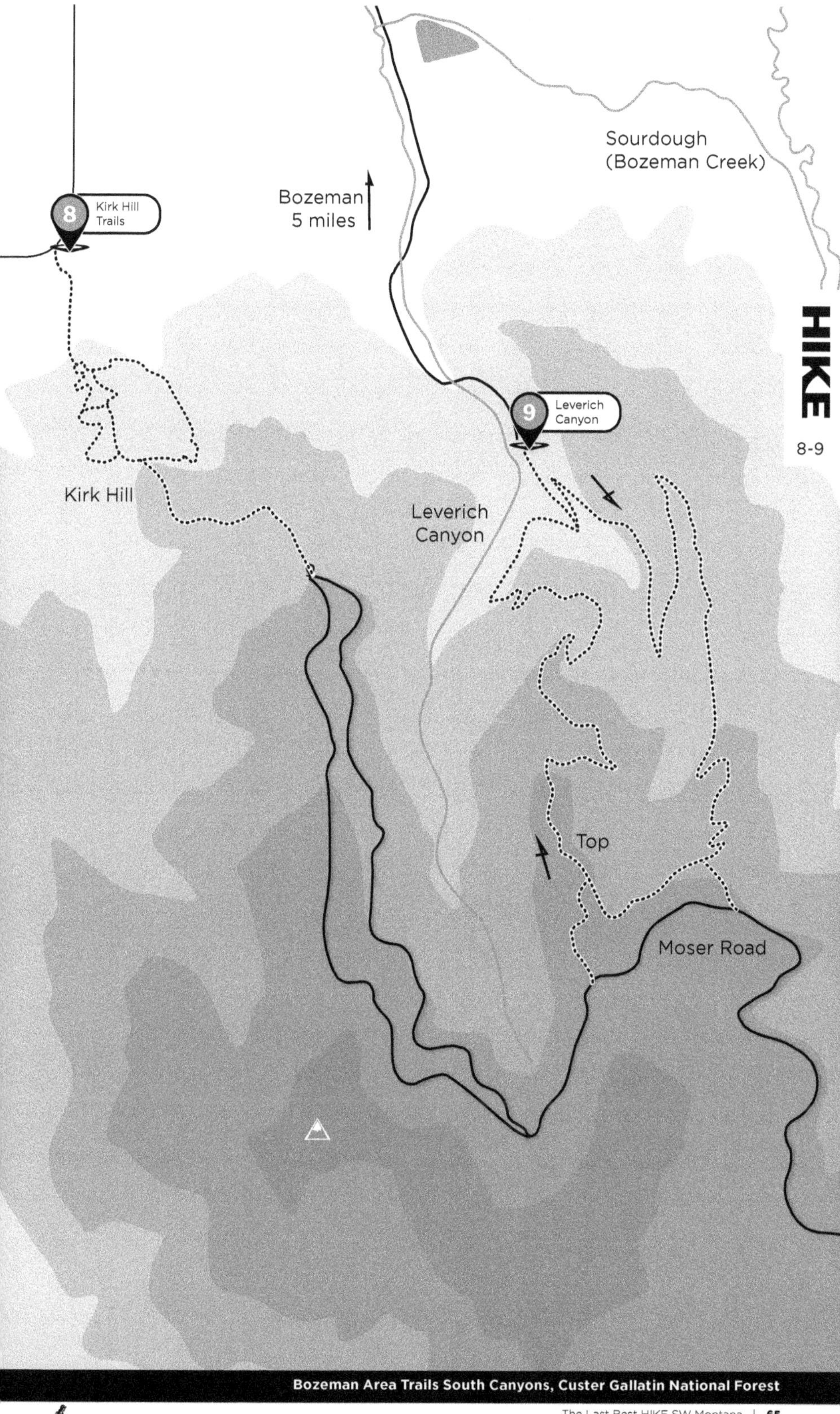

Bozeman Area Trails South Canyons, Custer Gallatin National Forest

BOZEMAN ON FOOT

10. South Cottonwood Creek

Search South Cottonwood Creek Trail
Custer Gallatin National Forest
Trailhead (45.54007,-111.09244)

Out-and-Back: 5 miles
Elevation gain: 524 feet
Top Elevation: 6,004 feet
Difficulty: Beginner
Land: Custer Gallatin National Forest

This pleasant year round, out-and-back trail ranges from a few miles to a 15 + mile shuttle to Hyalite. The wooded trail is often muddy at the start of the switchbacks, then it ascends and descends back to Cottonwood Creek. Along the creek are fun places for kids to take a break and great turnaround spots. This is a popular family hiking trail, running route and a mountain bike out and back. See bike trail #72 on page 174.

People of all ages hike and run the South Cottonwood trail any time of the year

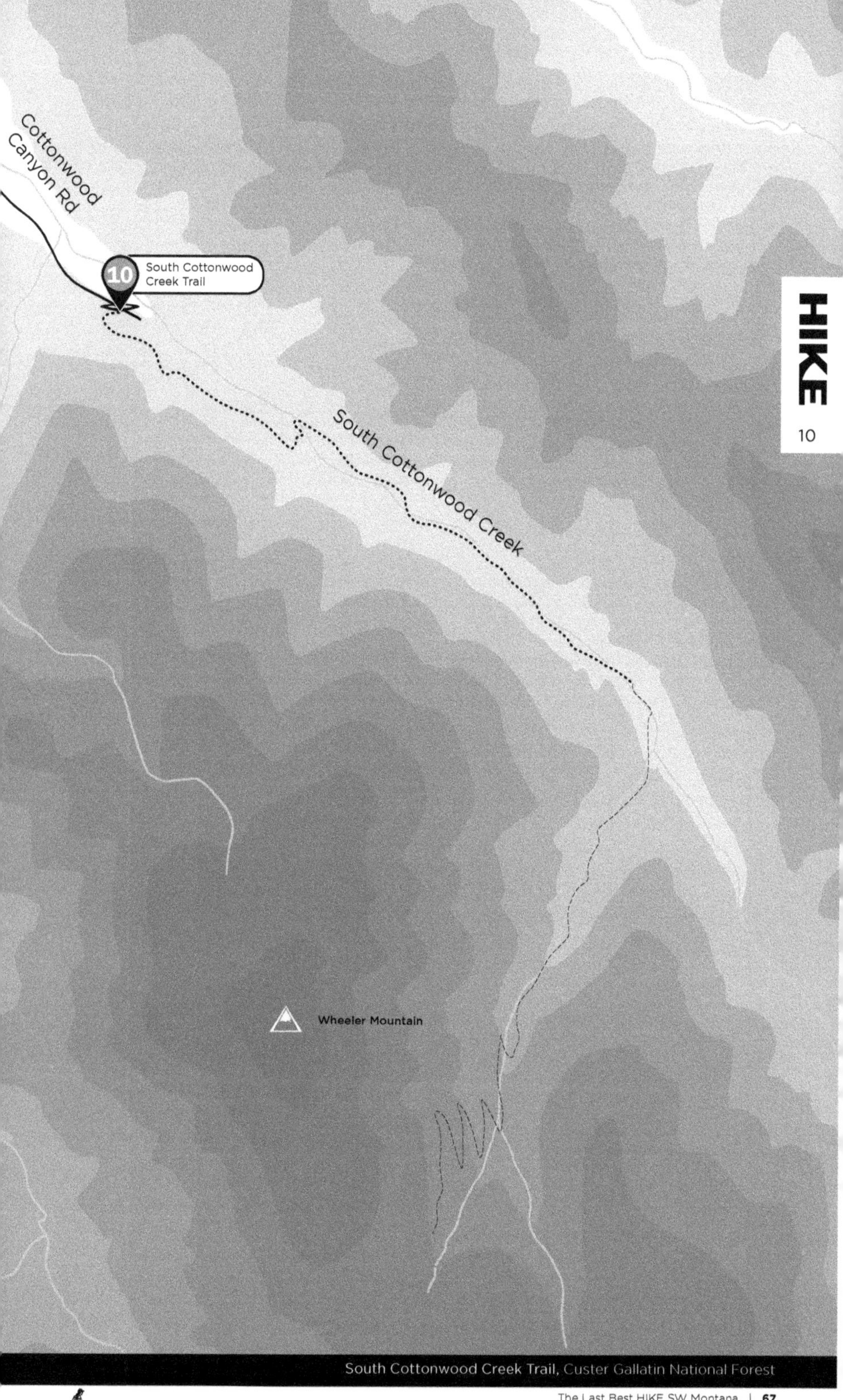

South Cottonwood Creek Trail, Custer Gallatin National Forest

THE BRIDGERS ON FOOT
Bridger Range

Called the Wolf Mountains by the Apsáalooke people (Crow), the Bridgers were later named after the famous mountain man Jim Bridger who led wagon trains through an eastern flank of the range into Bozeman. (See history section)

From short out-and-back hikes to long trail runs and peak bagging options, the Bridgers are packed full of mountain trails.

The most accessible point to the Bridgers from Bozeman is the iconic college "M" trail at the southwest corner of this range. Climbing above the white-painted "M" is the 20-mile Bridger Ridge trail that summits Mount Baldy, Bridger Peak, Saddle Peak and passes by Bridger Bowl and Ross Peak. It ascends Naya Nuki and Sacajawea Peak to the popular trailhead at Fairy Lake on the northeast side of the range.

The lower foothills trail, similar in length as the ridge trail, traverses the Bridgers on lower western flanks, rejoining the ridge trail near the summit of Sacajawea Peak. While the character of these trails is rough and rugged, some sections are suitable for biking as well as hiking.

Multiple finger ridges extend perpendicularly from the main ridge, forming canyon drainages. These western Bridger trails have a similar character of beginning in forested canyons and switchbacking up ridges. The more difficult trails like Sypes and North Cottonwood have eroded, exposing rough and rocky steep sections. Some of the more moderate trails have smoother single tracks but also have sections of exposed sidehill, like Johnson Canyon and Corbly Gulch.

All of these western Bridger trails are moderate to advanced, offering out-and-back or loop options and extending to bike and hike peak-bagging adventures.

The Bridger Mountains have nine registered summits, all accessible by trails. From north to south they are Hardscrabble, Pomp, Sacagawea, Naya Nuki, Ross, Saddle, Bridger, and Baldy above The College M at the south end.

It is possible to bike and hike all of these trails with the exception of Mount Baldy as the college "M" trail is off limits to bikes. There is a bike rack at the "M" trailhead for bike/hike options from town.

Bridger Range from town

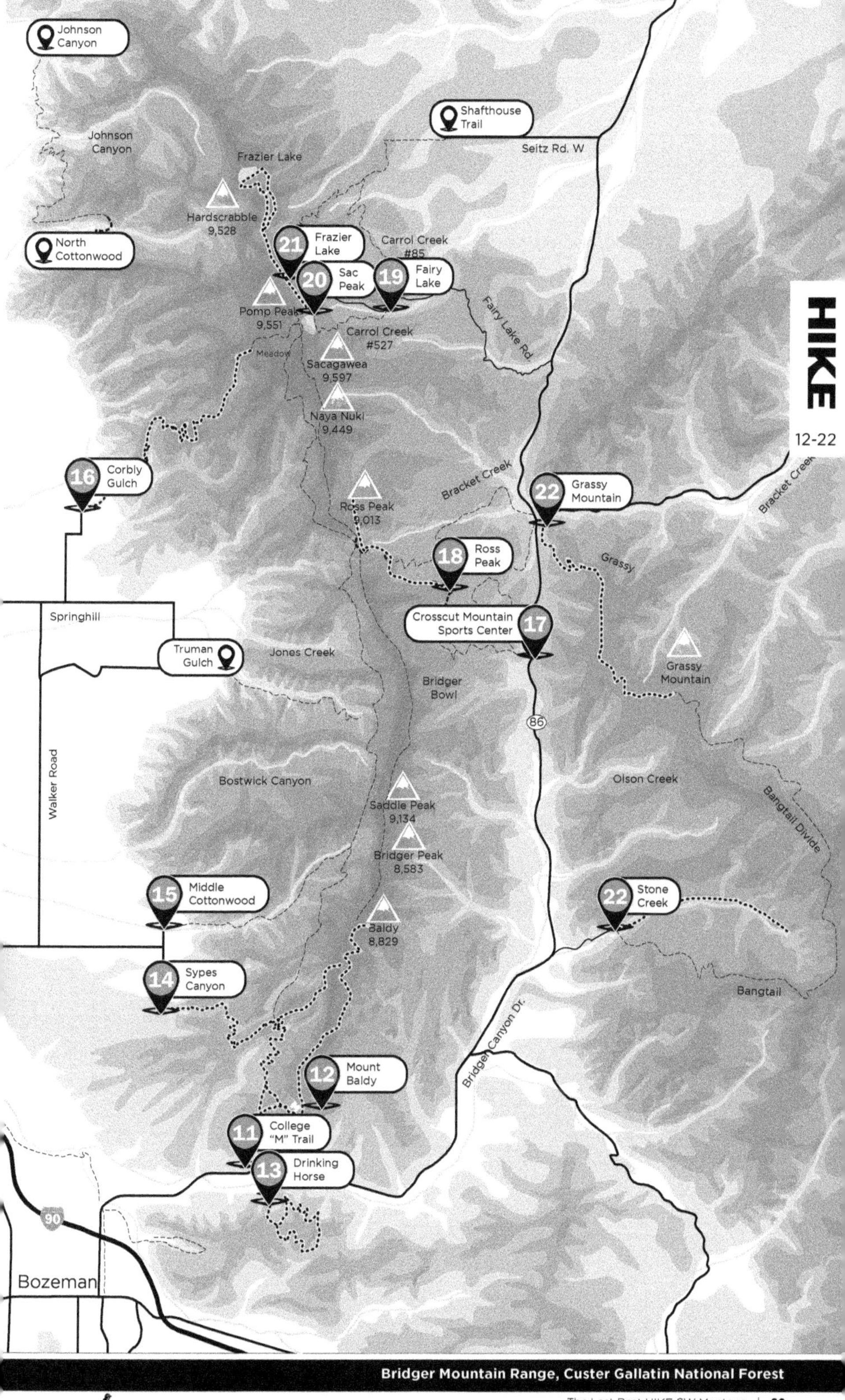
Johnson Canyon
Shafthouse Trail
Johnson Canyon
Frazier Lake
Seitz Rd. W
Hardscrabble 9,528
North Cottonwood
21 Frazier Lake
Carrol Creek #85
20 Sac Peak
19 Fairy Lake
Pomp Peak 9,551
Fairy Lake Rd.
Carrol Creek #527
Meadow
Sacagawea 9,597
Naya Nuki 9,449
HIKE
12-22
16 Corbly Gulch
Bracket Creek
22 Grassy Mountain
Bracket Creek
Ross Peak 9,013
18 Ross Peak
Grassy
Springhill
Crosscut Mountain Sports Center
17
Truman Gulch
Jones Creek
Grassy Mountain
Bridger Bowl
86
Walker Road
Bostwick Canyon
Olson Creek
Saddle Peak 9,134
Bangtail Divide
Bridger Peak 8,583
15 Middle Cottonwood
22 Stone Creek
Baldy 8,829
14 Sypes Canyon
Bangtail
Bridger Canyon Dr.
12 Mount Baldy
11 College "M" Trail
13 Drinking Horse
90
Bozeman

Bridger Mountain Range, Custer Gallatin National Forest

BRIDGERS ON FOOT

11. College "M" Trail

Loop: 3 miles (long version)
Elevation gain: 820 feet
Top Elevation 5,775 feet
Difficulty: Moderate
Land: Custer Gallatin National Forest

The "M" trail is the best-known Bozeman trail and most visible from anywhere around the valley. The viewpoint objective is the obvious white rock "M" on the south Bridger hillside. It is commonplace in many Montana towns to have an initial on the side of a hill. Many towns have the initial of the town, so while you may expect to see a "B" on the hillside, remember that this "M" stands for Montana State University, not to be confused by the Missoula "M" that stands for the University of Montana. Choose from three routes to make to make your hike a loop or out-and-back.

The right steepest path is a mile long and rough, rocky, steep and direct. Going back down on the left trail is a 1.9 mile loop.

The middle one-mile route tucks into wooded switchbacks with one steeper rock section near some bolted climbing routes.

The far left two-mile trail takes a wider swath across the Bridger foothills with open wildflower hillsides and benches along the way. This foothills trail is open to bikes while the others are not.

Search College M Steep Trail
Custer Gallatin National Forest
Trailhead (45.70998,-110.97692)

Bridger fire - September 2020, burning above the College "M" trail

BRIDGERS ON FOOT

12. Mount Baldy

Loop: 9.6 Miles out-and-back 15 miles loop
Elevation gain: 4,330feet
Top Elevation: 8,829 feet
Difficulty: Hard
Land: Custer Gallatin National Forest

Continue straight up from the "M" along "The Ridge" to the popular training summit of Baldy Mountain. Loop down through forest fire debris, taking a right at 8,367'. Offering more scenic overlooks to Sypes Canyon and the Bridger foothills trail, this trail returns to the parking lot in a loop. The Foothills trail continues westward from a switchback on the far left College "M" trail and climbs a steep, rugged section through limestone cliffs to the Sypes Canyon junction atop of the foothills ridge. The Foothills trail continues to climb and descend the lower fingers, extending north/south on the western flank of the Bridgers to the saddle between Bridger and Ross Peaks. While the Foothills trail may sound like a mellow traverse of the range compared to the classic "Ridge trail" that mainly crosses the top of the Bridger range, it is still plenty rough, rugged and adventurous. The well-known Ridge trail is the route of an annual, supported run which begins at Fairy Lake, climbs Sacajawea Peak, past Naya Nuki, Ross, Bridger Peak, then continues southward to Saddle Peak, and Mount Baldy, and, finally, descending steeply to the College "M" and to the parking lot below.

Note that water is unavailable for the most part later in the summer/fall, so bring plenty of water with you.

Search Baldy Peak Summit
Custer Gallatin National Forest
Trailhead (45.70998,-110.97692)

Dan Clark and son Shad moving to keep warm on a first-light Mount Baldy climb

BRIDGERS ON FOOT

13. Drinking Horse

Loop: 2.1 miles
Elevation gain: 656 feet
Top Elevation: 5,512 feet
Difficulty: Moderate
Land: Custer Gallatin National Forest

When viewed from Bridger Canyon traveling back to town, this hill really does look like a drinking horse. The trail is across the road from the College "M." A convenient tunnel under the highway gives access to bike or foot travel, so you can avoid the parking lot and make a bike and hike on this trail as well as the "M" trail. Otherwise park adjacent to the fish technology center. If you aren't in a rush, the fish pools are fun to check out. Similar character to the "M" trail, Drinking Horse climbs switchbacks through the forested hillside to reveal valley views at the top. Dogs and kids enjoy taking a shady break at the ornate bridge crossing Bridger Creek before the switchbacks begin. Loop the trail heading up left through switchbacks in pine trees. Then reach the "summit" with rocky outcroppings shaded by old evergreen trees. This is a popular viewpoint and play spot for kids. Enjoy the upper flower-filled meadows with views across the valley before continuing left to finish the loop on gradual switchbacks. This trail is for foot travel only. Bikes aren't allowed.

Search Drinking Horse Mountain Trail Custer Gallatin National Forest Trailhead (45.70775,-110.98019)

The view from the backside of Drinking Horse coming out of Bridger Canyon

Meghan Schaeffer taking in the wildflower and valley views on the Drinking Horse trail

BRIDGERS ON FOOT

14. Sypes Canyon

Out-and-Back: 6.2 miles
Elevation gain: 1,620 feet
Top Elevation: 6,824 feet
Difficulty: Moderate
Land: Custer Gallatin National Forest

The Bridger foothills are a handful of finger ridges that protrude perpendicular to the range's north-south backbone. The ridges descend westward onto plains that drop gradually to the valley floor through ranches and neighborhoods that dot the hillsides. Sypes is a canyon hike that crests onto a ridge and highpoint junction with the Bridger Foothills trail. This trail's rocky sections grow increasingly rougher and looser as they are worn away by weather and human use. It is a popular and challenging mountain bike trail and can be traveled as an out-and-back hike/trail run or extended by making a loop with the connecting section of Bridger foothills trail.

Shuttle cars to the "M" trailhead to the east or connect to Middle Cottonwood Trail or Truman Gulch to the west.

Truman Gulch, Middle Cottonwood, Corbly Gulch, and Johnson Canyon are all trails of a similar character and worth checking out.

Search Sypes Canyon
Custer Gallatin National Forest
Trailhead (45.74528,-111.008)

13-14

Sypes Canyon Trail, Western Bridgers

BRIDGERS ON FOOT

15. Middle Cottonwood

Out-and-Back: 2.8 miles
Elevation gain: 480 feet
Top Elevation: 6,004 feet to Junction
Difficulty: Moderate
Land: Custer Gallatin National Forest

The Middle Cottonwood trail ascends towards Saddle Peak from the west Springhill road. There are multiple creek crossings and waterfalls in lush foliage that keep this hike interesting and cool on hot days.

Extend the hike by continuing steep switchbacks to the summit of Saddle Peak in just over ten miles round trip and 4,000 feet vertical gain.

Search Middle Cottonwood Trail 586
Custer Gallatin National Forest
Trailhead (45.86076,-111.03998)

16. Corbly Gulch

Out-and-Back: 8
Elevation gain: 1,596 feet
Top Elevation: 7,063 feet at Meadow
Difficulty: Moderate
Land: Custer Gallatin National Forest

This farthest gulch to the west was rebuilt to make the contours more enjoyable. Enjoy long, flowing switchbacks and scenic overlooks on the way up to the meadow. This trail is popular for mountain biking (see trail #76 on page 182). Above the lookout the trail gets rocky and rooty. Cross a stream into the meadow. This is a great picnic and turnaround spot. The trail climbs through avalanche paths into open alpine meadows where switchbacks lead to the Sacagawea Summit Trail.

The Corbly trailhead can be impassable in the spring/fall when wet. The gumbo mud should be avoided until it dries out. Four-wheel drive and high clearance vehicles are recommended for the last few miles to the trailhead.

Search Corbly Gulch Trail
Belgrade, MT
Trailhead (45.86076,-111.03998)

Kiersten,Meghan and Loki hiking to Sacagawea Peak from the western Corbly Drainage

17. Crosscut Mountain Sports Center

Foot Trail Single-track : 10 miles
Elevation gain: 3,619 feet
Top Elevation 6,780 feet Loggers Loop
Difficulty: Easy
Land: Custer Gallatin National Forest

Sitting adjacent to Bridger Bowl alpine ski area is the Crosscut Mountain Sports Center. This area is a year round mountain hub for human-powered recreation. (See ski book and bike book.) It is used by athletes of all abilities, from elite Nordic and Paralympic skiers to elementary-high school mountain bike training. It is also a fun, convenient trail system to explore on foot.

The groomed Nordic trails in the winter have a summer complement of hiking and mountain biking-specific trails. A network of trails connects from the outer double-track Loggers Loop that spans the outskirts of the area to the north. Adjacent to Bridger Bowl and to US Forest Service lands, Crosscut is a non-profit organization committed to fitness and the appreciation of nature. Upper trails connect to the Northern Bridgers from the ski area to Ross pass. Although there are no lakes, major water features or other destinations, it is a popular place for easy-to-access hiking and trail running.

Visit Crosscutmt.org for info
& trail opening dates
Trailhead (45.82870,-110.88404)

18. Ross Peak Saddle

Out-and-Back : 8.4 miles
Elevation gain: + 3,619 feet
Top Elevation: 7,645 saddle- 9,004 Summit
Difficulty: Moderate, Hard scramble to summit
Land: Custer Gallatin National Forest

A more apt name for Ross Peak might be "Wizard Hat" or "Dragon's Head." The peak rises dramatically like a snake head emerging from a spiny rock backbone that contours along the ridge of the Bridger Mountains.

Drive up the South Brackett Creek road to a small parking lot and trailhead. From here are nice views of Banana Couloir located on the approach to the saddle below Ross Peak. A single track trail climbs to the saddle, connecting with the Ridge trail. From here, take the obvious climber's path directly to the base of the rock-filled gullies. The official trail ends here at the Ridge Trail intersection at 7,645 feet.

To continue to the summit, follow a mountain goat trail that connects gullies and rocky passageways to the exposed summit. This section of the hike does not require technical climbing but can be exposed in places. Rockfall, route finding and exposure are risks of summiting Ross Peak.

Search Ross Peak
Custer Gallatin National Forest
Trailhead (45.84584,-110.9008)

Looking up Ross Peak from the Ridge Trail Saddle, Bridger Range

19. Fairy Lake

Lollipop Loop: 1-5, 5 Miles lower parking
Elevation gain: 100 around lake 977 feet
Top Elevation 7,579 feet
Difficulty: Beginner - Moderate
Land: Custer Gallatin National Forest

The notoriously bad road winds up seven miles from the Bridger highway to reach the Fairy Lake parking lot and a .5 mile access to the lake. Fairy Lake sits in a northeastern basin on the flanks of Sacagawea Peak. If your vehicle can't handle the bumpy, rutted last few miles of the road, park at the lower lot and hike up the dual track section of the Shafthouse loop (see mountain biking #78 p.184).

The trail around the lake is about one mile, skirting the shoreline and providing plenty of swimming spots and areas for lounging with friends or hanging hammocks and rope swings in the trees. It is no wonder that Fairy Lake is a Bozeman classic alpine lake hangout spot.

The main parking lot by the lake is also used for access for climbing Sacajawea Peak. (See next page)

Search Fairy Lake
Custer Gallatin National Forest
Trailhead (45.90889,-110.92821)

HARDSCRABBLE
9,528"

Torrey flying over Fairy Lake

20. Sacagawea Peak

Out-and-Back: 5.2 Miles
Elevation gain: + 1,975feet
Top Elevation: 9,579 feet
Difficulty: Advanced
Land: Custer Gallatin National Forest

Extend your hike by climbing Sacagawea Peak or shuttling cars to the "M" trail and hike or run the entire 20-mile ridge route. The summit trail ascends to the northwest of the lake, gaining a snow-filled bowl in the spring and switchbacks to the ridge. Take a left heading south at the saddle to the switchback summit trail. It is common to see families of goats at the summit. Give them plenty of space as those horns are sharp. Towards Naya Nuki is the popular skiing chute that typically holds snow until mid summer. See Chris Kussmaul's book "Peaks and Couloirs of Southwest Montana" for more details.

Search Sacagawea Peak
Custer Gallatin National Forest
Trailhead (45.90679,-110.96029)

Rocky Mountain Goat

(Oreamnos americanus)
With striking white coats and pointy horns, these sure-footed goats call the Bridgers home. Often traveling in families, they can be seen on or near the summits of Sacajawea Peak, Naya-Nuki Peak, as well as Pomp and Hardscrabble peaks to the north.

These goats frequent areas where hikers have urinated as salt is a scarce necessity in the high mountains.

Ranging in size from 99 to over 300 pounds, the males are larger with longer beards and horns than their female counterparts. Their dense fur helps them withstand harsh cold winter conditions and winds, which are common in the high mountains throughout the year.

Mountain goats forage on low-growing shrubs, lichen and conifers.

A kid I met on the summit of Sacagawea, Bridger Range

BRIDGERS ON FOOT

21. Frazier Lake

Lollipop Loop: 2.8 Miles
Elevation gain: + 1,437 feet
Top Elevation: 8,563 feet
Difficulty: Moderate
Land: Custer Gallatin National Forest

Competing with its next-door neighbors, the ultra-popular Fairy Lake and Sacajawea Peak, the less-visited region of the northern Bridgers holds Frazier Lake beneath granite rock walls.

The trailhead to Frazier Lake is past Shafthouse, although it can also be reached via Shafthouse trail if you want a longer, more roundabout way to get there. Otherwise you can find the trailhead just off the parking lot opposite the Fairy Lake trailhead.

This trail goes pretty much straight up and may be discontinuous. Continue upward until cresting a ridge where the lake will be visible. Frazier Lake catches snow from the rugged and steep Bridger peaks. (See the section on Back Country Skiing - Bridgers for more information) Snow melt fills the lake, and, by August, it can be completely evaporated and filled with mosquitoes. So choose your time wisely to see this gem in its full alpine splendor.

Search Frazier Lake
Custer Gallatin National Forest
Trailhead (45.91132,-110.96057)

Rough-legged Hawk

(Buteo lagopus)
Rough-legged Hawks are frequently seen perching on telephone poles and fences, hunting small rodents, field mice and voles.

The Rough-legged Hawk is the most common of the Buteo Hawks. Taking advantage of beneficial updrafts, thousands of hawks migrate over the Bridger Mountains every fall.

Check out the annual Bridger Raptor Festival at Bridger Bowl Ski Area in October.

Rough-legged hawk taking a break while migrating north

BANGTAILS ON FOOT

22. Grassy Mountain

Out-and-Back: 5.7 Miles
Elevation gain: + 1,725 feet
Top Elevation: 6,689 feet
Difficulty: Moderate
Land: Custer Gallatin National Forest

The ultra-classic Bangtail Divide trail is a long day on foot but done more commonly as a point-to-point mountain bike ride from Stone Creek trailhead to Grassy Mountain trailhead at Bracket Creek (see bike trail #80 on page 186). Both trailheads have out-and-back day hikes through forest canopy switchbacks to scenic overlooks of the Bangtail Range that runs parallel to the Bridgers to the east.

Search Green Mountain Trail #94
Custer Gallatin National Forest
Trailhead (45.76397,-110.85441)

23. Stone Creek

Out and Back: 4.4 Miles
Elevation gain: + 498 feet
Top Elevation: 6,135feet
Difficulty: Easy
Land: Custer Gallatin National Forest

On the south end of Bangtail Divide is the Stone Creek trailhead. The trail begins immediately climbing switchbacks over rocky terrain through an evergreen forest. Take the forest road 480 along Stone Creek for a mellower out-and-back trail that is friendly for hikers of all ages. This is less traveled than the Bangtail route; however, the parking lot is very busy. This trail is dog friendly as well.

Search Stone Creek Trail
Custer Gallatin National Forest
Trailhead (45.76397,-110.85441)

Single track on Grassy Mountain, the Bangtails

HYALITE FOOT TRAILS

Hyalite Canyon

Welcome to the state's most popular US Forest Service recreation area - Hyalite Canyon. Like Mystic Lake to the north, Hyalite Reservoir is the center of outdoor activities in the area. Hyalite Creek and the trail following the creek is the best hike in Hyalite Canyon.

The trail ascends along Hyalite Creek past a dozen waterfalls to alpine Hyalite Lake and Hyalite Peak at 10,300 feet. The Gallatin crest travels further 20+ miles to the southeast from here.

The road is paved to Hyalite Reservoir and continues to the reservoir's northeast side. Expect difficult road conditions in the winter. The Friends of Hyalite plow the road, but in between storms and the plowing, the road can become rutted, icy, and treacherous despite the high traffic volume.

The Schaeffer family enjoying the golden hour while camping at Hyalite Reservoir

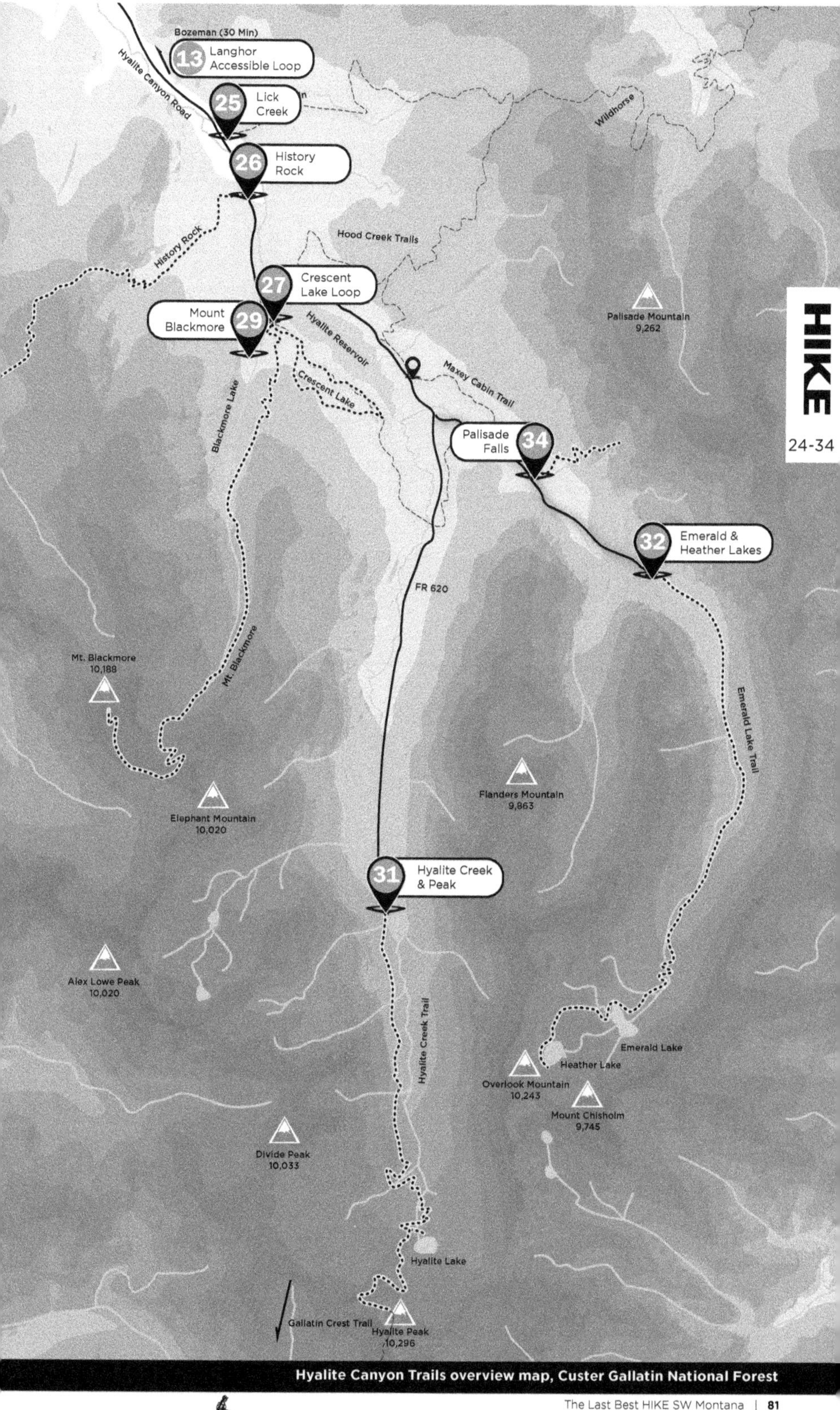

Hyalite Canyon Trails overview map, Custer Gallatin National Forest

HIKE
24-34

24. Langhor Loop Accessible Trail

Loop: .3 to 2 miles
Elevation gain/loss -5 + 5 feet
Top Elevation 5,246 feet
Difficulty: Beginner
Land: Custer Gallatin National Forest

At Langhor Campground the wheelchair accessible Hyalite Creek Interpretive trail begins at the bridge crossing Hyalite creek. Often ignored by Langhor campers and the crowds driving past on their way to Hyalite Reservoir, this loop follows along the south side of Hyalite Creek, providing access points for fishing, interpretive signs for learning and benches for resting. This is a great place to bring kids as well as grandparents to stretch the legs and do some forest bathing along the creekside.

There is another Langhor Meadows road/trail up the paved road that can be used as an out-and-back trail for hiking, biking, or skiing.

Search Langhor Creekside Trail
Custer Gallatin National Forest
Trailhead (45.53381,-111.01497)

25. Lick Creek Loop

Loop: 4.7 miles
Elevation gain/loss + 813 feet
Top Elevation: 6,759 feet
Difficulty: Moderate
Land: Custer Gallatin National Forest

Drive past the cattle gate and up the gravel road to the trailhead. This trail is also a good snow hike, ski or snowshoe trip, as well as a great mountain bike ride or hike/trail run in the summer. This loop passes through an evergreen forest into open grasslands, crossing over several cattle guards. The trail connects to Buckskin and Moser trails to the north or Hyalite trails to the south for a longer trip. From the Moser jump off road, cross an intersection to Moser Creek Road and loop back on the FS6220. This loop is less popular and crowded than other loops closer to the lake. There are several parking spots at the gate entrance, and additional spots across the road to the south.

Search Lick Creek Loop
Custer Gallatin National Forest
Trailhead (45.5371,-111.01642)

Anne and Torrey taking a winter walk up Lick Creek

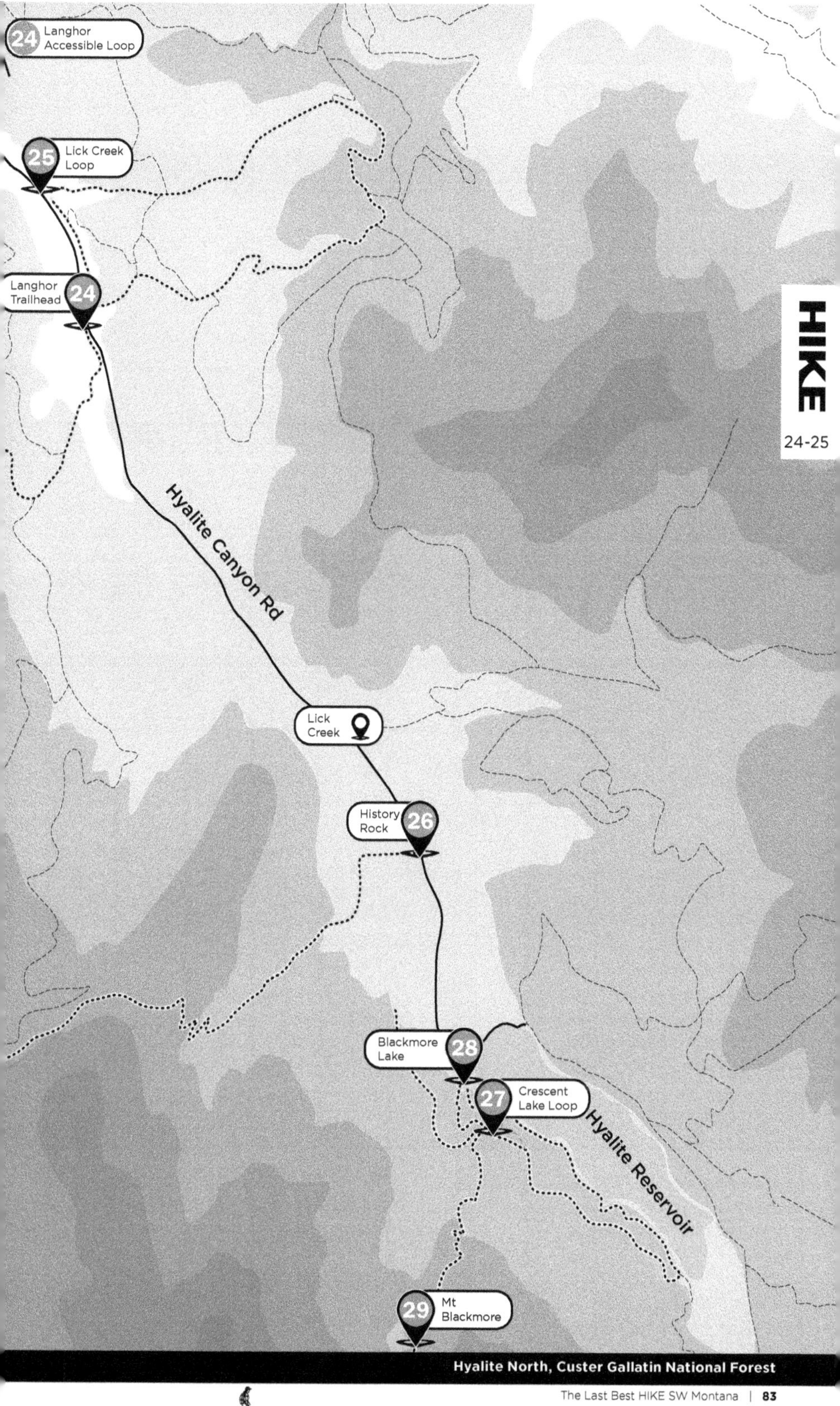
24 Langhor Accessible Loop
25 Lick Creek Loop
Langhor Trailhead 24
Hyalite Canyon Rd
Lick Creek
History Rock 26
Blackmore Lake 28
27 Crescent Lake Loop
Hyalite Reservoir
29 Mt Blackmore
HIKE
24-25
Hyalite North, Custer Gallatin National Forest

26. History Rock

Out-and-Back: 6.5 Miles
Elevation gain/loss + 1,496feet
Top Elevation 7,973 feet
Difficulty: Easy
Land: Custer Gallatin National Forest

A trailside protrusion of limestone rock covered with the carvings of early settlers is the attraction of this stretch of trail - a pleasant hike for all ages. This out-and-back is a short 1.2-mile hike to the actual History Rock which crosses an open meadow and climbs switchbacks up to the rock.

Continue up switchbacks to an overlook of Blackmore Peak at the junction to the South Cottonwood trail to complete the full distance. (see trail#72 on page 174).

Search History Rock Trail, Langhor Park, Custer Gallatin National Forest Trailhead (45.49856,-110.98457)

Trailside limestone-autographed History Rock

HYALITE ON FOOT

27. Crescent Lake Loop

Loop: 3.3 Miles
Elevation gain: + 347 feet
Top Elevation: 6,890 feet
Difficulty: Easy
Land: Custer Gallatin National Forest

Walk alongside two lakes, Hyalite Lake and the much-smaller Crescent Lake, in this short loop from the main parking lot at Hyalite Reservoir. Although there is minimal elevation gain, the trail is a fun, interesting loop, popular for snowshoeing and skiing in the winter or hiking, running and mountain biking in the summer.

This often overlooked loop begins at Hyalite Reservoir parking lot.

Extend the hike by going around to Langhor loop/Hyalite Lake or hike to Blackmore Lake and climb Blackmore Peak.

Search Westshore and Crescent Lake Loop, Custer Gallatin National Forest Trailhead (45.48476,-110.97982)

Great Blue Heron

(Ardea herodias)

Being the largest heron in North America, the Great Blue Heron lives up to its name. With a wing span ranging from five and a half to six and a half feet, the heron is a dominent prescence in marshy areas where it fishes and is often seen standing patiently looking for a meal.

In flight the neck is curved in an "S" shape.

Crescent Lake, Hyalite

HYALITE ON FOOT

28. Blackmore Lake

Out-and-Back: 4.3 Miles
Elevation gain: +905 feet
Top Elevation: 7,448 feet
Difficulty: Moderate
Land: Custer Gallatin National Forest

The trail to Blackmore Lake/Peak can be accessed from the Blackmore trailhead or a shorter route from Hyalite Reservoir. A few connector trails between the West Shore Trail and Crescent Lake Trail connect to the Blackmore trail along Blackmore Creek. This popular hike to the mountain lake is frequented by hikers, horseback riders and ambitious mountain bikers.

Connecting old logging roads to weaving single track, this trail rises before a short steep descent through a rocky trail to the lake basin.

The lake is shallow and may dry up later in the summer depending on the year.

Search Blackmore Trail
Custer Gallatin National Forest
Trailhead (45.48952,-110.98293)

MOUNT BLACKMORE
10,188"

Blackmore Peak viewed from Blackmore Lake - Hyalite

HYALITE ON FOOT

29. Mount Blackmore

Out-and-Back: 12.9 Miles
Elevation gain: + 3,756 feet
Top Elevation: 10,188 feet
Difficulty: Hard
Land: Custer Gallatin National Forest

The Blackmore trailhead is located up the road from the Hyalite and Crescent Lake access points, with a series of short access trails that connect to the Blackmore trail from the reservoir. The lake is more of a shallow pond later in the summer. Take a look to the east from the lake to see Blackmore Peak rising above. From here the rocky, rough trail climbs steeply, crossing streams, to emerge in high alpine meadows at the north basin of the peak. Switchbacks crest the ridge at the saddle junction. Take a right to the trail that makes a diagonal swipe up to the summit of Blackmore Peak with views of Hyalite Reservoir and nearby peaks; Elephant, Alex Lowe Peak and the South Cottonwood drainage to the south.

Bikes are not allowed from the saddle to the summit. So make a great hike and bike by stashing your ride in the tree line.

Search Mount Blackmore via Blackmore Trail, Hyalite Trailhead (45.48952,-110.98293)

Ridge to summit of Blackmore Lake, Alex Lowe Peak in the background, Custer Gallatin National Forest

HYALITE CREEK WATERFALLS

1. Grotto

2. Twin Falls

5. Silken Skein

6. Champagne

8. Shower

9. Apex

3. Arch

7. Chasm

11. Alpine

Photo Reference Courtesty
- Sebastian Petzing

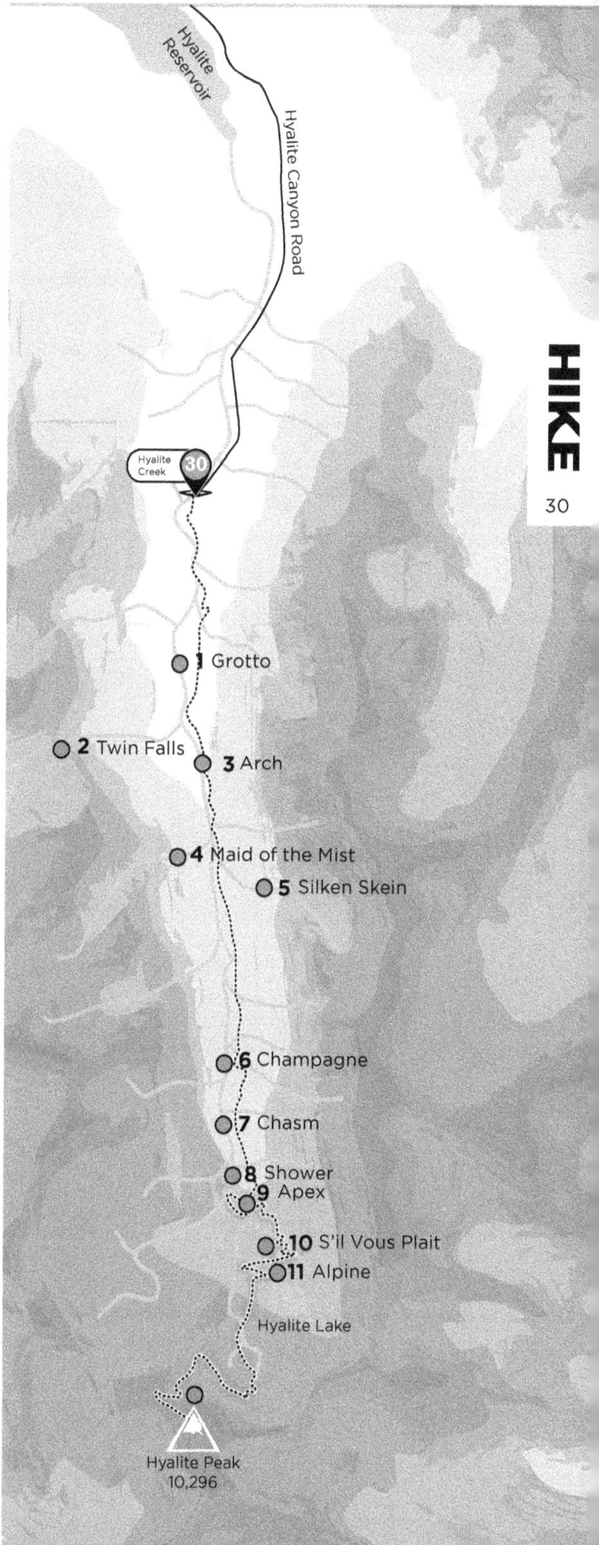

Hyalite Reservoir

Hyalite Canyon Road

Hyalite Creek 30

1 Grotto

2 Twin Falls

3 Arch

4 Maid of the Mist

5 Silken Skein

6 Champagne

7 Chasm

8 Shower

9 Apex

10 S'il Vous Plait

11 Alpine

Hyalite Lake

Hyalite Peak
10,296

HIKE
30

Hyalite Creek, Custer Gallatin National Forest

HYALITE ON FOOT

30. Hyalite Creek to Hyalite Lake

Out-and-Back: 10.9 Miles
Elevation gain/loss +2,139 feet
Top Elevation 8,892 feet
Difficulty: Hard
Land: Custer Gallatin National Forest

At the southeast edge of Hyalite Reservoir, the road ends at the parking lot for the Hyalite trailhead.

The trail is used year-round. In the winter, boot-packed climber trails lead to various frozen waterfall ice climbing routes throughout the area. The primary path is the summer hiking trail along Hyalite Creek, passing a series of waterfalls on the way to the high alpine lake. The information sign, posted by the outhouse at the trailhead, dates when motor bikes and mountain bikes can share the trail with foot travel. Hyalite Creek flows by the parking lot into Hyalite Reservoir, one of the main fresh water sources for the City of Bozeman, along with Bozeman Creek. The trail follows Hyalite Creek all the way to its source, Hyalite Lake in the basin below Hyalite Peak.

Eleven waterfalls are visible from the Hyalite Creek Trail. Grotto Falls at a mile and a quarter in, is the most visited and a great out-and-back hike for kids.

Twin Falls can be seen trail right high above the trail partially obscured by trees. The side by side falls drain from high Palace Lake.

At 2.5 miles reach a signed resting spot and the viewing area for Arch Falls. While there is a trail to the brink of the falls (watch your footing), the best views of the arch are from below. Down climb/ scramble to reach the creek side and straight on view of the magnificent arch. Do not attempt if trail is wet or frozen.

Silken Skien cannot be seen from the trail. There is a sign at 3.5 miles marking the short trail to view this falls. The trail can be a bit of a bushwack and requires a stream crossing. The lower falls are viewable a fourth of a mile in. Climb to another vantage point to see the larger higher falls. This has a potentially exposed rock area to reach the upper falls. Don't attempt if the trail is wet or frozen.

Maiden of the Mist falls is across the valley and, depending on the season, numerous cascades can be seen on the face of Hyalite Peak. *Cont. next page*

Search Hyalite Creek to Hyalite Lake Trail Hyalite Trailhead (45.44742,-110.96229)

Arch Falls, one of several spectacular waterfalls along Hyalite Creek.

HYALITE ON FOOT

31. Hyalite Peak

Out-and-Back: 14.5 Miles
Elevation gain/loss +3,487 feet
Top Elevation 10,296 feet
Difficulty: Hard
Land: Custer Gallatin National Forest

Cont. from previous page

A log bridge crosses the creek above the stone sidewalk to Apex Falls. S'il Vous Plait and Alpine falls greet you on the final switchbacks into the alpine lake basin of Hyalite Lake beneath the 10,298' Hyalite Peak. All of the waterfalls along the way make for a great turnaround points.

Arch Falls is next past Grotto Falls. A steep scramble down to the trail's right offers a viewpoint of the falls through the arch.

Silken Skien, a small but pretty waterfall, is a short distance for viewing. Champaign Falls is right off the trail as well as Chasm Falls and Shower Falls. Crossing a foot bridge, the switchbacks steepen, passing S'il Vous Plait Falls. Alpine Falls gains the final switchback into the lake basin.

In the early summer after the snow melts, enjoy wildflowers on the summit. The summit offers a fantastic view back across Hyalite Canyon. Snow fills the entire basin and the northern aspect can keep much of it through mid-summer. The switchbacking trail beyond the lake can stay snow-covered through the spring and mid-summer.

Although Hyalite Peak isn't the tallest peak in the range, its prominent position is perhaps the most aesthetic.

Views extend to the Bridgers, Absaroka-Beartooths across Paradise Valley, the Spanish Peaks and Madison Range to the south.

The summit of Hyalite Peak is also a starting point for the Gallatin Crest trail. This backpacking route travels southward, towards Big Sky, in the high country. The 42-mile trail can be backpacked in 2-4 days.

Search Hyalite Creek to Hyalite Lake Trail Hyalite Trailhead (45.44742,-110.96229)

Sebastian Petzing on the summit of Hyalite Peak photo reference - Sebastian Petzing

HYALITE ON FOOT

32. Emerald Lake

Out-and-Back: 9.5 Miles
Elevation gain/loss +2,165 feet
Top Elevation 8,924 feet
Difficulty: Hard
Land: Custer Gallatin National Forest

A sister drainage to Hyalite Creek, Emerald Lake is a ten mile out-and-back trail with similar elevation gain to the Hyalite Lake hike. This trail is closed to mountain bikes on Sundays and Mondays during summer peak trail season (see trail#73 on page 175).

33. Heather Lake

Out-and-Back: 10.5 Miles
Elevation gain/loss +2,165 feet
Top Elevation 9,220 feet
Difficulty: Hard
Land: Custer Gallatin National Forest

Beautiful Emerald lake offers great camping sites, as does Heather Lake one mile up the trail in the top basin. Heather lake sits in a cliff-lined basin with no trail access to the top of the ridge. There is a rugged loop around the lake which passes a few campsites on the north side. No trip to Emerald or Heather Lake is complete without a dip in the water.

Search Emerald and Heather Lake Trail, Hyalite Trailhead (45.45831,-110.92132).

Butterflies grace cone flowers in the alpine lake basin that holds both Emerald and Heather Lakes

HYALITE ON FOOT

34. Palisade Falls

Out-and-Back: 1.1 Miles
Elevation gain/loss + 239 feet
Top Elevation 7,185 feet
Difficulty: Easy
Land: Custer Gallatin National Forest

The paved parking lot is large enough for tour buses that funnel people up the paved .6-mile trail to the base of Palisade Falls. This highly-photographed falls drops 80 feet over basalt columns. When frozen, the falls have ice climbing routes ranging from WI 3 to WI 4+. The boot-packed trail is hikeable nearly year-round. After feeling the misty spray along the stream bank, return via the steep, winding paved trail to the parking lot.

This highly-photographed falls is a scenic destination with an easy to moderate approach depending on the weather conditions.

It is a good choice for a family hike or winter hike to check out the forming ice columns and the possibly seeing climbers dangling from the ice.

Search Palisade Falls, Hyalite Custer Gallatin National Forest Trailhead (45.46887,-110.93906)

Angela Krey checking out a partially frozen Palisade Falls, Hyalite

GALLATIN CANYON FOOT TRAILS
Gallatin

A series of drainages on both sides of the Gallatin River offer hiking trails and climbing access at the mouth of the canyon and to old-school rock climbing routes on the Gallatin Tower, Skyline Buttress, Spare Rib and other formations that are visible from the highway.

Lava Lake captures more than its fair share of moisture and is lush traveling along Cascade Creek, a nod to the Pacific Northwest.

Storm Castle is a relatively short hike with incredible summit views across the Gallatin River and valley.

Bighorn Sheep
(Ovis canadensis)

Named for its pair of large curling horns that can weigh up to 30lbs, the Bighorn sheep is native to North America.

Males use the impressive curls to butt heads with rivals during the rutt. Their muscular, compact bodies (weighing up to 500 lbs) and cloven hooves make them natural climbers. They prefer steep rocky terrain, which gives them some natural protection against predators like wolves.

Females also have horns, but they are much smaller and straighter.

Bighorn sheep can often be seen along the roadside on the drive to Big Sky - Photo reference Steve Morehouse

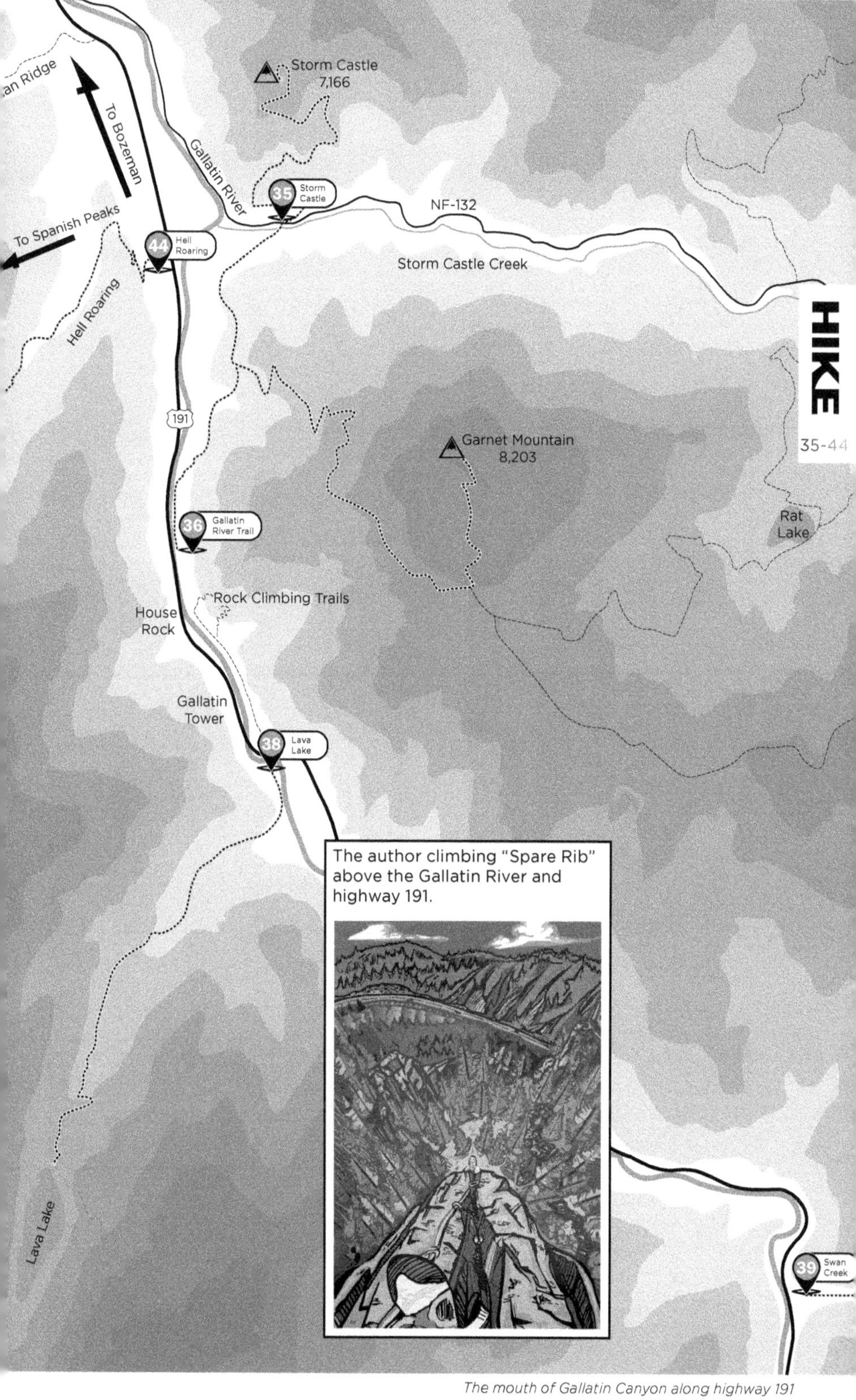

The author climbing "Spare Rib" above the Gallatin River and highway 191.

The mouth of Gallatin Canyon along highway 191

GALLATIN CANYON ON FOOT

Search Storm Castle Trail
Custer Gallatin National Forest
Trailhead (45.44125,-111.22323) 

35. Storm Castle Peak

Out-and-Back: 5.2 Miles
Elevation gain/loss +1860 feet
Top Elevation 7,166 feet
Difficulty: Moderate
Land: Custer Gallatin National Forest

This limestone-capped peak's rocky summit offers dramatic views over the Gallatin River. The stone window feels like a high fortress in the clouds. This is a great training hike/run to get the legs and lungs ready for peak bagging. Steep switchbacks, but not for a long distance, along with the payoff summit view, make this a popular hike near Bozeman at the mouth of Gallatin Canyon.

Loki looking through the limestone window to the Gallatin Valley below - the top of Storm Castle Peak

GALLATIN CANYON ON FOOT

36. Gallatin River Trail

Out-and-Back: 5.5 Miles
Elevation gain/loss + 200 feet
Top Elevation 5,446 feet
Difficulty: Easy
Land: Custer Gallatin National Forest

From the same trailhead as Storm Castle, cross the road and bridge over Storm Castle creek. The trail ascends a well-buffed single track through Douglas Fir to a junction. The trail to the right meanders through meadows and along the Gallatin River before it peters out among boulders and river bends.

The trail dead ends where the river bends and spring run-off erodes the bank. The middle section has no trail.

Upriver is House Rock (in the river) and paths to climbing routes. Access the climbing area trails to the north of the river from the pullout just across the bridge on the highway and across the river from the Lava Lake trailhead.

Search Gallatin Riverside Trail, Custer Gallatin National Forest Trailhead (45.44125,-111.22323)

Explore the steep, loose approach trails to old-school "trad" climbs on a series of buttresses emerging from the hillside above the river. A nice, short and flat stretch of trail follows along the river to a viewpoint of House rock. These trails are mostly used for rock climbing and river access. Unfortunately they don't connect to the Gallatin Riverside trail farther downstream, but would be cool if it did.

Gallatin Tower and area climbs are on the highway's south side, accessed by a small pullout before reaching the bridge. These climber trails are short and direct to the tower's base, with many classic "trad" rock routes.

STORM CASTLE
7,165"

Storm Castle on a stormy autumn day from the Gallatin River, Gallatin Canyon

GALLATIN CANYON ON FOOT

37. Garnet Lookout

Out-and-Back: 7.7 Miles
Elevation gain +2,814 feet
Top Elevation 8,203 feet
Difficulty: Hard
Land: Custer Gallatin National Forest

From the same trailhead as Storm Castle, cross the road and bridge over Storm Castle creek. The trail ascends a well-buffed single track through Douglas Fir to a junction.

Take a left at the junction to climb increasingly steep and exposed switchbacks to a double-track junction, the right trail goes down to Rat Lake and trailhead shared with ATVs.

This is another short hike option from the trailhead past Storm Castle Creek road, and a loop option for mountain biking (see trail#75 on page179).

Go left up the steep double track to the fire lookout at the summit. The fire lookout can be rented year round and reserved online. From the summit, views of adjacent Storm Castle Peak, the Gallatin River and the wooded hills extend northeast to Moser/Hyalite.

Search Garnet Mountain Trail
Custer Gallatin National Forest
Trailhead (45.44125,-111.22323)

Fire lookout at the top of Garnet Mountain overlooking the Gallatin River and Storm Castle

GALLATIN CANYON ON FOOT

38. Lava Lake

Out-and-Back: 6 Miles
Elevation gain + 1,620 feet
Top Elevation 7,087 feet
Difficulty: Moderate
Land: Custer Gallatin National Forest

Despite the name and its popularity, Lava Lake is actually pretty cold most of the year. Reminiscent of a Cascades mountain alpine lake with rocky peaks rising above.

This hike ascends along Cascade Creek which drains into the Gallatin River just past the small trailhead parking lot. This lush drainage attracts more moisture than surrounding areas and it is home to ferns, mosses and other lush foliage.

The trail ascends to the right of the creek to a sidehill where it traverses to the last steeper switchback section that climbs into the lake basin.

Prominent campsites sit above the rocky shore. A ridge trail to the east ascends to other trails in the Spanish Peaks Lee Metcalf Wilderness.

This popular hike has a small trailhead, parking fills up fast, especially on summer day weekends. There is more parking across the river, but a sketchy bridge crossing on the highway might be something you would want to avoid.

Search Lava Lake Cascade Creek Trail
Custer Gallatin National Forest
Trailhead (45.4063,-111.22448)

Meghan and Loki approaching the rocky beach of Lava Lake, Gallatin Canyon

GALLATIN CANYON ON FOOT

39. Swan Creek

Out-and-Back: 7.7 Miles
Elevation gain/loss +2,814 feet
Top Elevation 8,203 feet
Difficulty: Hard
Land: Custer Gallatin National Forest

The Swan Creek trail meanders through forests, rock fields, hillsides, and bends in the creek. This scenic and peaceful trail can be traveled all the way to Hyalite Peak and the Gallatin Crest trail.

There are plenty of streamside rest spots to take a break before returning from a trip length of your preference.

Search Swan Creek Trail to South Fork Swan Creek, Custer Gallatin National Forest. Trailhead (45.37231,-111.17423)

40. Hidden Lakes

Out-and-Back: 5.5 Miles
Elevation gain +1,259 feet
Top Elevation 9,056 feet
Difficulty: Moderate
Land: Custer Gallatin National Forest

The cobblestone-like Portal Creek road provides access to the Hidden Lakes trailhead, as well as the trailhead for Windy Pass and Golden Lakes. Drive just over 6 miles on the road, taking a right at the first junction. The Hidden Lakes trail starts with a series of switchbacks on a double track shared with side-by-sides and other ATVs. The track levels out providing occasional views across the drainage of lakes that are hidden in the forested hillsides. There are eight lakes total. Cross Hidden Creek to climb the trail access of the two least-hidden of the lakes. The other lakes require more adventurous off-trail orienteering but promise solitude.

Pack some topo maps, a compass, and your GPS to explore off trail to find the other hidden lakes.

Search Hidden Lakes Custer Gallatin National Forest Trailhead (45.28224,-111.15205)

Torrey and Anne checking out a colorful old growth tree on the way to the Hidden Lakes

GALLATIN CANYON ON FOOT

41. Golden Trout Lakes

Out-and-Back: 6 Miles
Elevation gain/loss + 1,620 feet
Top Elevation 7,087 feet
Difficulty: Moderate
Land: Custer Gallatin National Forest

This trail shares the same trailhead as the Windy Pass trail and is accessed via the Portal Creek road. Take the trailhead to the right, continuing on the road grade, the single track trailhead to the left goes to Windy Pass.

Pack a fishing pole to spend some lazy hours casting at the lake.

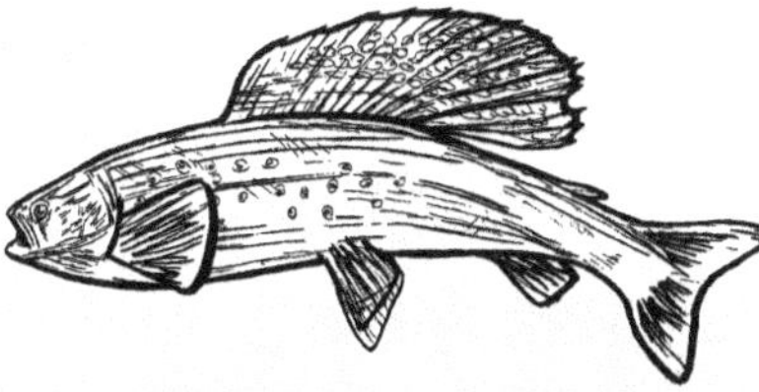

Artic grayling; one of the native species found in some of Montana's alpine lakes along with Golden Trout, Rainbow Trout, Brown Trout and The State Fish - Cutthroat Trout

Search Golden Trout Lakes Trail
Custer Gallatin National Forest
Trailhead (45.258,-111.12789)

42. Windy Pass

Out-and-Back: 7.7 Miles
Elevation gain + 1,994 feet
Top Elevation 9,941 feet
Difficulty: Moderate
Land: Custer Gallatin National Forest

This trail begins in the forest, descends to a creek crossing then switchbacks beautiful stream pools and a scenic waterfall.

This is the perfect spot to refill water before emerging from the forest into grassy hillsides. View the rentable cabin to the left and take a right to gain the Gallatin Crest trail where the views start to open up.

This ridge trail that connects Hyalite to Big Sky is over 40 miles and is a popular 2-4 day backpack shuttled route, that stays in the high country for the most part. Explore to the north or south before returning on the route if you haven't arranged a shuttle.

Search Windy Pass Trail
Porcupine-Buffalo Horn
Trailhead (45.25822,-111.12779)

Windy Pass trail looking towards Golden Trout Lakes

THE SPANISH PEAKS ON FOOT

North Madison Range

Access to the Spanish Peaks is near the entrance to Gallatin Canyon from the north where Spanish Creek joins the Gallatin River. The public access road goes through Ted Turner's Flying D Ranch where bison graze in the fields. If you see bison along the road, give them plenty of space and stay on the road as this stretch is through private land. Watch for other wildlife along the road - deer, elk, foxes, coyotes, and, possibly, bears and wolves. Drive nine miles from the highway to a parking lot and the Spanish Creek trailhead (and entrance to the Lee Metcalf Wilderness). In the summer the trailhead is used for wilderness horse packing, backpacking and the approach for the hike to ski the "blaze." In the winter the road is gated four miles from the trailhead and can be skied, hiked or biked, depending on snow coverage. The gate typically opens in May.

The Spanish Peaks mountain range is a backpacker's paradise with lakes, peaks and plentiful wildlife. The range includes the highest mountain in the area, Gallatin Peak at 11,015 feet, numerous rock climbing routes and the "blaze" - a backcountry skiing destination in the summer (see page 258 of Chris Kussmaul's "Peaks and Couloirs of Southwest Montana" for details in backcountry skiing.)

A variety of two to three-day backpacking trips can be completed in the Spanish Peaks, with loops or incorporating shuttles to the Hell Roaring trailhead, North Fork/Bear Basin or Beehive Basin trailheads.

With its numerous lakes and scenic campsites, the Spanish Peaks is an area worth exploring.

North American Bison raised on Ted Turner's Flying D Ranch.

GALLATIN PEAK
11,015"

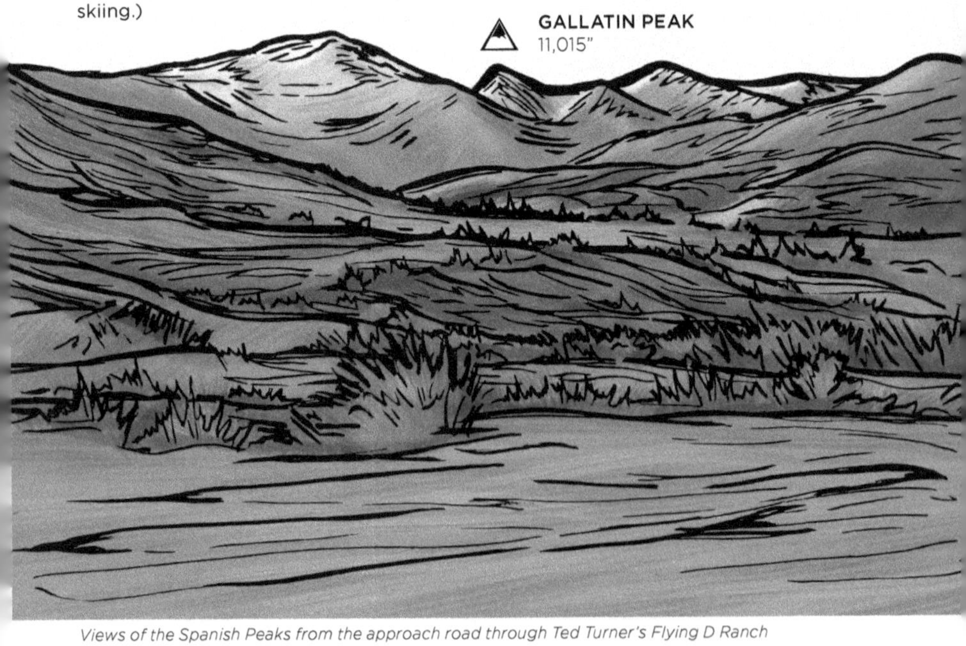

Views of the Spanish Peaks from the approach road through Ted Turner's Flying D Ranch

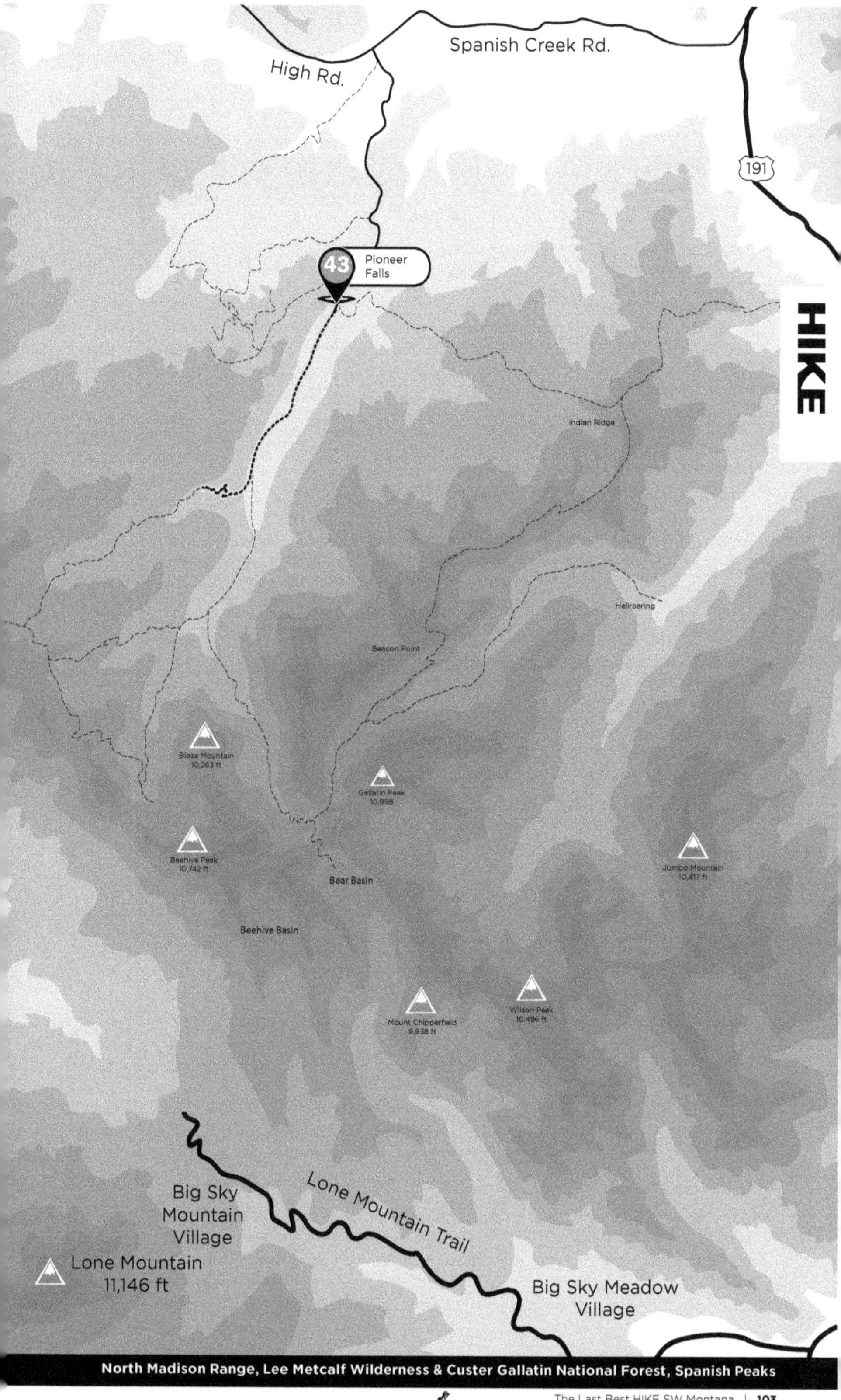

North Madison Range, Lee Metcalf Wilderness & Custer Gallatin National Forest, Spanish Peaks

SPANISH PEAKS ON FOOT

43. Pioneer Falls

Out-and-Back: 6.5 Miles
Elevation gain +810 feet
Top Elevation 6,890 feet
Difficulty: Easy - flat to switchbacks
Land: Custer Gallatin National Forest

The Pioneer Falls hike makes a great introduction to the Spanish Peaks. Begin the hike by crossing the South Fork of Spanish Creek near the trailhead. Be sure to carry bear spray as this is grizzly country.(see page 32 "Bear Country")

The first three miles to the trail junction follows the creek with little elevation gain. There are many shaded spots and stream-side hitching posts for horses; yield to horse packers and riders that you meet by stepping off to the side of the trail. At the meadow junction take a right towards Jerome Lakes. Switchbacks climb 450 vertical feet to a viewpoint and resting spot at the top of the 40' falls and a turn around point for a day hike. Enjoy cool, shaded pools between the boulders in Pioneer Creek.

Extend the trip by continuing to Jerome Lakes to camp or make a loop passing by Lake Solitude the Spanish Lakes, and returning to the trailhead along Spanish Creek.

44. Hell Roaring

Out-and-Back: 4.5 Miles
Elevation gain + 744 feet
Top Elevation 5,873 feet
Difficulty: Easy
Land: Custer Gallatin National Forest

Further up the Gallatin Canyon highway is the Hell Roaring Creek trailhead. The trail starts with switchbacks on a forested hillside before dropping to Hell Roaring Creek and crossing a substantial bridge. Continue on to a flower-filled meadow and seasonal blueberry picking. If your motivation for the hike isn't limited to berry picking, continue hiking to Hell Roaring Lake or take the trail to the right towards Summit Lake at the base of Gallatin Peak.

Gallatin Peak, at 11,015', is the highpoint of the Northern Madison Range/ Spanish Peaks. This peak is deep in the rugged Spanish Peaks and the approach is long from any direction. The common approaches include Hellroaring to Summit Lake, or Bear Basin via the North Fork Trail or Beehive Basin, descending and climbing again to get on the east ridge of Gallatin Peak.

Backpacking between Thompson and Summit Lakes at the foot of Gallatin Peak

Sandhill Crane

(Antigone canadensis)

The Sandhill Cranes travel in pairs or in family groups. These pre-historic looking birds frequent open fields where they scratch for corn and wheat seeds while migrating through Montana in the spring and fall.

These birds are large like Blue Herons but they fly with their necks and legs fully extended. Their distinctive call is positively prehistoric.

Sandhill Crane making a pit stop in the Spanish Peaks, Custer Gallatin National Forest

BIG SKY ON FOOT

Town Center to Moonlight Basin

Page 106 - Driving south through Gallatin Canyon, the terrain opens up to dramatic views of Lone Mountain, the home of Big Sky Resort - the largest ski area in the United States.

Big Sky has numerous trails that are easily accessed from the town trail network. Listen to the Podcast episode about the Big Sky Community Organization's master trail plan on page 199.

Ousel Falls is a popular trail with easy access from the town center. Up the road, just past the Big Sky Ski Resort and towards Moonlight Basin is the trail to Beehive Basin. At 8,500 feet, an unnamed lake sits in the alpine basin at the base of a rock outcropping and steppingstone to Beehive Peak, which is the southern border of the Spanish Peaks.

At a popular spot for backcountry skiing, the author skins up Beehive Basin

Kiersten, Meghan and Loki approaching Beehive Basin on a bluebird summer day

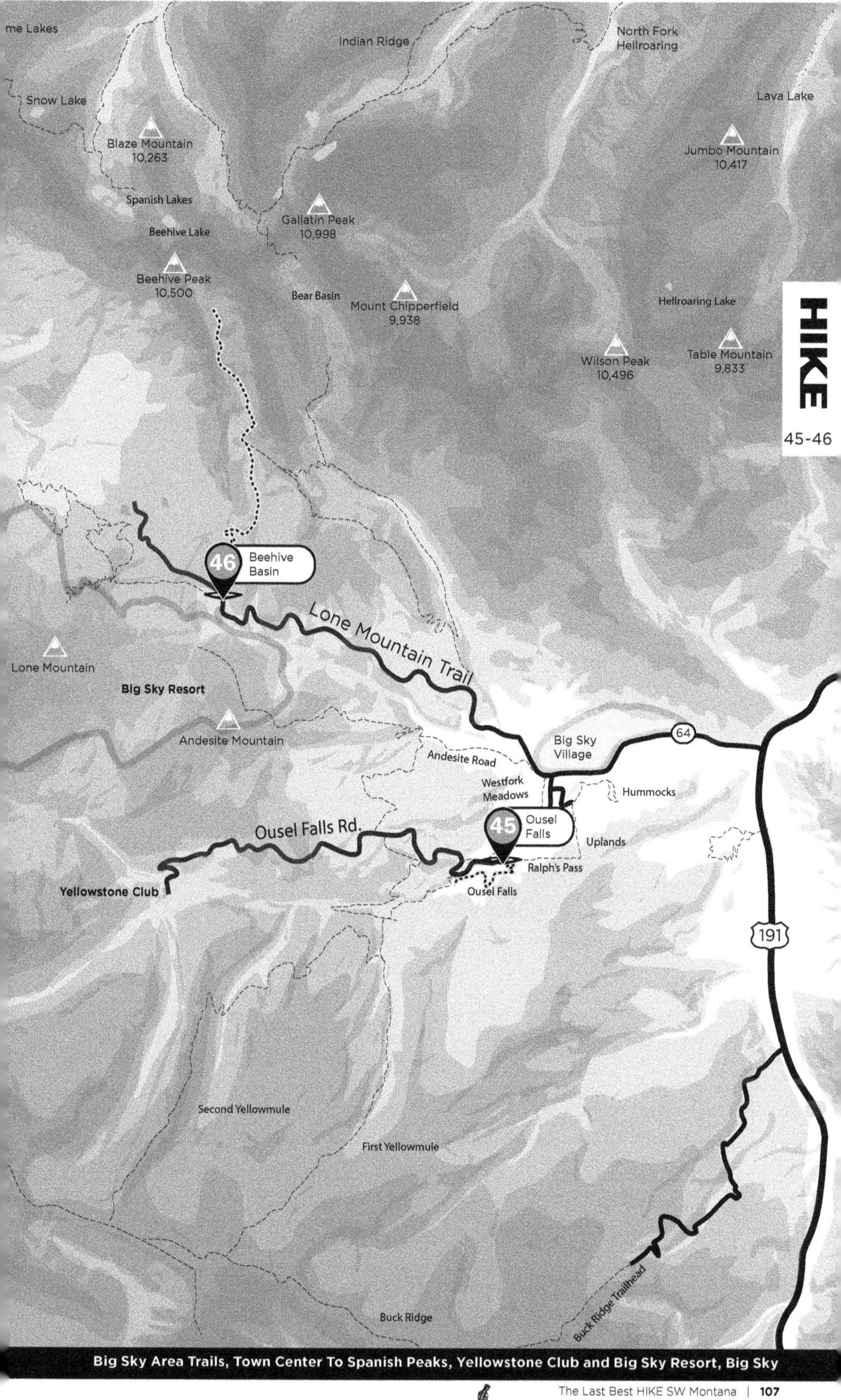

Big Sky Area Trails, Town Center To Spanish Peaks, Yellowstone Club and Big Sky Resort, Big Sky

BIG SKY ON FOOT

45. Ousel Falls

Out-and-Back: 7.7 Miles
Elevation gain/loss +2,814 feet
Top Elevation 8,203 feet
Difficulty: Hard
Land: Custer Gallatin National Forest

American Dipper, AKA the Water Ousel - Photo Reference Kiersten Schaeffer

Big Sky's most accessible and popular trail is just a few miles from the town center. It is accessible via bike path along the South Fork of the West Fork of the Gallatin.

This short and well-constructed trail descends a supported path from the parking lot diagonally down the hillside to the first bridge crossing. The trail follows along the water to another bridge crossing as the cliff walls narrow. Climb a short rise to the Ousel Falls overlook.

There is an open spot at the base of the falls where you can observe the power of the 35' cataract and maybe spot one of its namesake feathered friends too.

Search Ousel Falls Park Trail
Big Sky Montana
Trailhead (45.24414,-111.33237)

North American Dipper

(Cinclus mexicanus)
The North American Dipper, or Water Ousel, lives in Montana year round. Locating clean, fast-running streams in winter months, they dip their heads under the water or dive for insects. Ousels, very sensitive to water pollutants and are commonly seen at pristine mountain streams. These entertaining birds appear to be flying underwater when hunting.

Ousel falls from trail overlook

46. Beehive Basin

Out-and-Back: 7.1 Miles
Elevation gain/loss + 1,650 feet
Top Elevation 9,515feet
Difficulty: Moderate
Land: Lee Metcalf Wilderness

This popular trail is accessed through Moonlight Basin Ski Area. Arrive early in the day to the small parking lot at the trailhead as it fills up fast in hiking season and, also, in the winter as a backcountry playground (see trail # 96 on page 246).

The hike climbs to an elevation of 9,515 feet, but the reward is being in a sublime alpine basin. This is a great place for a picnic and/or a turn around spot for a day hike.

Extend the trip by hiking the path above the unnamed lake in the basin through rocky outcroppings and alpine hillsides to higher basins at the foot of Beehive Peak - recognizable by horizontal black stripes in the rock. There are a handful of quality multi-pitch rock climbing routes up the face.

The standard descent rappel route for climbers is Fourth of July couloir on the left. The couloir is also the standard winter climbing route to the peak. For the hiker, the saddle further to the left /south can be ascended to a notch and a talus slope that descends on the other side of the peak to the true Beehive Lake, making an interesting/challenging access to the Spanish Peaks.

Search Beehive Basin Trail 40
Big Sky Montana
Trailhead (45.30666,-111.38516)

North Madison Range, Spanish Peaks, Beehive Basin trail, Lee Metcalf Wilderness

Gallatin to West Yellowstone

As it leaves the canyon, the Gallatin River, flows through rolling terrain on the western edge of Yellowstone National Park. There are many great hikes in this area - Fawn Pass being, perhaps, the most notable, and a popular ski tour in the winter.

West Yellowstone is Montana's western entrance to Yellowstone National Park.

Bobcat
(Lynx rufus)

Smaller than the other resident big cat in Montana, the Mountain Lion, the Bobcat is recognizable by its short "bobbed" tail which is how it got its name. Solitary and residing in wooded areas where it hunts rabbits, rodents, and birds, the Bobcat is reclusive, and sightings are rare. But you may run across winter tracks on Nordic ski trails.

The Bobcat is also the mascot for Bozeman's Montana State University.

Bobcat stalking prey

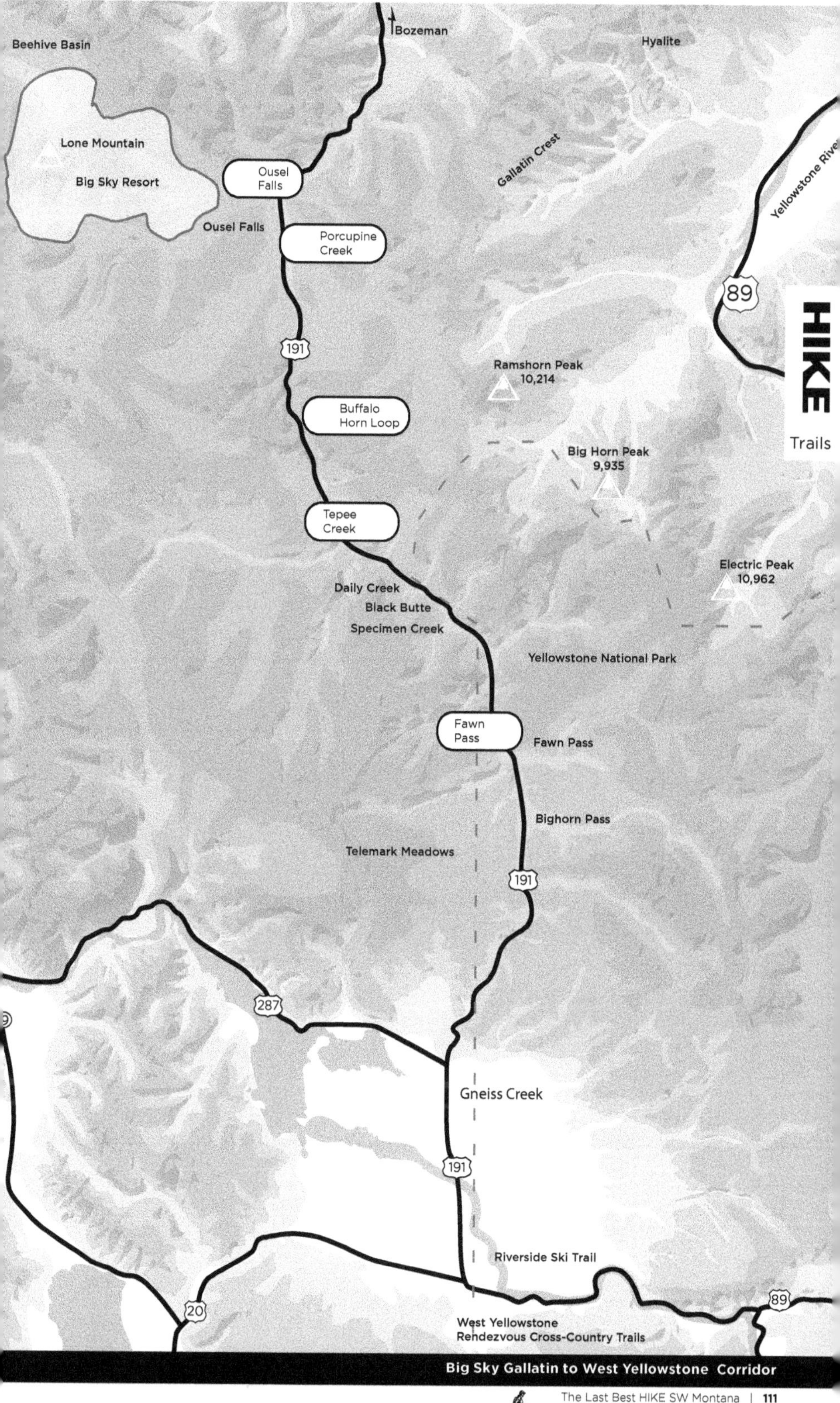
Bozeman
Beehive Basin
Hyalite
Lone Mountain
Big Sky Resort
Gallatin Crest
Yellowstone River
Ousel Falls
Ousel Falls
Porcupine Creek
89
191
HIKE
Trails
Ramshorn Peak 10,214
Buffalo Horn Loop
Big Horn Peak 9,935
Tepee Creek
Electric Peak 10,962
Daily Creek
Black Butte
Specimen Creek
Yellowstone National Park
Fawn Pass
Fawn Pass
Bighorn Pass
Telemark Meadows
191
287
Gneiss Creek
191
Riverside Ski Trail
89
20
West Yellowstone
Rendezvous Cross-Country Trails

Big Sky Gallatin to West Yellowstone Corridor

YELLOWSTONE CORRIDOR ON FOOT

47. Porcupine Creek

Out-and-Back: 3.5 Miles
Elevation gain +390 feet
Top Elevation 6,398 feet
Difficulty: Easy
Land: Custer Gallatin National Forest

The lollipop loop meanders through horse hoofed packed meadows along a rise with views of Lone Mountain and crosses Porcupine Creek at the apex to return along the other side of the stream. There is a bounty of wildflowers in the spring. There is no bridge across Porcupine Creek at the top of the loop, so use caution crossing during spring runoff.

Extend your hike to an eight mile loop continuing through fir forests on the west side of the drainage. There are other connections to more remote trails in this NW corner of Yellowstone National Park.

(For meadow and crust skiing in late winter/ early spring see trail#97 on page 248)

Search Porcupine Creek
Custer Gallatin National Forest
Trailhead (45.2233, -111.242)

48. Buffalo Horn to Ramshorn Lake

Loop: 7.4 miles
Elevation gain+ 2,633 feet
Top Elevation 8,748 feet
Difficulty: Moderate
Land: Custer Gallatin National Forest

The 320 Guest Ranch is the starting point connecting Buffalo Horn Pass to Tom Minor Basin in Paradise Valley to the east. The trail climbs steadily to Buffalo Horn Pass. This trail is commonly hiked as an out-and-back, but there is a network of trails for longer treks and loops.

Take a right to loop back to Wilson Draw or continue to Buffalo Horn Pass and Ramshorn Pass over to Tom Miner Basin in the Paradise Valley to the east and Tepee creek to the southwest.

This area is a migration corridor for wildlife from Yellowstone National Park; as always in these areas, carry bear spray and travel in groups.

Search Tepee Creek Trail
Custer Gallatin National Forest
Trailhead (45.06288,-111.16829)

Hiking along a swollen Porcupine Creek in spring run-off, Porcupine photo reference: Christopher Moriaty

YELLOWSTONE CORRIDOR ON FOOT

49. Tepee Creek to Daily Creek

Out-and-Back: 10 Miles
Elevation gain/loss + 1,050 feet
Top Elevation 7,218 feet
Difficulty: Moderate
Land: CGNF & Yellowstone NP

Tepee Creek sits at the northwest edge of Yellowstone National Park. This hike is also a pleasant backcountry ski tour in the winter (see trail # 98 on page 248).

The trail climbs gradually along the creek to open meadows. Cross over to the Dailey Creek drainage on a grassy ridge and along a forested section before descending. Shuttle a vehicle two miles down the highway.

If you bring your dog, stay on the Tepee Creek side for the return hike as dogs are not allowed on trails in Yellowstone National Park.

Search Buffalo Horn Creek - Wilson Draw Loop
Custer Gallatin National Forest
Trailhead (45.1057,-111.9834)

50. Fawn Pass to Big Horn Pass

Out-and-Back: 10 Miles
Elevation gain + 1,000 feet
Top Elevation 7,842 feet
Difficulty: Hard
Land: Yellowstone National Park

Fawn Pass is a classic backcountry ski tour destination (see trail #99 on page 249). To make a loop , hike south from Fawn Pass to Big Horn Pass and take the Big Horn trail back to the highway. (Shuttle a vehicle to the Big Horn trailhead.)

Extended trips can be made from this trailhead connecting all the way to Mammoth hot springs. The open flowing landscape has a Yellowstone feel of open expanses filled with wildlife, snow capped peaks in the distance. Climb gradually to the Pass taking a right to return on the Big Horn drainage to the south.

Search Fawn Pass
Yellowstone National Park
Trailhead (44.95067,-111.05895)

Fawn Pass trail from Trailhead pull-off

PARADISE VALLEY FOOT TRAILS

Livingston to Gardner

> "Montana is the landscape that generations of dreamers, despots, adventurers, explorers, crackpots and heroes fought and died for. It's one of the most beautiful places on Earth. There is no place like it."
>
> *-Anthony Bourdain while traveling, eating and filming in the Paradise Valley*

An interesting and scenic drive to Paradise Valley from Bozeman follows Trail Creek, which is an exit off I-90 between Bozeman and Livingston just west of Bozeman Pass. Spectacular views of the Absaroka/Beartooth Mountains , including Black Mountain directly across the valley, make this shortcut drive to Paradise Valley worth taking. However, the gravel road can be muddy in spring, rough and dusty in summer and icy in winter.

Bald Eagle

(Haliaeetus leucocephalus)
The national bird and largest true raptor in North America lives near large water sources with plentiful food.

The Bald Eagle build large platform nests in old-growth trees, generally near good fishing. Juveniles have dark brown plumage with white streaking until they reach sexual maturity (approximately five years) when head feathers turn white in both males and females.

Mature females eagles are about 25 per-cent larger than the males. Eagles are effective predators, snatching fish out of the water. Their lower talon punctures prey while the upper talons secure it.

Bald eagles are commonly seen fishing along the Yellowstone River throughout Paradise Valley

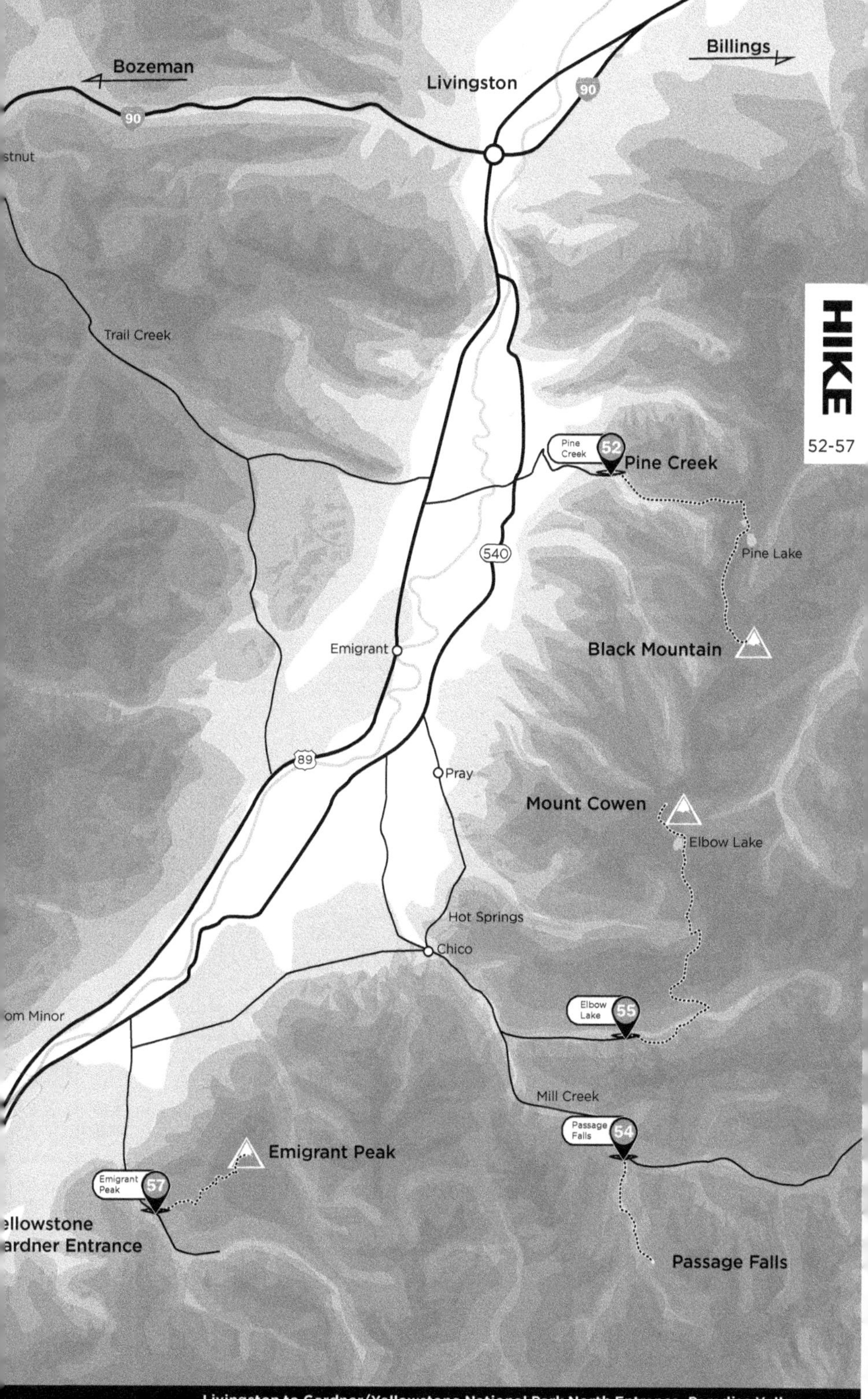

Livingston to Gardner/Yellowstone National Park North Entrance, Paradise Valley

PARADISE VALLEY ON FOOT

51. Pine Creek Falls

Out-and-Back: 2.57 Miles
Elevation gain +2,90 feet
Top Elevation 6,070 feet
Difficulty: Easy
Land: Custer Gallatin National Forest

This is the most popular family hike in Paradise Valley. The Pine Creek area has a campground, nearby lodge, concert area for summer music and trailhead access into the rugged Absoroka Beartooth wilderness.

The easy version of the hike travels through forest, meandering along Pine Creek, crossing it once on a mile-long hike to the falls. A log bridge with handrail spans the creek and offers views of the attractive falls. This is a popular resting spot for families.

Please keep dogs on leash.

Search Pine Creek Lake Rec Area
Livingston Montana
Trailhead (45.49735,-110.51853)

52. Pine Creek Lake

Out-and-Back: 10.5 miles
Elevation gain/loss + 3,635 feet
Top Elevation 9,056 feet
Difficulty: Hard
Land: Custer Gallatin National Forest

Beyond the falls the trail abruptly changes character as it switchbacks up the steep-walled canyon. A key creek crossing past brushy growth in an avalanche path puts the hiker on the left side of the creek. The spring run off is impressive, and hikers and dogs need to take care maneuvering over slippery rocks in the powerful current.

The hike continues steeply up hill, cresting at a dramatic viewpoint of Jewel Lake with its waterfalls and Black Mountain in the background.

Note the rocky slabs rising out of the lake. The hike to this point is an impressive 3,400' vertical gain.

Search Pine Creek Lake Rec Area
Livingston Montana
Trailhead (45.49735,-110.51853)

Crossing the bridge at the base of Pine Creek Falls

53. Black Mountain

Search Black Mountain
Livingston Montana
Trailhead (45.49735,-110.51853)

Out-and-Back: 12.56 Miles
Elevation gain/loss + 6,064 feet
Top Elevation 10,994 feet
Difficulty: Hard - scrambling at elevation
Land: Custer Gallatin National Forest

At the junction of Pine Creek Lake and Jewell Lake, note the prominent drainage at the flanks of the mountain that holds snow until late summer/fall and a stream that leads to a southwest facing snow/talus field. Ascend these snow/talus fields on the western flank of the peak to the upper ridge.

As there is some fairly complex topography on the upper peak, it is a good idea to bring along a topographical map.

After a short section at the saddle, climb down the rock buttress to the right and continue upward over rocks and talus to make your way to easier ground to attain the summit. From the summit there are views into the Absaroka-Beartooth, Including Mount Cowan and Emigrant Peak to the south and across Paradise Valley. Descend on the same route.

The northeastern aspect of the peak is exposed, providing a chute skiing experience in the winter. (See Chris Kussmaul's "Peaks and Couloirs of Southwest Montana")

View of Black Mountain above Jade Lake, Pine Creek trail, Custer Gallatin National Forest

PARADISE VALLEY ON FOOT

54. Passage Falls

Out-and-Back: 5.10 Miles
Elevation gain +623 feet
Top Elevation 6,529 feet
Difficulty: moderate - steep by falls
Land: Customer Gallatin National Forest

The deepest road access into the Absaroka-Beartooths from the west side is the Mill Creek Road. In the winter the road is gated and becomes an out-and-back ski and dog sledding track. Passage Falls can be reached in the winter via skis. In the summer, drive to the parking lot at the Wallace Creek trailhead off the Mill Creek road. The trail follows along the creek that is lined by massive boulders, leading to an open meadow and crossing a few tributary streams. Bear right up the Passage Creek drainage.

Take a right at the bridge (don't cross). A slight rise of switchbacks go to an overlook above a private cabin. The steep trail descends on exposed switchbacks into Passage Creek. Mind your footing and be especially careful if the trail is snowy or icy. Enjoy the spectacle of Passage Falls inside the narrow canyon. Extend the trip hiking the Wallace or Grizzly Creek trails of which both go all the way south to Gardiner and Yellowstone National Park.

Dogs should be kept on leashes as the area leading to the falls is steep and exposed.

Search Passage Falls
Custer Gallatin National Forest
Trailhead (45.27396,-110.50124)

A steep, short drop into Passage Creek reveals the tucked away Passage Falls

55. Elbow Lake

Out-and-Back: 15.7 Miles
Elevation gain/loss + 4,206 feet
Top Elevation 8,629 feet
Difficulty: Hard - challenging route finding
Land: Customer Gallatin National Forest

Just north of the Mill Creek road is the East Fork road which ends at the East Fork trailhead of Mill Creek. Start on this trail taking a left at the junction.

Cross Upper Sage Creek and Elbow Creek. This is a long, challenging climb that may not be well marked in places.

If the 15.7 miles and elevation gain of 4,206 feet out & back isn't enough of a physical and navigational challenge, extend the trip by climbing Mount Cowen.

Search Elbow Lake
Custer Gallatin National Forest
Trailhead(45.31694,-110.53654)

56. Mount Cowen

Out-and-Back: 20 Miles
Elevation gain/loss + 7,000 feet
Top Elevation 11,054 feet
Difficulty: Very Hard - exposed rock
Land: Customer Gallatin National Forest

As the Grand Teton of the Absoroka Beartooths, this 11,212' peak is the high point of the range. The peak holds many quality alpine climbing routes on steep granite faces and crack systems that range from ice and snow couloir routes to 5.11 rock routes. Ten miles one way with nearly 6,000 feet of elevation gain.

Ron Brunckhorst's "Alpine Rock and Ice Guide to Montana" is the best reference for those planning to climb one of the numerous rock climbing routes in the Cowen Cirque.

Search Mount Cowen
Custer Gallatin National Forest
Trailhead(45.31694,-110.53654)

MOUNT COWEN
11,054"

Mount Cowen in the morning light from Elbow Lake - Photo reference, Jamie Bolie

PARADISE VALLEY ON FOOT

57. Emigrant Peak

Out-and-Back: 7.5 Miles
Elevation gain +5,082 feet
Top Elevation 10,916 feet
Difficulty: Hard
Land: Custer Gallatin National Forest

Emigrant Peak is a prominent mountain viewable from much of the Paradise Valley. Mount Cowen trail is accessed crossing through private land, but from the parking area Emigrant Peak and the route are plainly visible.

This peak is 57 Miles from Bozeman in the Paradise Valley. Drive by Pray Montana, near Chico Hot springs to begin the hike.

Hike through brush, climbing more steeply on a road grade double track through forest before gaining the upper steep grassland fence line. Trails in the forest switchback up to prominent talus and ridge lines.

The final exposed rock ridge slabs are exciting but not too technical. My dog was able to navigate without assistance. Wrap-around views from the summit of the Paradise Valley, Absoroka Beartooths and south to Yellowstone.

There are skiable lines on the peak when conditions are right. See Chris Kussmaul's "Peaks and Couloirs of Southwest Montana" for more details.

Search Emigrant Peak Trail
Custer Gallatin National Forest
Trailhead(45.26031,-110.76714)

EMIGRANT PEAK
10,916"

Straight ahead and up - trail to Emigrant Peak from the parking area

HIKE 57

Elk

(Cervus canadensis)

This ungulate is called "wapiti" by indigenous people and, to many tribes, the Yellowstone River was known as the "elk" river. In Paradise Valley the river corridor serves as a major migration route for several large herds that migrate into Yellowstone Park to higher ground to spend the summer through the fall rut. The Greater Yellowstone ecosystem is home to 20,000 to 30,000 elk.

Bugling elk during the rut at Mammoth Hot Springs; elk are commonly seen in the Paradise Valley

MADISON RIVER ON FOOT

58. Bear Trap Canyon

Out-and-Back: 1-15 miles
Elevation gain/loss 1,515 ft
Top Elevation 4,790 ft
Difficulty: Easy - Moderate
Land: Lee Metcalf Wilderness

The Madison River, southwest of Bozeman, is the immensely popular with river rafters, fishermen and inner tubing party floats. Originating in Yellowstone National Park, the Madison flows into Ennis lake where the river is dammed (final hike turnaround point). The river travels through a section of the Lee Metcalf Wilderness before connecting with the Norris Hot springs Creek at the highway. The trailhead is large and used by hikers, runners, and fishermen. It travels riverside in open sagebrush country, passing multiple fishing access points in the river with boulders strew riverside.

Cross Beartrap Creek, climbing a slight rise where the trail flows left, following the river bend into the canyon. Rock Walls steeply rise from the river, offering rock climbing. Continue as far as you like. There are many scenic viewpoints and resting spots for turnaround locations. At 7 miles is the Madison pump house the dam at 9 miles. Keep an eye out for rattlesnakes. This is a great shoulder season hike as it is typically drier and warmer than Bozeman.

Keep dogs on a leash. Near Norris, Ennis.

Search Bear Trap Canyon
Lee Metcalf Wilderness
Trailhead (45.57767,-111.59539)

Prairie Rattlesnake

(Crotalus viridis)

A member of the viper family, the prairie rattlesnake can be up to five feet long with the unmistakable rattle at the end of the tail. If you are bitten, seek emergency medical care.

Suns out, snakes out. Keep an eye out and listen for the rattles of poisonous rattlesnakes sunbathing.

Bear Trap Canyon Trail, Lee Metcalf Wilderness

MADISON RIVER ON FOOT

59. Madison Buffalo Jump

Loop: 3.6 Miles
Elevation gain/loss +721 feet
Top Elevation 4,725 feet
Difficulty: Easy
Land: State Monument

Out of the native populations, young men with exceptional skills of speed and stamina were chosen as runners. The requirements of a runner required a heightened level of peak performance. One can only imagine how a young brave would prepare for such a task. Sprinting speed, navigating obstacles, running alongside large animals and jumping the precipice at the exact predefined crevice as the bison charged overhead, falling to their demise. This must have required incredible focus and timing to perfect the moment for the desired outcome. If any bison survived, it was feared they would remember and become skittish in future opportunities, making the technique no longer usable.

While the practical purposes of these experiences were crucial for the survival of ancient Montanans, weren't seen as recreation there is something innately human about sewing our wild oats. Exploring what is unknown and pushing past the edge of the familiar into the unknown pushing physical limits of human strength and endurance.

Today you can visit the Madison Buffalo jump on foot, hiking, trail running, horseback riding or mountain biking. Hike the loop or series of trails up, over and around the historical site. It is also great mountain biking in the shoulder season. While there is no longer the danger of being stampeded by a heard of bison, look out for rattlesnakes and prickly pear cactus. Be mindful of the limestone cliff exposures and the hot, dry conditions in the summer. Pack more water than you think you will need.

Step back in time a few hundred years and explore the location of an ancient "pushkin" or buffalo jump. Archaeological digs in the 1980s reveal the site had been used by many first nations dating back at least 2,000 years. It was primarily used by the Shoshone but also several other tribes through the ages. The prominent cliffs can be seen from the parking lot. A .5 mile trail to the interpretive viewpoint is a great introduction to the area and history. Make a loop around the jump, starting from the left trail and climbing up around the west side of the jump. Follow contours around the top of the cliff (watch your step) to the eastern edge where the trail connects to a path through wooded area. The trail can be harder to follow connecting back to the parking lot, but open sight lines will let you know which way to go. This area is a good early season mountain bike spot (see bike book p?). Be cautious of prickly pear, rattlesnakes, and extreme heat in the summer.

Search Buffalo Jump State Park Loop Trailhead (45.79474722198833, -111.47198170804859)

Approaching the Madison Buffalo Jump from the parking lot. See map for location of viewpoint

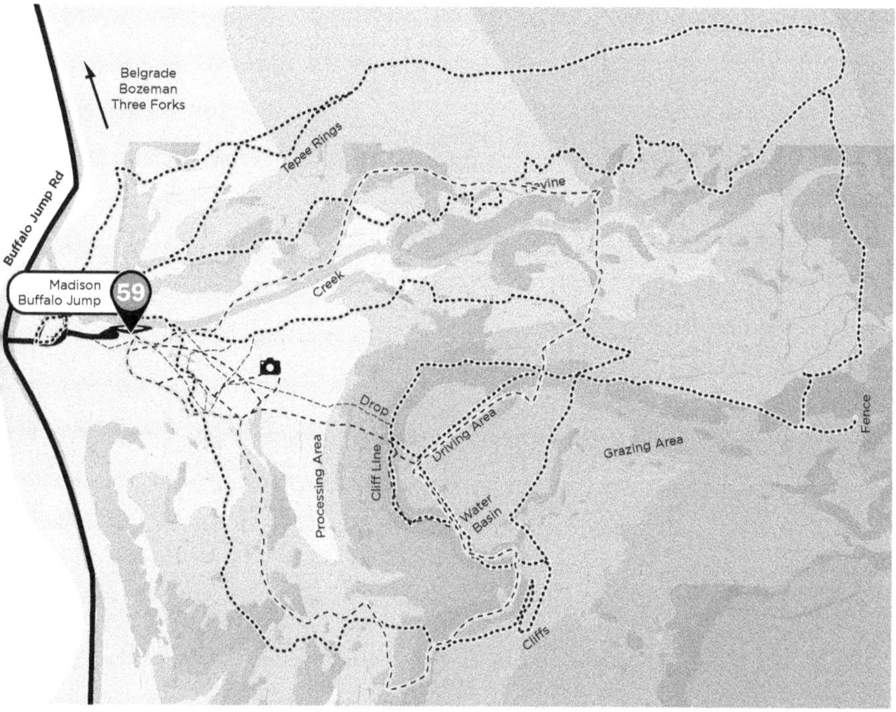

HIKE 59

Loop trail network, Madison Buffalo Jump State Monument

MADISON RIVER ON FOOT

60. Lewis & Clark Caverns

Search Danmore Gypsum Mine, Middle View & Eastside Trail Loop Trailhead (45.82311231012737, -111.85072188551514)

Distance: 6.3 Miles
Elevation gain/loss 1,519 ft
Top Elevation 5,438 ft
Difficulty: Moderate
Land: Lewis & Clark Caverns State Park

The state park has trailheads at the lower camping area and up the hill side at the cavern entrance. Take a 2 mile, 2 hours guided tour through one of the largest known limestone caverns in the northwest. The caverns are open May 28th through September 30th. The trail systems are open year-round for hiking and mountain biking (see trail#83 on page 195). From the lower parking lot, hike Greer Gulch Trail to Middle View, topping out at the cavern entrance. Take a left at Cave Gulch Trail to return to the parking lot on the east side trail. There are lots of hiking and biking loop options. Stay on the trails as prickly pear cacti are common on the dry hillsides.

Autumn hillsides on the dry and warm Lewis and Clark Caverns loops.

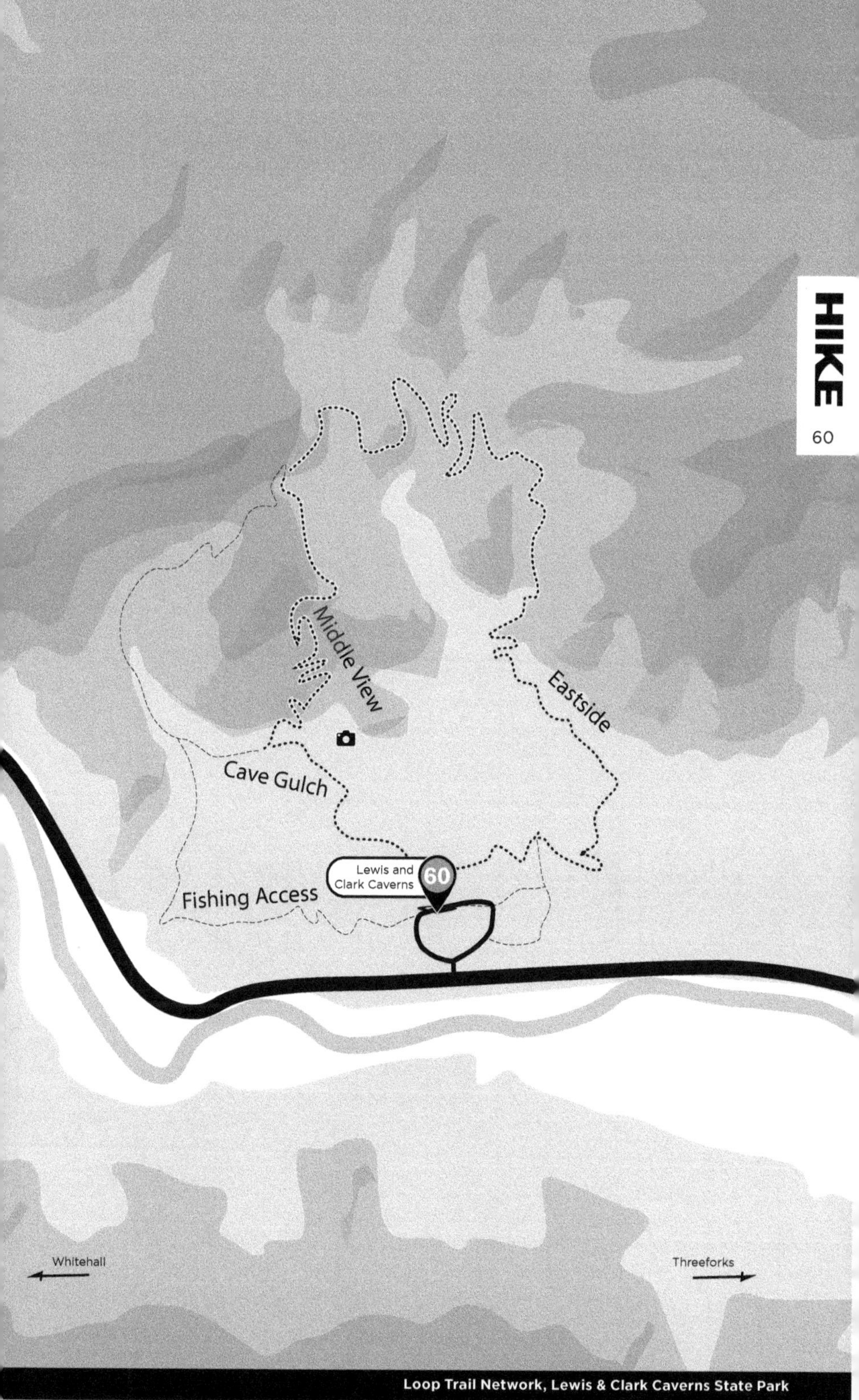
HIKE
60
Middle View
Eastside
Cave Gulch
Lewis and
Clark Caverns
60
Fishing Access
Whitehall
Threeforks
Loop Trail Network, Lewis & Clark Caverns State Park

MADISON RIVER ON FOOT

61. Missouri Headwaters State Park

Direction: South of Bozeman 30 Min
Elevation gain/loss 3,559 ft
Top Elevation 11,105 Gallatin Peak
Spanish Peak Trail: 15.7 Miles
Land: Lee Metcalf Wilderness

This area is historically important as the location where the Shoshone, Crow, Blackfeet and other tribes met to trade. Lewis and Clark made camps here on both directions of their expedition. The state park offers camping, paved bike trails and river access to the Jefferson, Madison, and Gallatin Rivers.

This 2.8 mile loop edges the river, ascends a bluff viewpoint and passes through grasslands and the interpretive areas.

The John Colter run is an annual trail run put on by Bozeman's Big Sky Wind Drinkers running group. It was inspired by Colter's historic run as he escaped death by the Blackfeet Indians who captured him near the headwaters of the Missouri in 1808 (See page 21).

The course at the state park is 7.5 miles on rough trails, gravel roads and asphalt, with two river crossings. The land looks much as it did when Colter ran for his life while being chased by Indians.

Single track and paved bike trails extend from the Headwaters State Park to the town of Three Forks. There is plenty to see and do here and it is an especially nice place to visit in the shoulder season when the mountains are still snowed in.

Search Missouri Headwaters
State Park
Trailhead (45.933374,-111.49457)

Drift fishermen and hikers enjoying a spring day in the Missouri Headwaters State Park

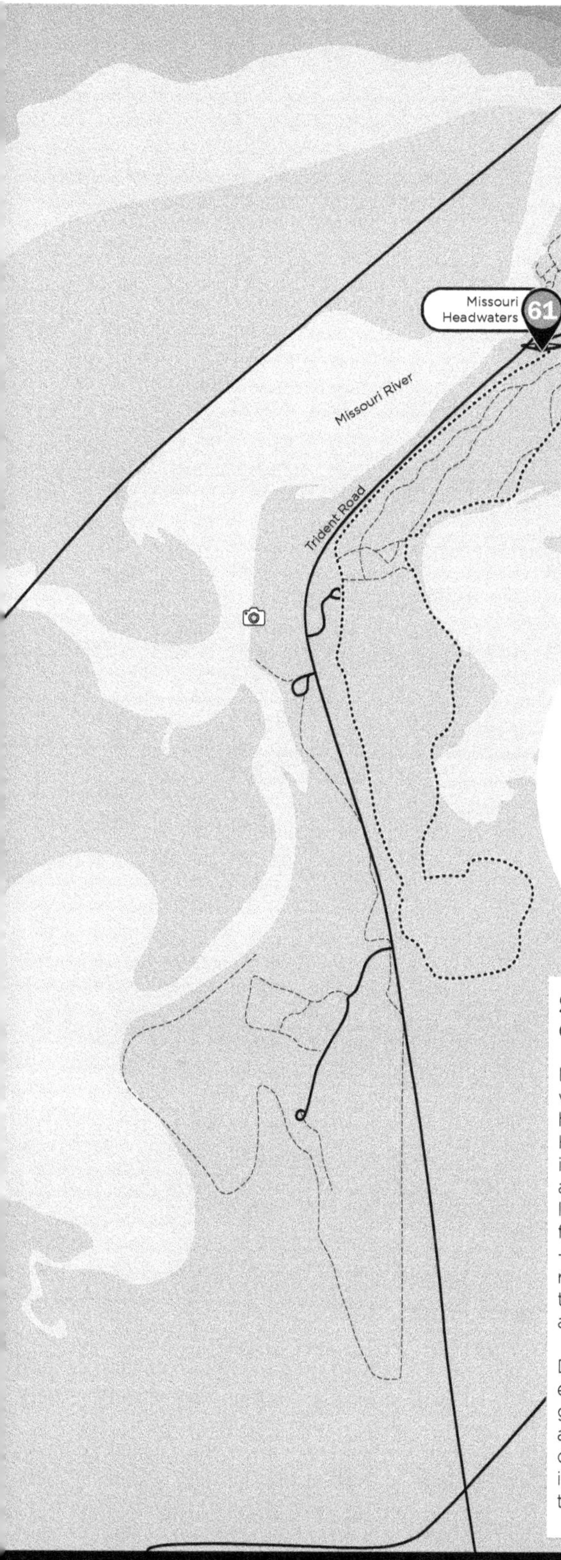

Clarkston

Missouri Headwaters 61

Gallatin River

Missouri River

Trident Road

HIKE

61

Sage Grouse strut display

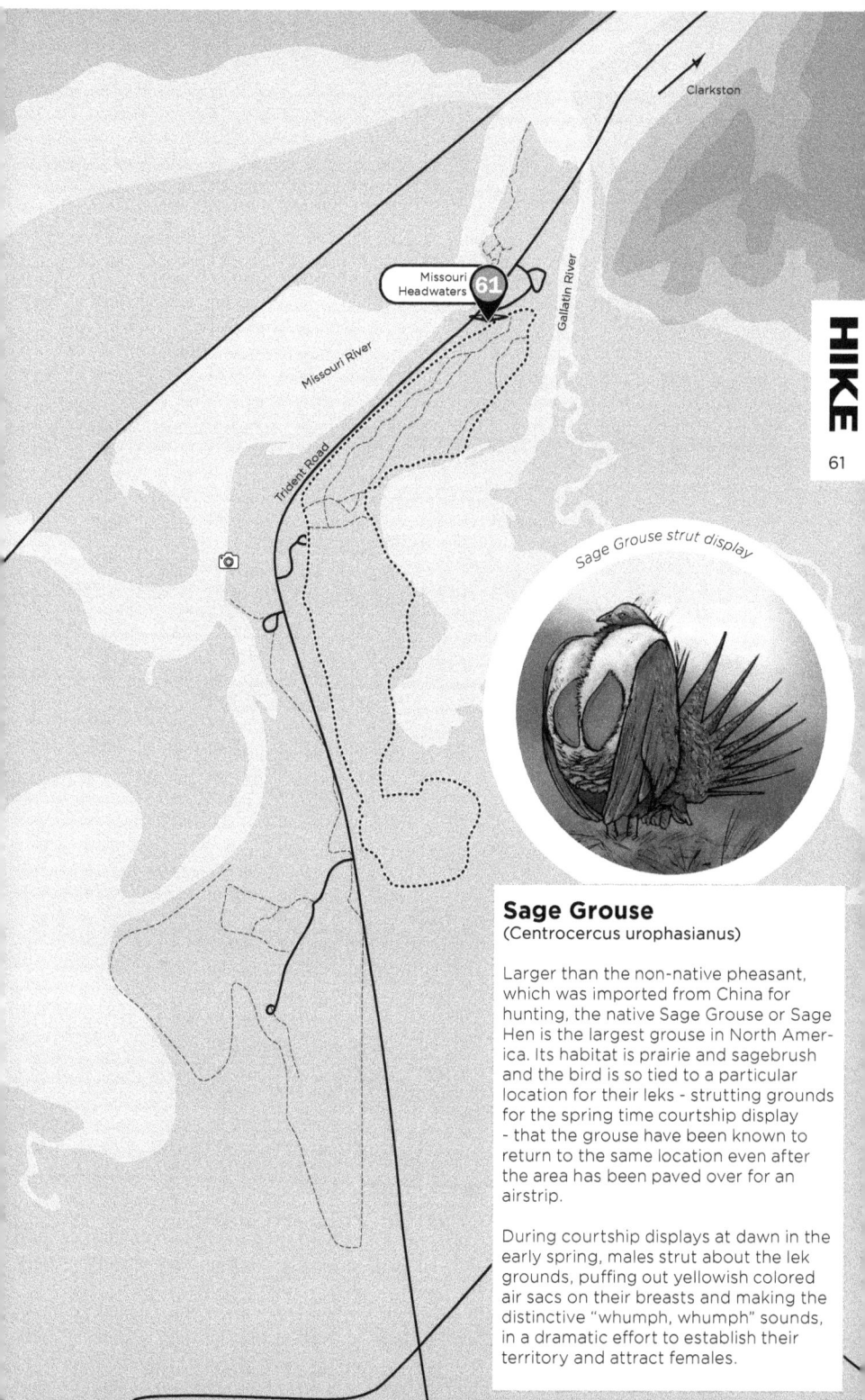

Sage Grouse
(Centrocercus urophasianus)

Larger than the non-native pheasant, which was imported from China for hunting, the native Sage Grouse or Sage Hen is the largest grouse in North America. Its habitat is prairie and sagebrush and the bird is so tied to a particular location for their leks - strutting grounds for the spring time courtship display - that the grouse have been known to return to the same location even after the area has been paved over for an airstrip.

During courtship displays at dawn in the early spring, males strut about the lek grounds, puffing out yellowish colored air sacs on their breasts and making the distinctive "whumph, whumph" sounds, in a dramatic effort to establish their territory and attract females.

Hiking trails and paved bike paths, Missouri Headwaters State Park

BEARTOOTHS ON FOOT

62.The Beaten Path (East Rosebud)

Distance: 26 Miles
Elevation gain/loss + 3,326 ft
Top Elevation 10,191
Difficulty: Hard
Land: Absaroka-Beartooth Wilderness

The Absaroka Beartooth Wilderness is at high elevations with rugged landscapes and many alpine lakes. Most of the land mass is above 10,000 feet, including 30 peaks over 12,000 feet.

While the wilderness has numerous connecting trails, there are few access points to trailheads from outside the wilderness, the predominant ones being Mill Creek road from the west in Paradise Valley, Boulder Creek road south of Big Timber, the West Rosebud trail southwest of the town of Absarokee, and the East Rosebud trail south of Absarokee.

From the South, access to the wilderness is near Cooke City, and from the southwest, near Gardiner.

Access points to the wilderness are on the southeast side, near the Red Lodge area.

Connecting Cooke City with Red Lodge is the Beartooth highway. This 69-mile scenic drive is closed during winter (generally from October to Memorial Day. The pass' highest elevation is 10,947 feet. Pass rugged peaks like "The Bear's Tooth" on the winding route. U.S. Route 212 is a famous cycling road and home to the Beartooth Basin Summer Ski Area.

The East Rosebud trailhead is the beginning of what has become known by trail runners as the "Beaten Path." It is

a 26-mile route through the Beartooth high country to Cooke City. This trail along East Rosebud Creek is popular for day hiking, backpacking, and fishing.

Search East Rosebud
Custer Gallatin National Forest
Trailhead (45.19729, -109.63536)

Photo reference courtesy of Arlin Ladue

Granite Peak 63

W Rosebud Rd.

Saddleback Mountain 10,876'

E Rosebud Rd.

The Beaten Path 62

Granite Peak 12,087'

Glacier Peak 12,320'

Snowbank Mountain 12,089'

Bear's Tooth 11,920'

Cooke City

212

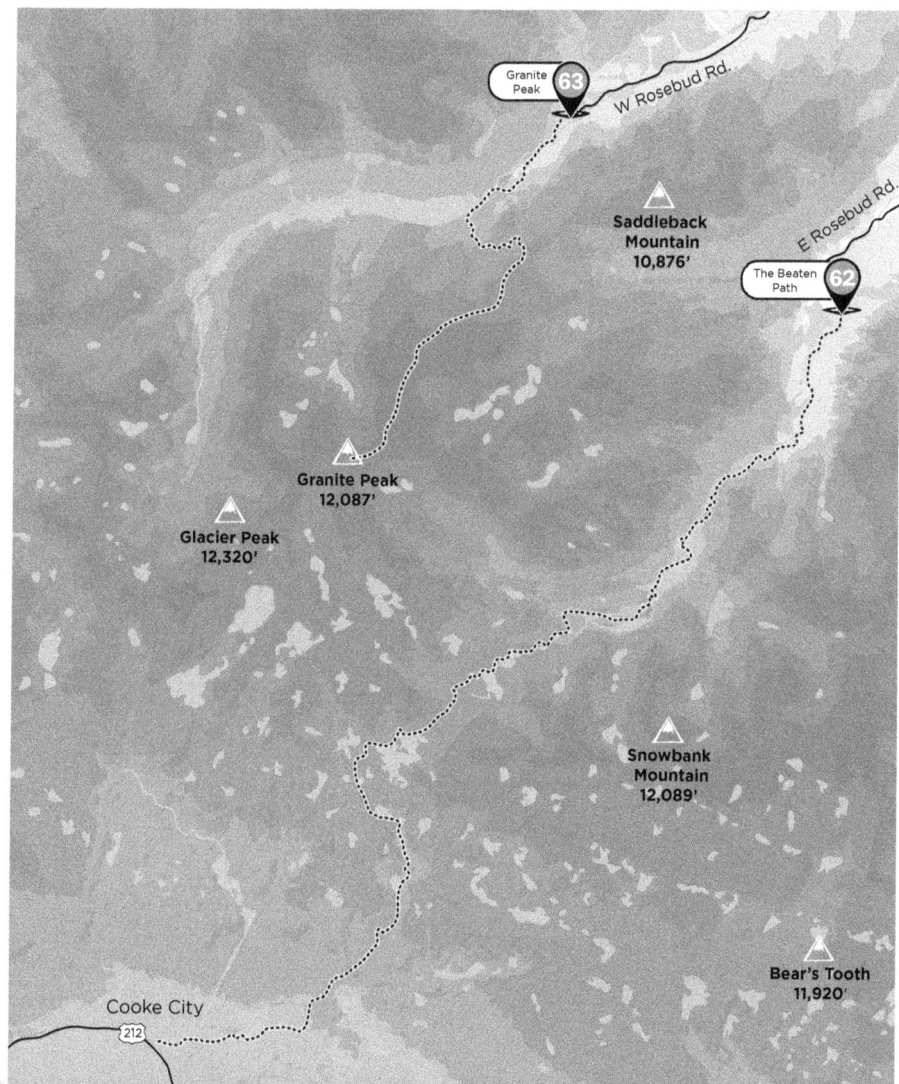

West and East Rosebud Drainages, Absaroka-Beartooth Wilderness

Mourning Cloak Butterfly

(Nymphalis antiopa)

Originating from the spiny elm caterpillar, the Mourning Cloak Butterfly is one of the longest living butterflies, living from 11 to 12 months. Its beauty and resilience earns it the title of Montana's state insect.

BEARTOOTHS ON FOOT

63.(West Rosebud) Granite Peak

Out-and-Back: East of Bozeman 90 Min
Cumulative Elevation Gain +9,960 feet
Top Elevation 12,799 feet
Difficulty: Low 5th Class
Land: Absaroka-Beartooth Wilderness

A trail on the east side of West Rosebud Lake begins the approach to climbing Granite Peak, Montana's highest peak, with switchbacks to Froze to Death plateau. The trail on the plateau (at 10,000 feet) for a few miles is over rough talus. Look for the cairns passing marshy areas (and good places to refill water bottles).

Take in astounding views of 12,000' Beartooth Peaks accompany you on the journey to the first overlook of the peak itself. From the large cairns at the viewpoint, descend 1,500' on talus trail to a notch, then regain the elevation to the steep, snow-saddle crossing. This is where most parties rope up. The final stretch is a mix of low 5th class to 3rd class chimney climbing through rocky blocks, finally topping out on the rocky summit of Granite Peak.

Congratulations on reaching arguably one of the most challenging peak ascents in the U S, with its lengthy approach, consistent exposure above 10,000 feet, challenging route finding, and its infamous temperamental weather that often prevents successful summiting.

Reach Granite Peak, the high-point of Montana via a lengthy approach, with consistent exposure above 10,000 feet and challenging route finding to the rocky summit.

Infamous for it's temperamental weather, we threaded the weather needle between snow storms and were fortunate to get possibly some of the last best conditions of the season.

Scan the QR code on the opposite page to watch the Climb Granite Peak video.

Search Granite Peak Trail
Absaroka-Beartooth Wilderness
Trailhead (45.24533,-109.73033)

GRANITE PEAK
12,799"

Climbers scoping out the approach to Granite Peak, the high point of Montana

PEAK BAGGING

Trail accessible summits listed
in order of elevation

Grassy Mountain - 6,689" Page# 79

Storm Castle - 7,166" Page# 96

Chestnut Mountain - 7,481" Page# 58

Mount Ellis - 7,726" Page# 232

Garnet Lookout - 8,203" Page# 98

Mount Baldy - 8,829" Page# 71

Ross Peak - 9,004" Page# 75

Naya Nuki - 9,449" Page# 69

Saddle Peak - 9,159" Page# 186

Hardscrabble - 9,528" Page# 69

Pomp Peak - 9,551 " Page# 69

Sacagawea - 9,579" Page# 77

Mount Flanders - 9,961" Page# 80

Alex Lowe Peak - 10,036" Page# 87

Mount Blackmore - 10,188" Page# 86

Hyalite Peak - 10,296" Page# 91

Mount Bole - 10,333" Page# 87

Jumbo Mountain - 10,412" Page# 99

Beehive Peak - 10,742" Page# 109

Emigrant Peak - 10,916" Page# 120

Mount Black - 10,994" Page# 117

Gallatin Peak - 11,015" Page# 102

Mount Cowen - 11,054" Page# 119

Lone Mountain - 11,167" Page# 243

Granite Peak - 12,799" Page# 132

Climb Granite Peak

63

The author training for peak bagging

ADDITIONAL RESOURCES

OUTDOORS WITH BRYAN SCHAEFFER PODCAST

The Simplest thing we can do to improve our physical & mental health for ourselves, our family and the planet is to exercise outdoors in nature every day. This Podcast is getting outside and offline with accomplished skiers, hikers, runners and mountain bikers.

With expert tips on fitness, planning, gear and how to have the best experiences exploring year-round trails, this is your trailhead to adventure. Join us as we explore the thriving communities within these life-long sports.

Scan QR codes to listen.

Watch Buffalo Jump Reenactment
Short animated film by Bryan Schaeffer
North American bison herds were legendary. Numbering in the tens of millions, bison migrated to the best grazing sites throughout the year. Indigenous people followed these migrations and gathered annually at buffalo jumps to harvest the bison.

Dr. Shane Doyle, Apsáalooke
- Teacher, Scholar, Performer
Montana's human stories go deeper than the dominant narrative - the turmoil of the 1800s. Montana is unique in the US. Its indigenous people historically had no permanent camps. The intense seasons created nomadic cultures with annual migrations for hunting, gathering, and interacting with other groups.

Tami Asars
- Guidebook Author, the Mountaineers Books
Tami has authored "Hiking the Wonderland Trail" and "Hiking the Pacific Crest Trail Washington" and many other books. Join us as Tami shares about her latest long hiking adventures on the Arizona Trail and the Continental Trail.
https://tamiasars.com

Bryce Stevens
- Co-Founder Trails.com and Guidebook Author
Guidebook author Bryce Stephens and I talk about digitizing maps and materials for one of the early online trail platforms, Trails.com. Bryce has authored hiking guidebooks and, more recently, a guidebook to backcountry adventure/dirt biking routes across northwest US. www.topozone.com & www.mountainzone.com

John Zilly
- Guidebook Author and Shoe Innovator
John takes his creative/innovative side to another level, co-founding a new running shoe company that builds personalized models attuned to each runner's individual running mechanics.
https://vimazi.com

Hannah Brattenrud
- Mental Health Benefits of Social Outdoor Exercise
Being in nature can restore connections in your brain, unload stress and help you recenter and refocus. Research indicates that we are hard-wired for the trifecta of physical exercise in nature and with other people.
https://multipliersale.com

Mary Erickson
- Forest Director Custer Gallatin National Forest USFS
Mary Erickson's team just wrapped up the first Land Management Plan in over 30 years for the Custer Gallatin National Forest. Mary discusses what these plans are, how they are developed and what impacts they have shaping policy for the Forest Service.
https://www.fs.usda.gov/main/custergallatin/landmanagement/planning

Corey Lewellen
- District Ranger, Custer Gallatin National Forest
Corey and Marna discuss the creation of the Land Management Plan - with local feedback - and how the plan affects popular recreation areas around Bozeman.
Closures and alerts: https://www.fs.usda.gov/main/custergallatin/home
https://www.facebook.com/CusterGallatinNationalForest

EJ Porth
- Associate Director, Gallatin Valley Land Trust (GVLT)
The Gallatin Valley Land Trust's Main street to Mountains trails connect Bozeman to local mountain biking adventures right from town.
https://www.crosscutmt.org

Jacob Zimmerer - Ph.D. student in Indigenous and Rural Health at Montana State University
I met Jacob at an indigenous edible plant walk a few weeks ago. I invited him to share some of his foraging wisdom with us.
http://ecologicalhuman.com/
https://www.facebook.com/ecologicalhumanproject

Adam Johnson
- Big Sky Community Organization
Park & Trails Director
Big changes are in the works for connecting communities in the Big Sky area with the Big Sky trail system.
https://bsco.org

Graham Zimmerman
- American Alpine Club President
Protect Our Winters
"The Greater Yellowstone region is very close to my heart. Yellowstone is, for most Americans, an iconic place of wilderness. It is a zone that really represents wilderness in the American ideology."
https://americanalpineclub.org

Scott Secor
- SAR Commander
Gallatin County Sheriff Search and Rescue
"Bringing a communication device, going with a partner and dressing for the conditions are the big three."
https://gallatincomt.virtualtownhall.net/search-and-rescue
https://www.friendsgcssar.org

THE LAST BEST
BIKE
BOZEMAN
BIG SKY
BEYOND
MONTANA

For updates, more info and links go to: ***www.thelastbestbike.com***

SELECT MOUNTAIN BIKE TRAILS

64. Highland Glen Trail
65. Painted Hills Connector Trail
66. Triple Tree Loop
67. Bear Canyon
68. Chestnut Mountain Trail
69. Shootout Park Meadow
70. Sourdough Canyon (Bozeman Creek)
71. Leverich Canyon
72. History Rock
73. Emerald Lake
74. Garnet Mountain
75. Spanish Creek Road
76. Corbly Gulch
77. Sypes Canyon
78. Shafthouse
79. Crosscut Mountain Sports Center
80. Bangtail Divide Trail
81. Mountain to Meadow Ride
82. Madison Buffalo Jump
83. Lewis & Clark Caverns
84. Copper City Loop

SHOULDER SEASON TRAILS

Copper City Trails, Lewis & Clark Cavern rails, Madison Buffalo Jump Trials

EARLY SUMMER TRAILS

Highland Glen Trails, Painted Hills Connector Trail - Bozeman
Hyalite Road, Storm Castle Road, Yellowstone National Park - West Yellowstone
Spanish Creek Road - Spanish Peaks

Corbly Gulch, Sypes Canyon - West Bridgers

BUILT FOR MOUNTAIN BIKING

What goes up & Must Come Down - Crosscut Mountain Sports Center
Mountain to Meadow - Big Sky

LATE SUMMER TRAILS

Bear Canyon, Chestnut Mountain - Bozeman
Shafthouse, Bangtail Divide Trails East Bridgers/Bangtails
Shootout Park, Emerald Lake, Hyalite

BEGINNER TRAILS

GVLT Main street to Mountains 80 miles gravel and paved - Bozeman
Green Eagle - Copper City
Langhor Loop - Hyalite

MODERATE TRAILS

Crescent Lake Loop, Hyalite
Higland Glen, Painted Hills Connector, Triple Tree - Bozeman
High Ore - Copper City Trails
What Goes up & Must Come Down - Crosscut Mountain Sports Center
Mountains to Meadow - Big Sky

ADVANCED TRAILS

OLD-SCHOOL
Emerald Lake, Garnet Lookout, StoneCreek - Bangtail Divide, Shafthouse, Leverich (strenuous)

MANUFACTURED
Big Sky Resort, lift-accessed downhill trails
Never Sweat - Copper City Trails

THE LAST BEST BIKE MONTANA

Drew Lakowski getting in the active ready position for a technical stretch of trail.

THE FUN KIND OF ZOOM MEETINGS

FOREWORD

by Tim Hawke

Co-Author Southern Montana Single track & Architect of Copper City Trails

You have probably heard Montana referred to as "The last, best place."

If you're one of the lucky natives like Bryan, you probably had to live elsewhere for a while to truly appreciate that. The 406 has a way of bringing its children home.

If you're one of the many newcomers, then I'm guessing that the awe is still fresh in your heart. This book hopes to stoke that fire for old and new alike.

Biking is not easy around here. Sure, the advent of e-bikes, and the Copper City trails project have made local pedaling a bit more feasible, but you still have to work hard for it. And that's awesome. It makes the effort that much more rewarding.

But with that reward comes responsibility. Personal and social. Both of these duties are paramount to not only having a great adventure, but also for the sake of the sport!

Know that whenever you put your tires onto a backcountry Single track in SW MT, you have entered the wilds of the greater Yellowstone ecosystem. You are a temporary visitor, and you have to keep your wits about you. I pack a rain shell all year long. Even if the forecast is for a sunny, 90 degree day. And bear spray will do you no good if it's in your pack. Or you're not trained on how to use it!

A lot of folks have moved here recently to enjoy the mountains, and the quality of life in this valley. A vast majority of those folks head out to the trails often. It's imperative that we all play nice. Not simply in the name of advocacy and safety, but to maintain the friendly nature of people in the mountains. It's part of our heritage here.

Say hello to other trail users, and don't startle them! Stop when you see a horse, and step below them on the trail. Talk calmly so they know you're not a threat.

Offer up the 2 finger wave to other drivers on the dirt roads when you're coming and going.

Just be nice dammit. It's the Montana way!

And get involved. If you plan on sticking around, then try and make a difference. Join a local bike club. Show up for trail work days. Pack a hand saw on your rides and clear downfall with your friends. It makes the ride out that much better.

I've witnessed the closure of over 700 miles of some of our greatest rides in the last fifteen years. I've heard of less than 50 new miles being built. The onus is on us- the riders, to preserve the legacy of riding here in Montana. Tell your friends.

Ride smart. Ride kind. Have fun.

May this book send you on some world class adventures.

Tim Hawke riding Copper City in the winter

Jason Lunden cresting the Continental Divide

A bike is more than a series of connected metal tubes and two wheels.

It is a time machine.

With a couple pedal strokes and the sudden "whoosh" of air through the helmet vents, riding a bike has the power to transport you back to that to that "ah ha" moment when you first learned how to ride. During childhood a bike was the ticket to freedom. It was the passport to roam, explore, be part of the pack. It still is.

Biking puts you In the moment - focusing on where you are, where you're going and who you're with. Biking is both an individual sport and a group activity. From packs of kids roaming the neighborhood, haphazardly flinging their bikes onto the lawn of a friend's house to biking in a streamlined peloton, this machine draws us together.

This book is designed to guide you to the right gear to the right trails at the right time.

We have interviewed program directors, trail builders, and bike shop owners to help you and your crew get the most out of your trail days in SW Montana and beyond.

Let's go ride!

The author learning to ride his new BMX bike, circa 1982

After the storm - Climbing Chestnut Mountain with double rainbows across the Paradise Valley

PROLOGUE

Despite 2020 being a train wreck of a year, it forced many of us to slow down and take a look at what is truly important. I bought my first mountain bike from Chalet Sports in 1989 and have been riding in different intensities since then.

With the recent purchase of a lighter, faster and all-around better bike than I have ever ridden before, the 2020 mountain biking season became my best one yet.

Exploring further became easier with good equipment, more know-how and building fitness. I started skipping the crowded parking lots by riding more from town to my favorite local trails. I rode with high school athletes coaching NICA during the week and daydreamed of other trails to explore or routes to connect on weekends.

We rode with a group of dads on "Thursday Night" trails and completed some amazing virtual courses.

My favorite images riding with friends and family during this season became references for the sketches used in this book.

During the shoulder season I was able to relive these summer memories and collect what ended up being over 100 of my hand-drawn scenes of local bikers on local trails. Along the way I interviewed over a dozen program directors of trail systems, bike shops, and community mountain biking organizations. You can listen to the edited interviews by scanning the QR codes on the pages of this book.

I hope this hand-crafted book and short film inspire you to make some new friends on the trail and have your best season mountain biking in SW Montana yet.

This is not a definitive guidebook for mountain biking in this region or Montana in general.

There are many good guidebooks on the market (ie. "Southern Montana Single Track," by Beartooth Publishing and apps like "Trailforks.")

This book is similar to a trailhead; it's a starting point and a guide to obtaining additional information from local organizations, shops and experts. Visit **TheLastBestBike.com** for updated links to trail conditions, community organizations, gear shops and more.

See the Additional Resources pages at the end of this section for Podcast interviews with local biking experts and links to organizations, gear shops and more.

THE LAST BEST BIKE FILM
WATCH
SINGLE TRACK MIND
BIKE
Film
Scan to watch
animated film
Single Track Mind

BIKE FITTING

A bike that fits well will ride well.

Just as each person is unique, so are bikes. Different types of mountain bikes have different geometry, particularly with the stem angle (slack) and the seat angle on a bike (the distance between the two is the reach). Cross country bikes tend to have a longer reach and steeper angles on the stem and seat (less slack) with emphasis on forward climbing position. Trail bikes, enduro, downhill and freestyle have progressively shorter reach, lower seat height and slacker head tube for that is farther back on the bike and ideal for descending.

The bike frame is the most important and, hopefully, the only part that won't wear out. Steel, aluminum, carbon fiber or titanium each have a different riding feel and price point.

Taking a bike out on the trail is the best way to get a sense of how the bike will perform for you when climbing, descending and cornering. Many of the local bike shops in Bozeman are close to Pete's Hill. If they let you take a test ride from the shop, that is a much better way to get the trail feel of the bike than riding in the parking lot alone.

The easiest adjustment to make on a bike is the seat height followed by saddle position.

The saddle should be at full height, leaving the leg 90% straight but not locked at the knee. If you experience side to side rotation, the seat is too high.

If your stance is too far over the handle bars, the reach is too short. This can be adjusted by repositioning the stem, changing stem direction or adding spacers for fine adjustments.

Other fine tunings include saddle angle, leaning it slightly forward or back. Pedal spacers are also available for wider hips.

An expert can help you with these fine tunings.

SAFETY

Mountain Biking can be dangerous

You can fall, things can fall on you. You could get hypothermia, frostbite, heatstroke or get sunburned. You could get lost or collide with a car, bike, animal, rock, trail or tree.

Using the right technique, wearing the correct gear and properly evaluating terrain and conditions are all important to having a fun and being safe on and off the trail.

While it is impossible to remove all risk from mountain biking, which would also remove the fun, safety should always be the priority.

Make the experience more fun and rewarding. Do your research. Get proper skills training (we will talk about progression of skills later), develop fitness and know how your bike works.

By their nature, mountain trails have obstacles like roots, rocks, loose soil, steep side-hills and deadfall.

Every trail should first be ridden with a cautious pre-ride and re-ride before embarking on a free-ride.

Packing the bike-specific ten essentials can help you get out of a jam. Make sure to take the time and read all of this.

RISKS

The more advanced trails have obstacles that are "higher consequence." These include ramps, drops, jumps and other features that often require catching some air or descending extremely steep sections.

It is a judgment call between going light and having more protection. Add body armor protection for high-consequence trails like knee pads, elbow pads, shoulder pads, shin guards, back braces and so forth. Some riders opt to do the climbing sections of a trail with just a helmet and don the rest of the protective gear at the top before beginning a fast and technical descent.

Mountain bikes optimized for trail performance often remove street-friendly reflectors and safety gear. If you are riding to the trailhead on city streets and highways make sure to wear reflective clothing and use flashing front and back lights. This is especially important in the early morning and evening when visibility is reduced. When transporting your bikes to and from the trailhead, make sure they are securely fastened and locks are set. Know the safety features of your rack. A bike falling off your vehicle in the parking lot or, worse yet, off the road, is a bad deal for the bike and for other drivers.

The most common injuries sustained while biking are road rash due to sliding, impacts to knees, elbow and shoulders and head injuries due to the impact of ejection over the handle bars.

PUT A LID ON IT

New technologies make helmets safer (and cooler looking) and come within a variety of price ranges. Buy a helmet that is ANSI certified. You can check this by looking at the tag inside the helmet.

Make sure your helmet is fitted correctly according to manufacturer's recommendations. This typically means that the strap is snug but not choking tight. You shouldn't be able to pull the helmet over the top of your head exposing your forehead. This is an area where many injuries occur due to the trajectory forces of an endo and the weight/velocity of your melon ejecting over the bars.

Make sure your forehead is covered.

Traveling in remote areas also requires first aid awareness and preparation for changing weather conditions.

INJURIES FROM TRAUMA

Have a plan for worst-case scenarios. Know basic first aid and learn where the nearest medical centers are.

COLD

Wear clothes in layers. Pack warmer insulation for stopping or in case of equipment failures. Use wind proof clothing, a neck tube or other coverings for the neck and ears and, also, under the helmet for cold weather riding.

TRAIL ETIQUETTE

Mountain bikers can sometimes be in a fragile position as to how they are perceived by other trail users. Do your part for the mountain bike community and be courteous to hikers, runners, equestrians and other bikers. When in doubt about the right of way, simply step off the trail and let the other party go by with a smile and a wave.

Bikers yield to horses.

Always step to the downhill side of the trail. It's less threatening to the horse. Talk to the horse, it assures them that you're a human. Talk to the rider.

Bikers yield to hikers.

If they see you speeding by and step off the trail, slow down and say thanks.

Bikers yield to bikers when descending (let the uphill rider, who is putting out the most effort have the right of way and cheer them on with an "atta way!"

THE DIRT

Soil is a combination of three main ingredients: clay, sand and silt. The texture of the soil is based on the percentage of each in the mix. Equal parts of clay, sand and silt makes a loam soil which can be ideal for riding (and plant growth).

Solids, water and air volume will also contribute to the tackiness, or stickiness of the trail. A dry trail will be dusty where a very wet trail will be muddy, especially with a heavy clay mix.

Clay feels sticky when wet and will glob on to your bike and components, turning stone-like when dry and making it difficult to remove. Silt feels silky smooth when wet while sand feels course and gritty like riding on slick ball bearings when it's wet. The rule of thumb is to give two days after a good rain to let the trails fully dry out before riding and risking damage to them.

TRAIL DOGS

Some dogs simply love to run with bikes. The four-legged creatures can outrun most humans, but a bike can level the playing field (at least on the downhills). Riding with your dog can be an amazing way to connect with your canine companion in the outdoors.

Check to see if dogs are allowed off leash where you are riding. All Bozeman trails (except for Pete's Hill Dog Park and the connector trail) require dogs to be leashed. It is possible to rig a bike leash. I've used a retractable leash connected to the stem of the bike with Velcro or ski straps. The leash mechanism allows for some expansion or contraction of the leash line so Fido is less likely to abruptly jerk the handle bars to the side, causing the rider to fly over the handlebars. Always wear a helmet as head injuries can be fatal. Avoid the leash being caught around the wheel which can ruin your day (and your bike) pretty quickly.

Advanced maneuvers

Teach your dog to heel on your right side, getting them off the trail so other hikers or riders can pass.

Get your dog to scope a line down between switchback descents so they can keep up on full-speed downhills.

Sustainable Trail Care

When riding in the mountain in the early season you may encounter water on the trail, deadfall, eye-poker snags and

other hazards. Bike photojournalist Bob Allen brings a trail kit to help keep the trails safe and running smoothly.

BOB ALLEN'S TRAIL KIT

1. A hand saw for cutting reasonably-sized dead fall and trail-blocking nuisances.

2. A pruning shears to clear water bars, and to cut eye-poker tree branches which tend to curl downwards as the season gets drier.

3. A collapsible trail hoe/shovel for draining puddles by cleaning up water bars and any other necessary digging to prevent water from running down the trail and eroding it.

Keep an eye out for travelers - invasive species and weeds, that is. Spotted knapweed grows like wild fire when introduced along trails. Pulling it out by the root before it flowers can go a long way in reducing the impact of this weed. Washing your bike as a part of your routine maintenance after a ride can also decrease the likelihood of transporting these unwanted travelers to other trails.

While land agencies typically have some budget for trail maintenance, it is up to every user to respectfully manage the sustainable use of trails. Our own actions - such as staying on marked trails will help reduce erosion. Give a hoot, don't pollute, pick up trash when you see it and, in general, leave the place better than how you found it.

Jason Lunden and Jason Erickson doing some field repairs far out in the mountains

MAINTENANCE- THE ABCS

A properly running machine will make your biking trips safe and enjoyable. Before each ride check the ABCs.

Air - Check tire pressures: tubeless tires can take lower pressures. Do some experimenting to decide how much air gives you the best grip or the smoothest roll.

Brakes - Check the levers and brake pads.

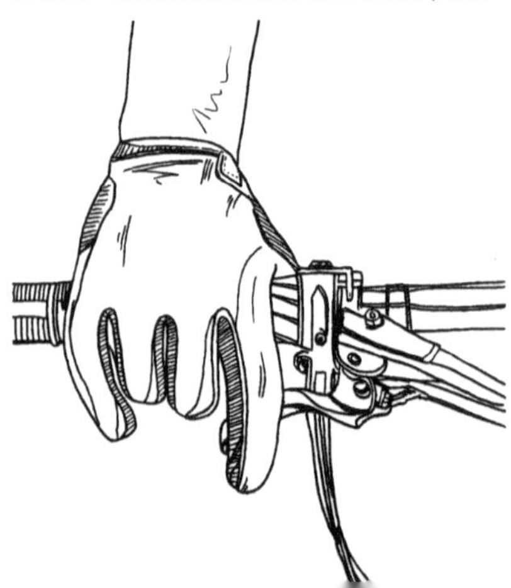

If your brakes squeak excessively (and aren't wet) it is likely past due time to swap out the brake pads.
Chain - A clean chain is a happy chain. Wash it after each ride (especially messy ones) ideally with a chain cleaning tool. A wet rag and brush will work too. This is a good time to inspect the chain and make sure there aren't any weak links, check that the drive chain is running smoothly, spin through gears and try shifting while the bike is on a stand or upside down. Finish by oiling up the chain and you'll be ready for the next ride. Carrying a quick link and a chain tool on long remote ride will get you out of a pinch if you need to fix a broken chain or remove it.

The more you ride and wear out parts, the more familiar you will become with making slight adjustments on all the systems and know when to turn off the YouTube videos and to have the pros work on it. It is a good idea to do an overhaul in the spring before you start putting tough miles on the trails.

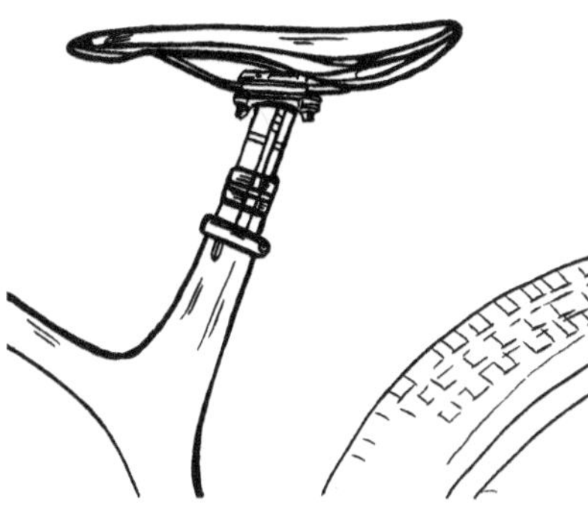

DROP IT

Seat posts can be adjusted with an Allen key (typically for lighter racing cross country bikes), a quick release for manual adjustment or with a hydraulically controlled dropper post that some bikes have. By using body weight and pressing of a lever on the handlebar the seat will lower to a fixed lower downhill position. By unweighting and pressing the lever the seat rises to the default up position for climbing.

Stopping the spinning wheel of a bike is achieved by compressing of padded calibers on the rims (caliper breaks) or compressing of brake pads on rotors that spin inside the wheel. Downhill bikes have larger rotors and break pads to distribute more heat.

DRIVE CHAIN

Gone are the day of the 21 speeds, 3 cogs in the front, 7 in the back and two shifter levers. The modern mountain bike set up runs a 1x10 or 1x12 which means one single cog in the front attached to the crank and ten or twelve sets of gears in the rear. This removes the need for two sets of shifting levers, leaving the shifting to the right handlebar and clearing space on the left for dropper post lever and suspension lock out grip twist, buttons or levers.

Drive chains are the parts that make your bike move forward from your pedaling force. This encompasses the front cog, hub and crankshaft, connected by the chain to the rear cogs, with shifting enabled through the rear derailleur and connecting cables and wires to complete the package. Eventually, after enough wear and tear, your chain will stretch and your gear teeth will wear down, requiring the replacement of the chain and eventually the replacement of the gears

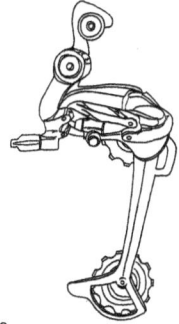

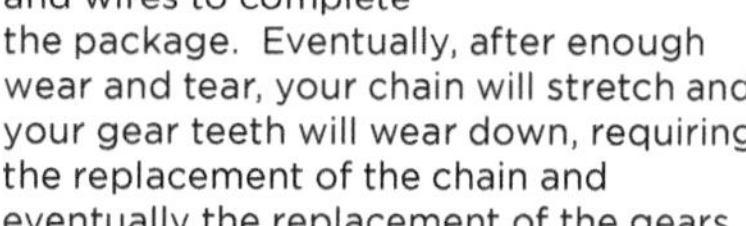

when they are all worn out.

RUBBER SIDE DOWN

Where the rubber hits the road, gravel, dirt and duff.

Mountain bike tires range from small nubby cross country tires designed for roll efficiency and speed to burly, knobby wide tires for downhill, rocks and snow. Ranging in width from 2" to the 4" fat bike tires there are many tire variations each one with a specific range of riding

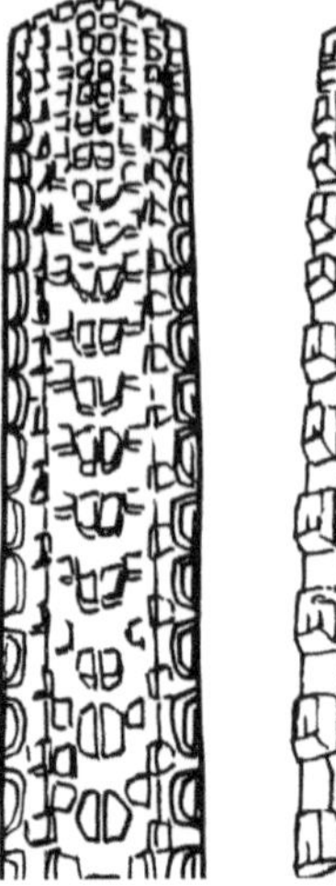

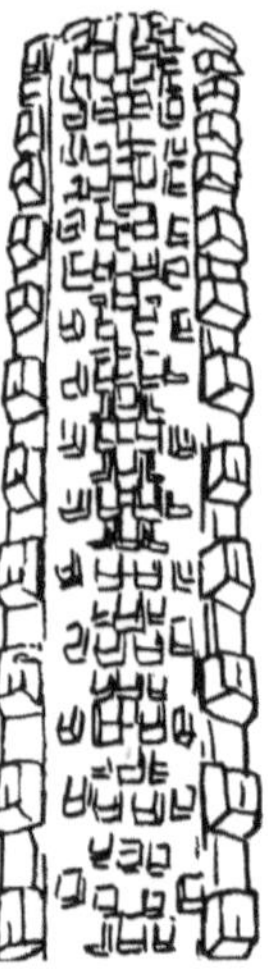

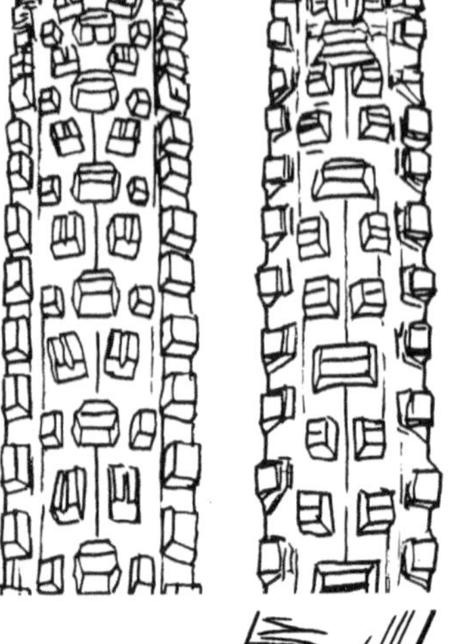

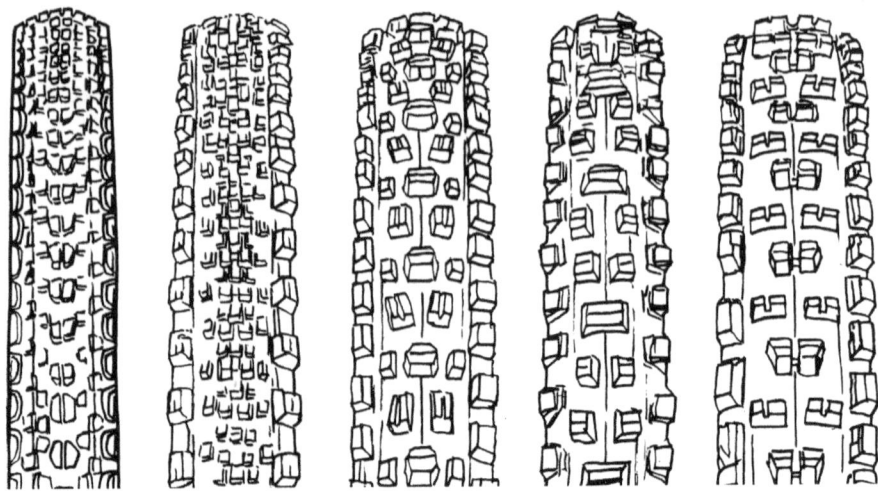

in mind.

Talk to your bike shop about the options your bike wheels have for tires. The standard mountain bike wheel size was 26" for ages. Now the larger 29" wheels offer more speed and cornering power utilizing the centrifugal force of the wheel size. 27.5" tires with wider sizes are popular smaller riders or to provide more traction and cushion for a fun ride on a hard tail.

Many wheels now have the option to go tubeless. This system seals the tire to the rim in a similar way that a car tire works. To give extra durability and puncture resistance, a slime or coating is applied inside the tire and spread evenly by spinning the wheels. On the occurrence of a small puncture, like a cactus, the wheel will self-seal and fix the leak.

"Bacon strips" can be used for larger punctures. Side wall gashes can be repaired with dollar bills.

Packing a five dollar bill serves two purposes: some emergency cash should you require a snack or energy beverage on the ride and as a makeshift patch to fix sidewall damage on tubeless tires.

It is still a good idea to pack a spare tube, patch kit and pump for emergencies. If one system fails, it is good to have a backup.

Double action hand held pumps work in the field, as well as pressurized single-use air canisters that will save some time pumping.

Tubeless tires can be run at less air pressure than a tubed rig. This allows for greater flexibility for tuning in for better climbing traction or shock absorption on descents.

There is no cut and dried rule for how much air to put into tires other than don't exceed what the label says on the tire. This is generally 40 psi for a tubed mountain bike tire. Tubeless generally run between 20 and 30 psi. It will take some experimenting, taking into consideration the terrain, your body weight and the temperature.

Just like car tires, bike tires will increase air pressure as the temperature rises and decreases in colder temperatures. That's why it is important to check tire pressure each time you pull the bike out of the garage before riding.

An air compressor you use for your car can be the easiest way to check tire pressures and refill. If you have the thinner valve (presta) a cheap adapter can be used to make the compressor work with the same type of valve that your car uses.

PROGRESSION OF SPORT

The best way to safely learn to mountain bike and get the most enjoyment is to progressively learn skills and build fitness. Start small by getting familiar with the bike trying basic maneuvers on short easy trails. Advance from there, riding longer and increasing difficult trails and features incrementally.

Pre-ride, Re-ride & Free-ride

Get familiar with the terrain of a trail by doing the first lap in a slower mind-ful pace. Look for obstacles, noting climbs, descents and key turns, etc. The next lap builds on the first lap, making the course more familiar by practicing poten-tial lines more assertively which should prepare you for the free ride.

After learning the course and where potential areas are for acceleration and caution you are ready for free ride. Free ride focuses on efficient riding with maximum speed and focus on performance.

SKILLS

• Bunny hop - compressing the bike and releasing with a spring of your legs to compel both tires to rise off the ground. Helpful in clearing obstacles like rocks and logs in the trail or jumping in and out of a rut.

• Wheelie - riding on the rear wheel while the front wheel is raised above the ground. Rear brake is applied to keep the rider from "looping out" or falling flat on their back.

• Manual - like a wheelie but riding on the back wheel without pedaling. Useful in descending rough terrain or preparing to drop off a rise.

• Endo - opposite of a wheelie; the rear wheel rises off the ground, rolling or stationary, on the front wheel only. An abrupt compression of the first brake will result in an over-the bar endo, ejecting the rider from the bike (this is bad). A more subtle movement is rising onto the front wheel and adjusting the position of the rear tire, which is useful for descending sharp switchbacks but also requires a great deal of skill to do without going over the handlebars.

Jump - both wheels rise off the ground, like a bunny hop, but as the result of propelling off a rise with speed. A pre-jump where the bike is compressed prior to the apex of the rise can be helpful in maintaining control and speed or avoiding unwanted air.

• Carve - cornering the bike to turn left or right on a berm. Enter the berm on the high side and cut in, leaning the bike pedals while evenly maintaining pressure and balance through the center of gravity under the rider.

• Bike body separation, carving - wind shield wipers, moving the bike left or right to engage the centrifugal force of the wheels (even more pronounced on 29" tires) this gives the turning knobs purchase in the ground to pull around corners with velocity. Shed speed prior to starting the turn, accelerate out of the turn looking further down the trail.

• Bike body separation, climbing and descending - as the grade steepens, sitting more forward in the saddle with your weight forward will help with climbing. An extreme example is rising fully out of the seat, leaning forward cranking pedals around. This is used on extremely steep hills while pumping the

NICA head coach Heidi Makoutz giving some enthusiastic feedback

bike side to side sprinting to provide a quick pick up to muscle activation on a long climb.

FITNESS

Just like the skills bits, fitness is an incremental build as well. Start each season getting reacquainted with your bike on short easy trails. With many GVLT town trails Bozeman is a great place for this. Many mountain bikers start off in the spring by riding road bikes while the trails dry out. Bike computers can be used to measure power wattage to tailor your training intervals. Apps like Strava can help you keep track of mileage and note who is riding what trails and when. This can also help you pick a route that is in season by noting what trails other people are riding from week to week.

The public lands in SW Montana are a treasure. Access to the trails that connect these wild places is something that mountain bikers shouldn't take for granted. The Montana Mountain Bike Alliance took a place at the table in 2009 when many areas were removing access to mountain bikes.

TRAIL ADVOCACY

Advocacy for responsible trail use has sprung up, appearing in other prominent community organizations like the Southwest Montana Mountain Bike Association (SWMMBA) which has groups in Bozeman and Big Sky.

There are more opportunities now than ever to get involved with mountain biking and the organizations that want to keep the sport accessible to everyone.

The author is Ready to Ride!

We hope this book inspires you to be your own action hero. Get out there and explore. Meet up with friends. Find a new trail. Drain a puddle, remove a trail-blocking deadfall tree, trim eye-poker branches, pull a weed. It is up to all of us to serve as positive examples of responsible stewardship for these local treasures.

Now get out there and make some mountain biking memories!

BIKING IS FOR EVERYONE

We all start somewhere. Regardless of our God-given abilities, we don't reach our full potential without the help of others. Consider what opportunities you have for improving your biking. Find a group to ride with. Evaluate your interests and specific strengths and weaknesses. Biking is a lifetime sport that is available to all, regardless of age or physical abilities. Both the very young and older adults can experience the joy of spinning on mountain trails.

The bike community here in SW Montana is made of many different groups with far-reaching impacts. These groups are all passionate about biking, trails and the incredible power of working together to provide recreation opportunities for everyone.

Biking makes us happier, not just as individuals, but within entire communities.

That is why we are building this book experience. We encourage you to explore the QR code links to interviews, videos, GPS maps and more. This resource is designed to help you start learning about a new aspect of the sport, if you desire to do that, by providing information on who to talk to about getting started, building skills, fitness, and where to go to have the best day on your bike throughout the season.

I hope this book inspires your family to get out and make some memories of your own.

Happy Trails

Be safe & enjoy riding!

Mountain biking adventures in the Lion's Head Range, overlooking Sheep Creek and steep switchbacks ahead

BIKE
Prep

SADDLE
SADDLE RAILS
SEAT TUBE
DROPPER SEAT POST
SHOCK
SEAT STAYS

Reach

DRIVE TRAIN
REAR DERAILLEUR
CASSETTE
CHAIN STAYS
CHAIN RING
CRANK ARM
PEDAL

BIKE ANATOMY

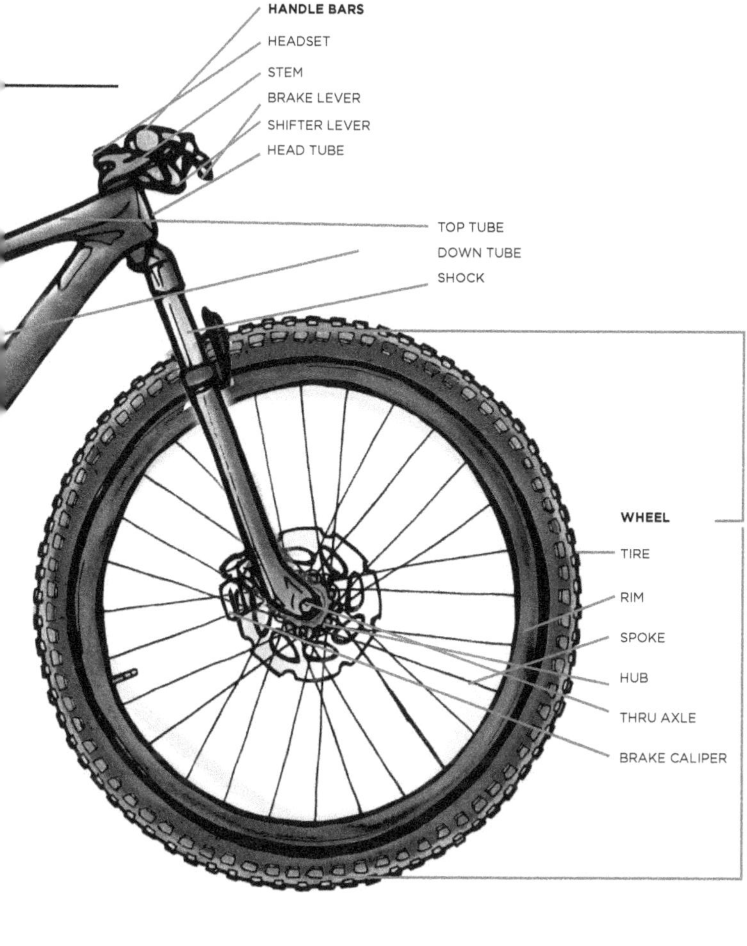

BIKE
Gear

GET THE GEAR

To enjoy this sport, you are going to need a bike.

The following pages will demonstrate different types of bikes and riding.

Beyond the frame, the performance and weight of the bike is determined by its components: drive chain, brakes and wheels. Each can be tailored for specific performance properties, factoring in the strength and weight of the materials they are made of.

TYPES OF MOUNTAIN BIKES

Wheel size, suspension and geometry are the differentiators between bikes for each riding style.

Differences you will find between bikes for different riding styles include fork angle and travel. The more "slack" the fork is, the more suited it is for aggressive downhill riding. Travel is the amount of suspension that a fork will allow. This is measured in millimeters, for example: 150 MML travel in front, 80 in rear etc. There are many different types of suspension layouts. Some are mounted in the top tube like in cross-country race bikes: enduro and trail bikes may have the suspension built into the lower bar and have different settings for adjusting dampening. Other suspension setups for downhill bikes include visible springs. Work with your bike shop to get the best suspension adjustments for your riding style and bike.

Adjustments should be made by your bike shop to fit your size, weight and riding style.

Support local businesses for the best service. See list of local bike shops in the Additional Resources pages at the end of this section.

Enduro jump

TYPES OF BIKES

TOWING RIGS

Suspension: Varied to accommodate weight
Frame Geometry: Large tube for battery
Weight: 40+lbs
Pedals: Flats
Wheels: 29" Small Knobs 2.4-4"

CHARIOT

Bike attachments for strollers, like the chariot handle, will collapse for storage and enable the entire family to get out together. As kids grow, replacing the enclosed chariot with a tagalong riding behind you and gives them the feel of biking with the folks.

TAGALONG

Attaching at the seat post, tagalong bikes have a rear wheel, drive chain and handlebars. These bikes help give kids a sense of being on a bigger pedal bike, with the assistance of the rider in the drivers seat. A modified tandem of sorts for one adult or larger rider and child, these bikes are a great progression from the enclosed chariot to a strider bike. The bikes are a way to have longer rides as a family where little legs might not be able do to the distance or difficulty.

TOW CABLES

Tow cables connect an adult bike to a child's bike by attaching the seat post of the adult bike to the handle bars of the child's bike. In most cases it is best to remove the tow cables for descents.

These specifically designed bungee cords allow a tow function. They do take a little practice so the rear rider doesn't run into the tire of the front rider or get ejected around a corner. Consistent steady riding is the name of the game for this type of device. They are more useful on flat or uphill riding. In most cases is best to remove for the descents.

STRIDER BIKE

Suspension: None
Frame Geometry: No drive chain
Weight: less than 10lbs
Pedals: None
Wheels: 20"

The days of running behind the child's bike, hunched over and holding on to the back of the seat, are gone. Strider bikes give better balance, engage the core and help kids to comfortably develop the sensation of inertia and balance. If you don't have a strider bike, taking the pedals off your child's bike and lowering the seat to where their feet firmly rest on the ground can work as a makeshift strider. GVLT trails and the start of Copper City are great for helping young kids get a trail feel on their tiny bikes.

Although it takes some work getting the family out on the trails, outings are almost always memorable.

It can be challenging to get the entire family out on bikes. It can be a challenge finding equipment that fits growing kids and also keeping track of helmets, gloves, coats, shorts and sunglasses for the entire crew, plus having spares in case gear is lost. It is exhausting to think about all this before the riding even starts!

Tagalongs taking a break at Copper City rocks

Torrey Schaeffer and Mom striding at Copper City

TYPES OF BIKES

CROSS-COUNTRY

Suspension: >120MML
Frame Geometry: Climbing Oriented
Weight: High teens to Mid-Twenty Lbs.
Pedals: Clipless or Flats
Wheels: 29" Small Knobs 2.2-2.4"

Most of us get started on a hardtail cross-country mountain bike. These are the least expensive (unless you go top of the line ultra-light custom race bike).

Cross country terrain consists of long climbs and relatively smooth trails. This is especially true for cross country mountain bike race courses where speed and distance are featured rather than extreme technical challenges, like on enduro or downhill courses.

Cross-country bikes are designed for efficient pedaling over smooth, rolling terrain.

Weight is the number one consideration. Lack of bulky rear suspension systems can save weight. making it easier for climbing, there are, however, high end racing models that feature top tube rear suspension as well.

Frame geometry is designed more for climbing than descending. Tires tend to be thinner with small knobs to give grip while reducing roll resistance.

TRAIL BIKE

Suspension: >150MML
Frame Geometry: Versatile
Weight: 20 - 30 lbs
Pedals: Clipless or Flats
Wheels: 29" Knobby Tires 2.4-2.6" wide

The most versatile and popular style of mountain bikes offer a balance of light weight and nimble feeling while having a slacker geometry suited for descending. Trail bikes can have up to 150mml of travel on front and rear suspension and a slacker geometry similar to an enduro bike.

The light weight and nimble feel makes these bikes a great choice for the full mountain biking experience of climbing and descending Montana trails.

The burlier geometry, higher stack height and relative slack angle compared to cross country bikes make trail bikes versatile for climbing and descending efficiently.

Typically lighter than enduro bikes, they tend to be more efficient at climbing while still being able to take a beating on the descent, making trail bikes feel nimble and playful.

Cole Bothner riding Crosscut single track

Carving Leverich corners

ENDURO BIKE

Suspension: >150-180MML
Frame Geometry: Downhill Oriented
Weight: 20s to 30 lbs
Pedals: Flats
Wheels: 29" Large Knobs 2.4-2.6"

Called the "all mountain" mountain bike, enduro bikes are built for steep and rough terrain, but they are still ridable both uphill and downhill.

Enduro bikes can take more of a downhill beating than a trail bike, but they are lighter and more responsive for climbing than a full downhill bike. With slack geometry, robust suspension and 150-180 mm of travel, these bikes are oriented for downhill performance. But because enduro courses have some cross country and uphill travel, the bikes can still be pedaled on the terrain that the courses cover.

DOWNHILL

Suspension: >180MML +
Frame Geometry: Downhill Optimized
Weight: 30+ lbs
Pedals: Flats
Wheels: 29" Large Knobs 2.4-2.6" wide

This bike is built entirely for descending.

Heavier dual-crown forks give the most suspension of all types of mountain bikes with over 180mm of travel.

Sturdily built to handle rough trails and compressions, the bike's weight is not a concern. Heavy downhill bikes are often either pushed uphill or ascend mountain courses via lift access or vehicle shuttle.

Riders descending a steep, curvy enduro course

Rider getting air on a downhill course

TYPES OF BIKES

E-BIKE

Suspension: Varied to accommodate weight
Frame Geometry: Large tube for battery
Weight: 40+lbs
Pedals: Flats
Wheels: 29" Small Knobs 2.4-4"

E bikes are built with a variety of configurations and electric assists, ranging from cross-country bikes with assists to fat bikes with full power mode.

Some models have a full power mode very similar to riding an electric motorcycle. Pedal boost will give pedal assistance, virtually making a steep hill feel like a flat zero incline. Batteries have different running lengths depending how far you go and how much power or assistance is used.

E-bikes aren't allowed on hiking trials and some specifically built mountain bike trails. They are generally allowed on any trail or double track where motorized vehicles are allowed; therefore, e-bikes are primarily ridable on gravel roads and ATV trails in Montana.

Check with each trail system before bringing an e-bike onto that trail.

Because they are self-propelled (to varying degrees) the US Forest Service considers all e-bikes as motorized vehicles. This category puts them in with motorized dirt bikes which have specific guidelines for trail use. Refer to the Motor Vehicle Use Map for Custer Gallatin National Forest trails to see where e-bikes are permitted.

There are timeshare trails for bikes and motorized bikes in the Bridger and Hyalite areas that apply from June 16th to September 4th.

GRAVEL BIKE

Suspension: None
Frame Geometry: Cyclo-cross
Weight: 20 - 30 lbs
Pedals: Clipless
Wheels: 700cc thin tires little knobs

Gravel bikes are basically a road bike with a few modifications to make them more durable and ridable on gravel roads, double track and some cross-country terrain.

Gravel bikes don't usually have suspension other than some custom systems that work like subtle dampeners. Caliper brakes are replaced with disc brakes, like in xc mountain bike riding, for better stopping power. Slicks are replaced with thinner knobby tires that have good roll speed and, also, some traction for, yes, gravel.

These are the bikes of choice for cyclocross events, stage races and some of the mellow trails on Bozeman's Main Street to Mountains trail system which are mostly gravel trails.

Being able to travel long distances with good traction and a smooth tire roll is the biggest attribute of this category.

It is common to see gravel bikes on the Painted Hills Connector trail and the Sourdough to Mystic section. Connecting Moser double tracks to Hyalite and beyond opens some fun options for a mix of gravel and pavement that is well-suited for these bikes.

Fat Tire Bikes, or Fat Bikes

Suspension: >150-180MML
Frame Geometry: Downhill Oriented
Weight: Premium Models less than 30 lbs
Pedals: Flats
Wheels: 29" 3.7 x 5.2"

Tires ranging from 3.7" to 5.2" wide and a sturdy frame give these bikes great traction through wintry conditions. Hard packed snow is the terrain of choice for fat bikers, who use hiking trails with the right inclines or custom packed routes specifically designed for fat biking. Tires in the 4" range should work well for packed snow. Wider tires do better in soft unpacked snow. Studded tires in 4.0" and 4.6" can provide better traction on icy terrain. They are expensive, but they allow riders to get out in extreme weather conditions. These can be set up tubeless which can run at very low tire pressure in winter conditions for maximum traction.

Fat bikes are as common around town in the winter as commuter bikes. While their bulk limits them from being especially fast, they are sturdy and have great stopping power on winter trails.

Fat bikes are not allowed on most Nordic groomed trails in the area. Look for specific fat bike trails like the narrow gauge trails at Crosscut or on packed winter hiking trails like the ice climbing approach trails in the Hyalite Grotto Falls area.

There are some snowmobile trails open to fat bikes on the national forest.

Check with the Gallatin National Forest for trail options and make sure to get a groomed trail pass from the Gallatin Valley Snowmobile Association.

Always yield to snowmobiles.

BMX BIKE

Suspension: None
Frame Geometry: Small Dirt Bike
Weight: 20-25 lbs
Pedals: Flats
Wheels: 26"

Smaller BMX bikes are nimble and make it easier to change body position on exaggerated features like dirt ramps, corners and jumps.

If a much shorter ride is in your plans, check out one of the local bike park pump tracks that are popping up in the Bozeman area. With short loops filled with dips, rises and berms, these BMX- reminiscent dirt or synthetic tracks are a great way to build skills like bike/ body separation and carrying momentum through the features. Some pump tracks like the new rubberized track in South Bozeman are designed with smaller riders in mind and use synthetic materials that won't get muddy.

Freeride bikes are the mountain bike version of BMX bikes, with full mountain bike components and a slack geometry. They are generally smaller - a more maneuverable size for aerial movement and bike control on jumps, ramps and extreme features.

Photo reference - Bob Allen

Photo reference courtesy of Mel Cronin SWMMBA - Gallatin County Bike Park

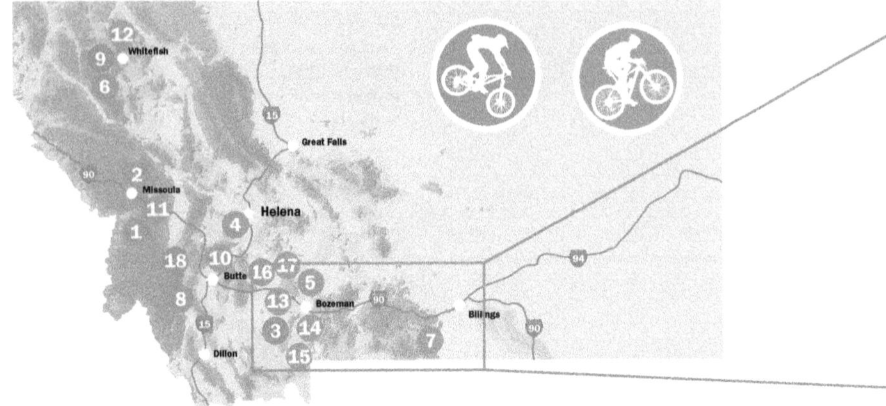

THE LAY OF THE LAND

Montana has endless legacy trails for mountain biking. Check with land management agencies to make sure biking is allowed before heading to a new place.

- United States Forest Service (USFS)
- Bureau of Land Management (BLM)
- National Park Service (NPS)
- City Parks and Municipalities

There are great resources online for taking your bike further, like bike packing the Gallatin to the Continental Divide. Check out bikepacking.com

Trail systems designed with mountain biking in mind are becoming more common especially in mountain biking hubs like Helena, Whitefish and Bozeman/ Big Sky.

This is by no means a definitive guide to all the mountain biking accessible in the state.

Montana has a variety of mountain biking destinations to explore.

Here are a few:

Mountain Bike Trail Systems

1. Warm Springs Trail Systems
2. The Rattlesnake Trail System - Fast and Flowy MTB
3. Big Sky Resort - Downhill MTB Playground
4. South Hills - Mt. Helena Ridge Miles of Mountain Bike Trails
5. Bangtail Divide - Bozeman
6. Beardance Trail - Kalispell
7. Line Creek Plateau - Red Lodge
8. Chief Joseph Pass Area Trails - Wisdom
9. Whitefish Mountain Resort
10. Thompson Park- Butte
11. Marshall Mountain- Bonner - Collegiate Mountain Bike Championship
12. Alpine #7 Mountain Biking Trail
13. Curly Lake Highline Trail - MTB to Over 10K Feet
14. Gallatin - Bozeman Emerald Trail
15. Madison Range - MTB Bliss
16. Pipestone Mountain Bike Trails - Kalispell
17. Copper City
18. Discovery

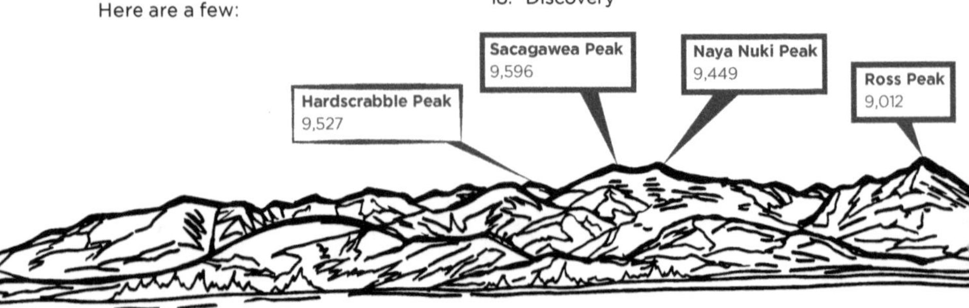

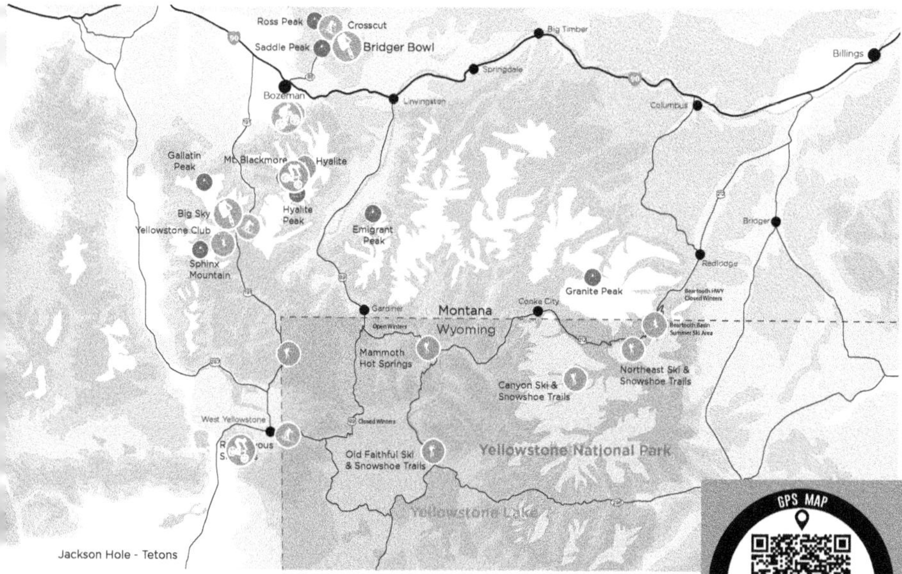

The Last Best BIKE GPS Regional Interactive Map

GPS MAP
GO
BIKE BOZEMAN

This book focuses on the greater Bozeman/Big Sky area (Bozone), including the Bridgers, Bozeman Town Trails, Hyalite and Gallatin Range, Big Sky and Madison Range, the Gallatin Corridor to West Yellowstone National Park and Paradise Valley.

It is a starting point with recommended trails in Bozeman, the Bridgers, Hyalite, Big Sky and the desert trails to the west like Copper City.

Visit the GPS map on the website for trailhead pins, GPS routes and locations of trail heads. This overview map shows the lay of the land and some pointers for finding more information for your next mountain biking adventure in the region.

Many local trails in Bozeman can be accessed by the Main Street to Mountains Trails developed by the Gallatin Valley Land Trust. Local trailhead parking lots fill up early and fast. So where there are bike to hike or loop options, this book will tell you about those, as well.

The website includes links for more information about trails and access points for the trail systems.

As of now there are no public shuttles available for the popular trailheads, so if you can't ride to the trailhead, consider carpooling with your friends.

Dig in deeper: check out "Southern Montana Single track" guidebook from Beartooth Publishing for more mountain biking routes in Southwest Montana.

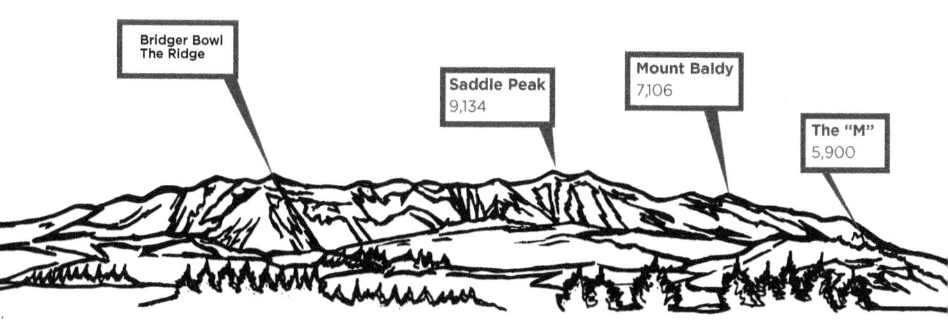

The Bridger Range looking north from Bozeman

LOCATIONS

BIKE
Trails

Kiersten and Meghan Biking GVLT Trails, Bozeman

BIKING BOZEMAN

Bozeman Area Trails

Main street To Mountains: 80+ Miles

The Bozeman area has access to a handful of trailheads via short drives or bike rides to trailheads. The Gallatin Valley Land Trust has been working on connecting trails between Bozeman's Main Street to the mountains over the past thirty years. Dirt and gravel trails wind through neighborhoods and connect to the main artery. Galligator Trail now extends from Triple Tree at the edge of the Gallatin Range through Bozeman and to the "M" trail and Bridger foothills.

These town trails provide access for commuters and cyclists of all ages and ability levels. The flat gravel trails wind through woods, along streams and can be chained together to form longer rides as skills increase.

The Main street to Mountains Trail is paved from Storymill Park to the "M" Trail. Downtown to Pete's Hill is the recommended starting ride for Bozeman. If the bike shops let you, this trail can also be the best place to test ride bikes to get a better idea of how they climb and descend on the trail.

A safe family-friendly grade on asphalt rises on rolling hills to meet the "M" and Drinking Horse trailheads for a bike and hike option. While the Drinking Horse and "M" trails aren't open to bikes, the Bridger Foothills trail is.

It is possible to make some adventurous mountain loops connecting one drainage to another right from the town trails.

This next section of the book will guide you to these trailhead access points. Many of them from town can be accessed on your bike on local trails and roads.

Many of these trailheads can be accessed from town by bike on local trails and roads. Many open up to multiple riding options. The out and back trails are labeled in the call out boxes, along with elevation gain, distance and difficulty. Many of these have options to extend the ride by looping or connecting with other trails. We encourage you to use these as starting points for your own explorations.

The alternates we list in this book are the ways we prefer to ride these trails after having explored the variations.

There are twenty main trail access points in this book, starting with downtown Bozeman and extending south to Big Sky and west to Copper City.

All of these trails are accessible as day rides from Bozeman.

Kiersten Schaeffer riding the bike path back from the "M" trail hike

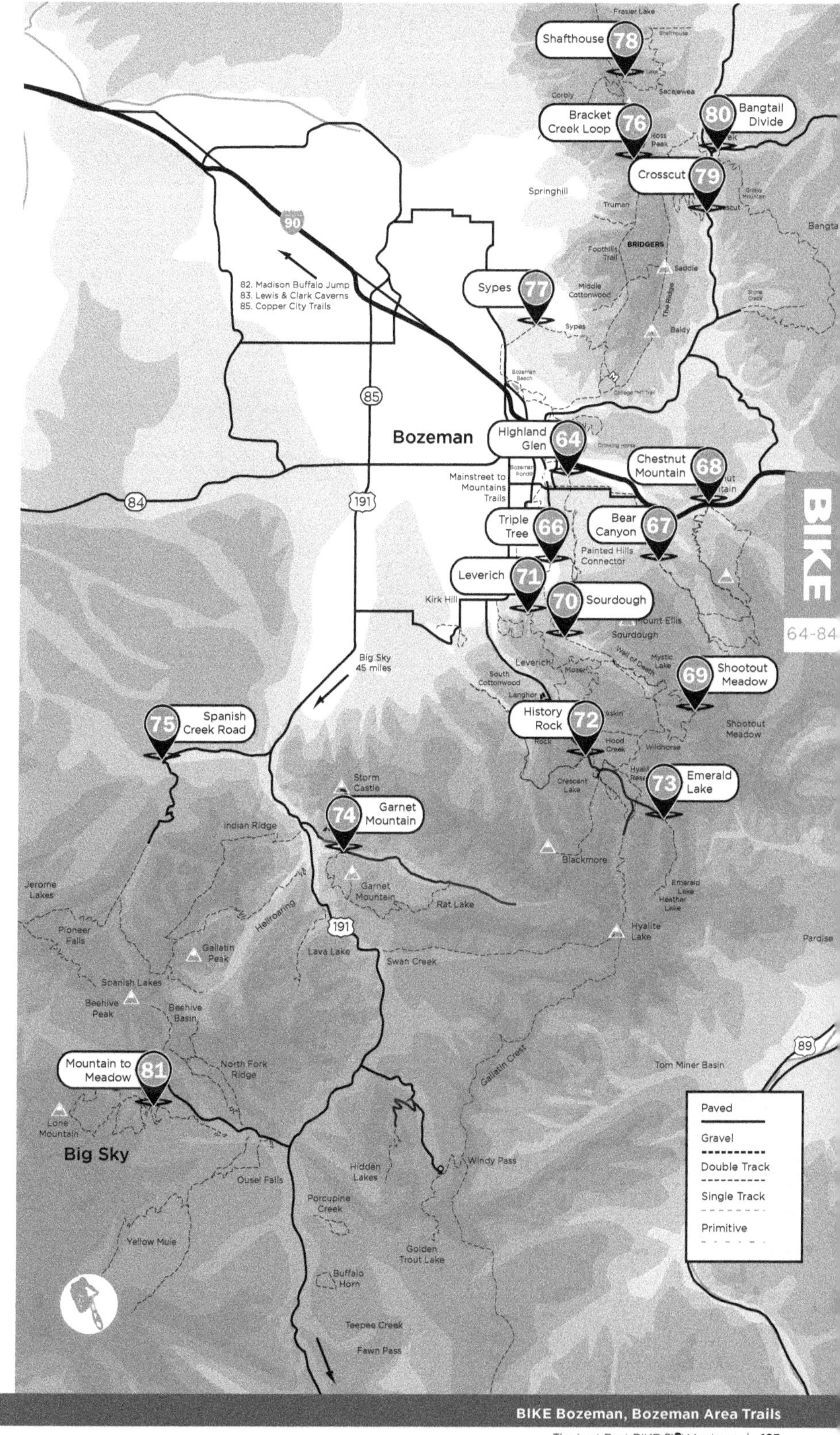

Shafthouse 78
Bracket Creek Loop 76
Bangtail Divide 80
Crosscut 79
Springhill
BRIDGERS
Sypes 77
82. Madison Buffalo Jump
83. Lewis & Clark Caverns
85. Copper City Trails
90
85
Bozeman
Highland Glen 64
Chestnut Mountain 68
Mainstreet to Mountains Trails
84
191
Triple Tree 66
Bear Canyon 67
Painted Hills Connector
Leverich 71
Sourdough 70
Kirk Hill
Mount Ellis
Big Sky 45 miles
Shootout Meadow 69
History Rock 72
Spanish Creek Road 75
Emerald Lake 73
Storm Castle
Garnet Mountain 74
Indian Ridge
Blackmore
Jerome Lakes
Rat Lake
Pioneer Falls
Gallatin Peak
Hellroaring
Hyalite Lake
Lava Lake
Swan Creek
Spanish Lakes
Beehive Peak
Beehive Basin
Mountain to Meadow 81
North Fork Ridge
Gallatin Crest
Tom Miner Basin
89
Lone Mountain
Big Sky
Windy Pass
Hidden Lakes
Ousel Falls
Porcupine Creek
Yellow Mule
Golden Trout Lake
Buffalo Horn
Teepee Creek
Fawn Pass
Paved
Gravel
Double Track
Single Track
Primitive
BIKE
64-84

BIKE Bozeman, Bozeman Area Trails

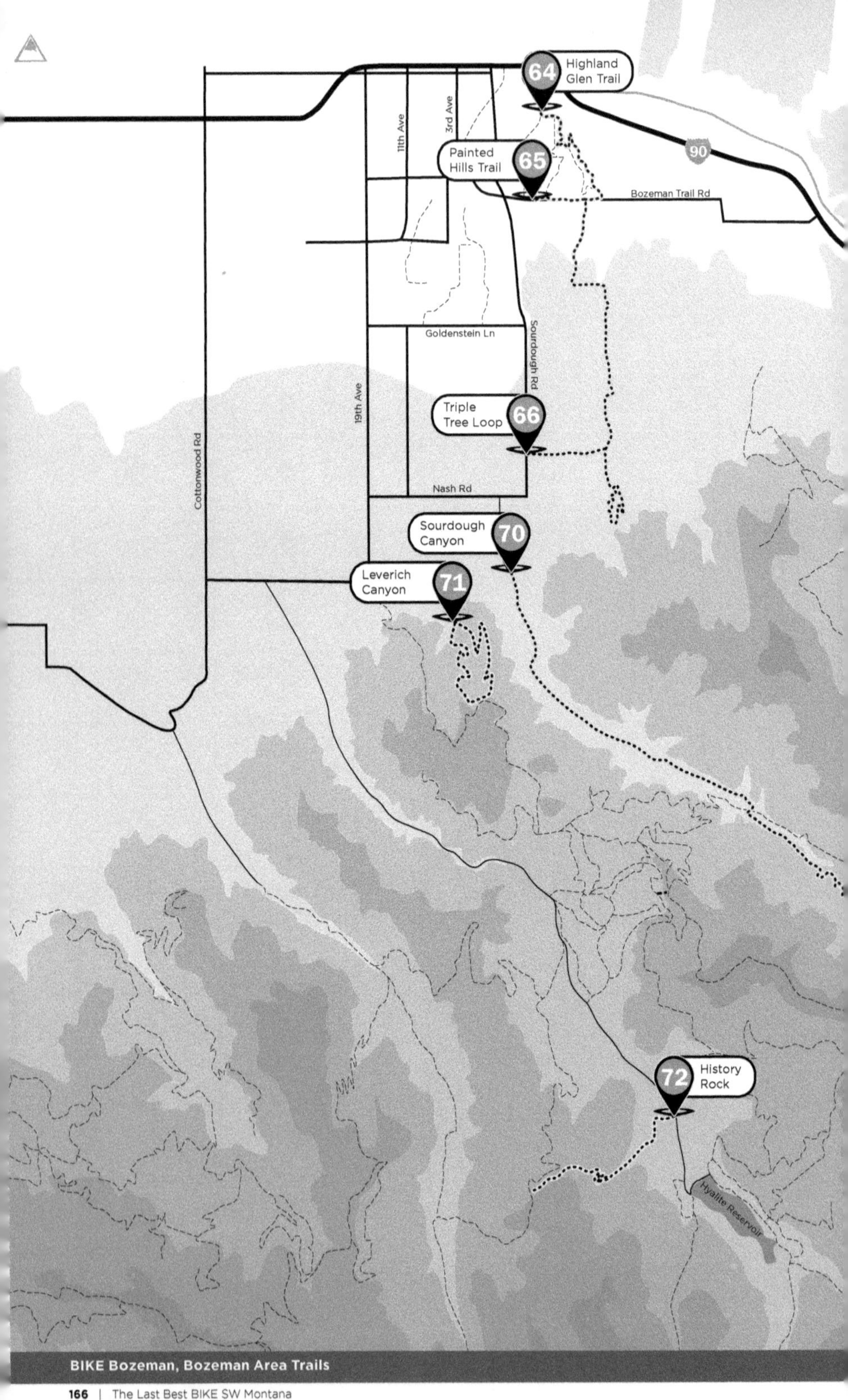

BIKE Bozeman, Bozeman Area Trails

BOZEMAN ON WHEELS

64. Highland Glen

Loop: 3.7 miles
Elevation gain/loss + 220 feet
Top Elevation 4,960 feet
Difficulty: Beginner
Land: *Gallatin Valley Land Trust*

Pete's Hill has multiple overlooks across Bozeman and the valley. Connecting from the library through Lindley Park and Sunset Hills are trails and a cyclocross course in the same area that has snow-making for groomed Nordic trails in the winter.

Highland Glen trails also mimic the Nordic trails in the winter with some variations. This is a popular practice spot for Bozeman Youth Cycling programs and other community-based training groups.

The outer loop at about four miles becomes rolling terrain followed by a short climb to a viewpoint looking across the valley.

Many other short loops can be made to practice mountain biking skills or to get out for a ride without having to drive out of town to a trail.

Highland Glen trails connect to Pete's Hill, the Galligator, Main street to Mountains trails and the Painted Hills Connector trail to Triple Tree Trail.

Search Highland Glen Trial, Bozeman
Trailhead parking at softball fields
(45.6724205,-111.0167652)

Riding Highland Glen above the switchback

65. Painted Hills Connector Trail

Out and Back: 8 miles
Elevation gain/loss +774 feet - 231
Top Elevation 5,282 feet
Difficulty: Moderate
Land: *Gallatin Valley Land Trust*

The Connector Trail connects Highland Glenn and Painted Hills to the Triple Tree Loop Trail via Painted Hills Trail and Painted Hills Gap with its many switchbacks.

This is a highly-trafficked out and back lolly-pop loop from town. Other loops can be made by linking a few roads and GVLT trails on a well-graded path that traces the contours of hills that rise gently from the edge of town. The riding is easy, other than a few steeper areas with tighter switchbacks that will get you breathing a bit harder.

Take in the views of the rolling Sourdough Hills and the mountains on the skyline.

This trail passes through private land easements; please keep your dogs under control and don't ride after dark.

Search Painted Hills Connector Trail
Bozeman, MT
Trailhead (45.6561792,-111.0064548)

Autumn haying along the Connector Trail

66. Triple Tree Loop

Lolly-pop Loop: 5.4 miles
Elevation gain/loss + 958 feet
Top Elevation 5,906 feet
Difficulty: Moderate
Land: *Gallatin Valley Land Trust*

This popular trail near town packs in interesting topography from a short distance.

The official starting point is from the parking lot on Sourdough Road. The trail climbs to a grassy open hillside with great farm-to-mountain views. Drop into a shady forested area and over a bridged stream crossing. Be watching for hikers; visibility is limited in some spots, especially near the stream. A gentle winding short climb leads to the road intersection and connection point to the Painted Hills Connector Trail.

Take a right down a few switchbacks to another shaded stream crossing. The trail then begins to climb steadily into the forest. Take a right at the junction to do the loop in the recommended clockwise direction. More switch backs and a few tight ones will get the blood pumping just in time for the trees to clear to open hillsides filled with wildflowers in the early summer.

Take a breather at the bench and see if you can spot the "Triple Trees" another 1,000 feet up a nearby hill.

The descent is bermed in places with nice flowing sections and water bars along the stream before reconnecting to the loop.

Be courteous to hikers and trail runners and, if in doubt, give them the right away.

Search Triple Tree Loop
Bozeman, MT
Trailhead (45.6130290,-111.0216160)

Erika Flowers riding near the top of Triple Tree

67. Bear Lakes Loop

Loop: 15.38 miles
Elevation gain/loss + 2,375 feet
Top Elevation 6,965 feet
Difficulty: Moderate
Land: Custer Gallatin National Forest

Bear Canyon below and to the southwest of Chestnut Mountain has a network of looping trails and connections to Mystic Lake and the Sourdough Trail.

Past New World Gulch the Bear Canyon trail is more bike friendly with re-graded single track sections and av double track that has been repaired after ATVs chewed it up in the muddy seasons.

This northeastern aspect is similar to the Chestnut Mountain trail and because it stays wet and muddy late into the summer season, it shouldn't be attempted if it has rained recently.

There are bears in this canyon, so be prepared. The trail also takes a very long time to dry out, but when dry it offers some fantastic loops that can be approached from town on more ambitious days.

The shorter Bear Canyon main trail is fun with some variations and a fast-rolling descent on a water-barred double track.

From Bear Lake take the climb up to the high ridge with a natural wall that is a great place for a refuel snack before heading down to the magical "Mystical Bear" trail. This steep trail that winds through rocky terrain and forests, meadows and countless rises is one of the best black diamond trails in the area.

Take Bear Canyon Trail 440, right on Bear Canyon Abbreviated 440, then Right on Bear Lakes Trail to loop back to parking lot.

Search Bear Canyon 440
Bear Lakes Loop Bozeman, MT
Trailhead (45.608768,-110.924000)

Bryan Schaeffer enjoying Bear Canyon rollers

BOZEMAN ON WHEELS

68. Chestnut Mountain Trail

Out and Back: 11.04 miles
Elevation gain/loss + 2,776 feet
Top Elevation 7,481 feet
Difficulty: Hard
Land: Custer Gallatin National Forest

East of town off I90 is the access point to the Chestnut Mountain trail.

When dry, this is a scenic trail close to town that has an amazing descent back to the trail head.

The trail from the parking lot to the connection with Bear Canyon climbs (steeply in places) past Frog Rock up Chestnut Mountain and past the GooseNut Cutoff trail and to the Bear Canyon trail.

The recommended route is a clockwise loop. Pass the trailhead for Trail Creek road and climb up the road that connects to a dirt road to the Goose Creek trailhead (also a popular backcountry skiing area in the winter).

The Goose Creek Chestnut Mountain loop or the "GooseNut" loop ascends above Bear Canyon and opens views of the Absaroka Mountains, as well as the "valley of flowers" to the west.

The descent is fast and steep with lots of winding turns and dramatic viewpoints as you pass Frog Rock and return to the trailhead.

Search Chestnut Mountain Trail
Bozeman, MT
Trailhead (45.645629,-110.882200)

Kiersten Schaeffer on Chestnut Mountain

69. Shootout Park

Loop: 1.6miles with 10+ mile approach
Elevation gain/loss + 95 feet - 405
Top Elevation 7,600 feet
Difficulty: Moderate
Land: Custer Gallatin National Forest

This new trail is in the high country of Bozeman's main water source - Bozeman Creek. It is just one of the scenic highlight sections from this area between the Bear Canyon and Sourdough trailhead access points.

Be sure to pack your 10 essentials and be prepared for wilderness riding in this area.

From the Mystic Bear/Mystic Lake junction the trails climbs steadily up a double track with views of open alpine meadows before cutting into the dark, winding new single track that opens up to the spectacular alpine meadows of Shootout Park.

Prior to the construction of this trail in the summer of 2020 the meadow was a walk-down in order to avoid damaging the flower-filled oasis. This trail addition is a brilliant path through alpine meadows that connects through Sourdough and Bear Canyon accessed by USFS Road 469. The distance to the start of this constructed Forest Service trail is over 10 miles from either direction. Shootout is just a shorter section of a much longer cross country ride.

The single track wraps around natural contours and several stream crossings to Bozeman Creek Crossing, with a double track past the Wildhorse Junction and back to the Sourdough double track.

Search Shootout Park Meadow
Bozeman, MT
Trailhead: (45.515849,-110.898536)

Jason Yager entering Shootout Park

70. Sourdough - The Wall of Death

Loop: 20 miles
Elevation gain/loss + 2,000 feet
Top Elevation 6,493 feet
Difficulty: Hard
Land: Custer Gallatin National Forest

Sourdough or Bozeman Creek is another major recreation access point near Bozeman. Grooming by the Bridger Ski Foundation in the winter connects the Sourdough trail over the bridge at about five miles to Mystic lake and Mosier. Popular year-round with hikers, dog walkers and trail runners, this trail system is open to bikes during the summer. Use caution especially on the first few miles, as this can be a congested area and is a good introduction to mountain biking on a wider, less technical trail. It's a moderate climb to Mystic Lake. The ominously named "Wall of Death" single track trail starts at the Mystic Lake outflow.

Return down the Sourdough double track or make a loop ride by descending the "Wall of Death" single track from the lake.

A short semi-technical climb leads to the exposed sidehill section which give this trial its intimidating name.

Fun, attention-grabbing corners and sections through rocks and drops follow along the sidehill and back down to the bridge on the Sourdough trail. Other extended routes include Moser dual track. Diaper Lane connects single track lines up and over the divide to forested Buckskin loops on the Hyalite side. A long, gradual climb going south from the Sourdough bridge leads to the top of a divide and, eventually, to the top of the Leverich Loop.

Search Sourdough Canyon
Bozeman, MT
Trailhead: (45.592258,-111.026241)

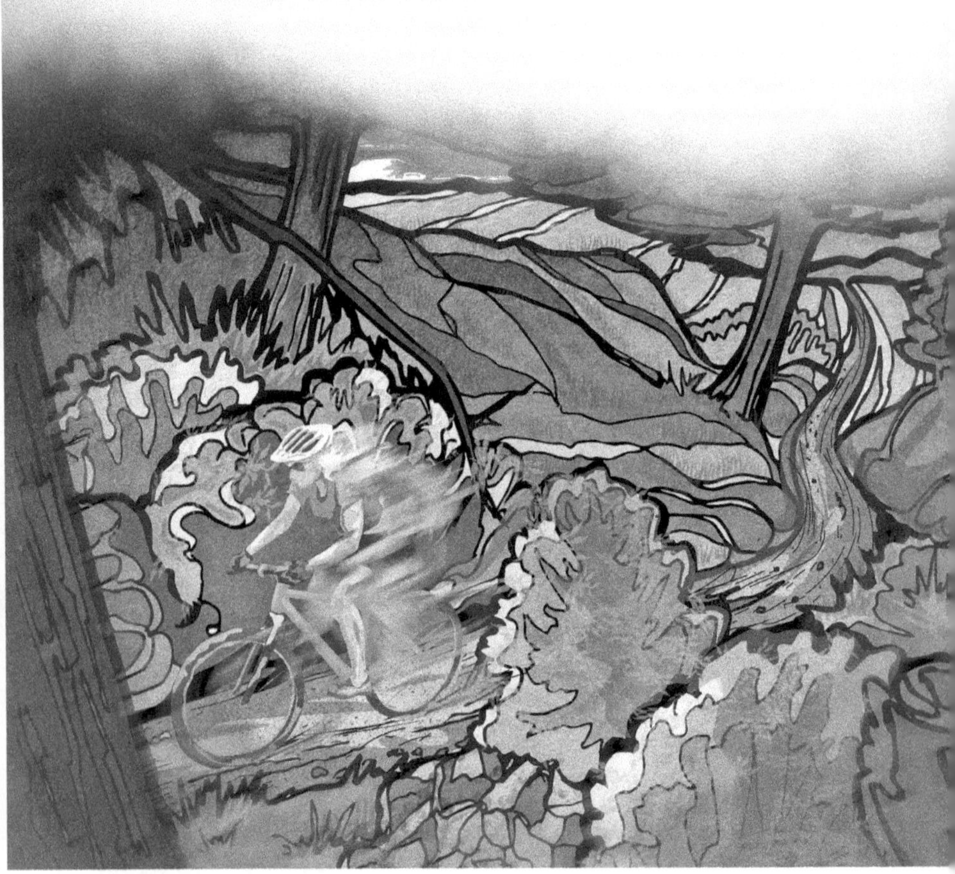

Anne Schaeffer riding the Wall of Death trail

BOZEMAN ON WHEELS

71. Leverich Canyon

Loop: 4.7 miles
Elevation gain/loss + 1,173 feet
Top Elevation 6,882 feet
Difficulty: Moderate/Strenuous
Land: Custer Gallatin National Forest

Leverich is a popular five mile multi-use loop trail south of town with a leg-burning, lung-busting climb and an awesome rough start to a flowy descent back to the parking lot. The recommended travel on the loop is clockwise.

Take the first sharp left at the junction a few hundred yards up the climb from the parking lot.

The long switchbacks get right to business. The right traversing switchback seems to be the most challenging.

Crest the top of the ridge and, descending briefly through Arrowleaf balsamroot and other wildflowers, the trail re-enters the woods for a final section of steep switchbacks, with rocks and roots thrown in for an extra challenge.
Many riders take a pause to collect the group (and their breath) at the top.

Don some pads and rip down the fantastic single track descent with its wide berms, flowing contours and sections that can carry speed.

This is a multi-use trail, so watch for hikers and give them the right-of-way.

The Leverich parking lot has limited space and the rough last mile to the parking lot doesn't allow space for passing, so vehicles have to back up to let other cars get through.

Riding from town is an option that reduces the traffic on the road while providing a warm-up ride.

Search Leverich Canyon
Bozeman, MT
Trailhead: (45.584034 -111.040666)

Jason Lunden cresting the top of Leverich

HYALITE ON WHEELS

HYALITE TRAILS

In April and early May the gate to Hyalite is locked, prohibiting vehicles from driving on the Hyalite road. It is open to bikes during this time, though, and is a popular road ride from the parking lot or from town to the reservoir. The road climbs steadily, with the steepest climbs coming at the end near the lake. This road ride is a great way to experience Hyalite before the mountain trails have melted out and dried up.

Hyalite Road is closed to motorized vehicles but open to bikes April 1 - May 15.

The only beginner loop in Hyalite is the gravel-pressed trail around the lake.

West Shore Path starts at the reservoir parking lot and traces the west shore of the lake. An offshoot to the south is a moderate single track section along Crescent Lake. The Mount Blackmore trail connects to the History Rock trailhead. Continuing on, the west shore path crosses, the road to Hyalite Creek trailhead and rolls though the trees on a well-graded path (Nordic trail in the winter), crossing a second road to the Palisade Falls parking lot. This connects to Hood Creek campground on the north side and a maze of trails in the Hood Creek area that finish the loop at the main parking lot near the dam.

Or climb up and over the steep Wildhorse trail, dropping into the Bozeman Creek/Sourdough trail. (Many Hyalite bike trails roughly follow Nordic skiing trails.)

The Buckskin trails that start from the Moser Creek trailhead are a moderate double track and single track trail system that connects Moser/Diaper Lane to Sourdough further west.

Riding past cabins with dramatic views of Hyalite Peak and the lake makes these trails a fun introduction to the area.

Mount Blackmore is a great hike and bike trip, providing steepness and technical challenges as it ascends the peak, with plenty of opportunities for pushing the bike uphill.

From the saddle, drop into the east branch of South Cottonwood or take a right to reach the summit. Bikes are not allowed on the stretch from the saddle to the summit. Hike to the summit.

Both Emerald Lake trail and Hyalite Creek trail alternate days for cycling:

mountain bikes are not allowed on Sundays and Mondays as part of the trail time share E bikes and motorcycles are allowed W,Th, F, Sat from July until September.

Check with the Gallatin Forest USFS website for updated information on trail time share for this and the popular Hyalite Lake trail to the west.

See if you spot Hyalite's gatekeeper - Crocodile Rock - above the road

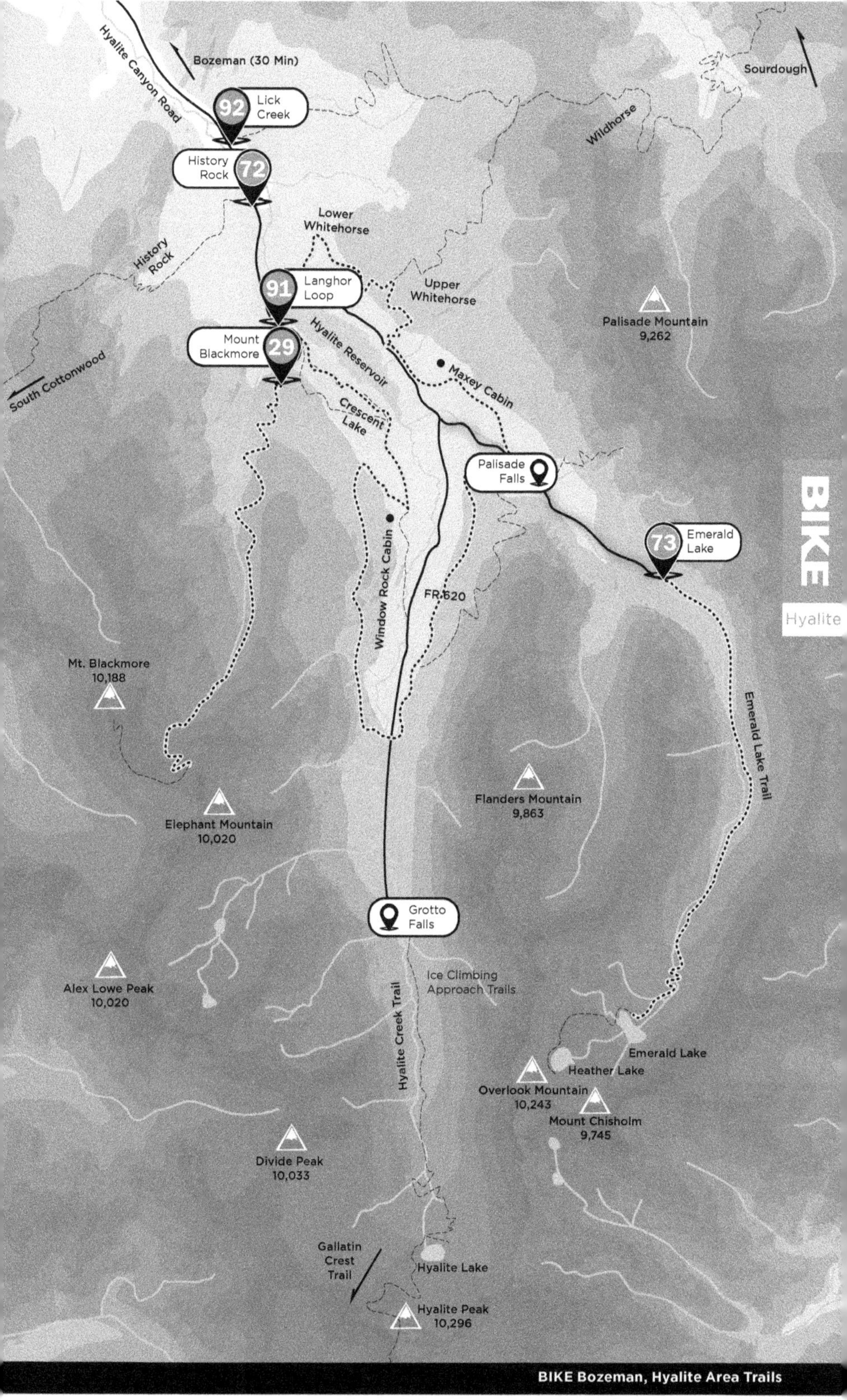
Hyalite Canyon Road
Bozeman (30 Min)
92 Lick Creek
History Rock 72
Sourdough
Wildhorse
Lower Whitehorse
History Rock
91 Langhor Loop
Upper Whitehorse
Mount Blackmore 29
Hyalite Reservoir
Palisade Mountain
9,262
South Cottonwood
Maxey Cabin
Crescent Lake
Palisade Falls
Window Rock Cabin
FR 620
73 Emerald Lake
Mt. Blackmore
10,188
Emerald Lake Trail
Flanders Mountain
9,863
Elephant Mountain
10,020
Grotto Falls
Alex Lowe Peak
10,020
Ice Climbing
Approach Trails
Hyalite Creek Trail
Emerald Lake
Heather Lake
Overlook Mountain
10,243
Mount Chisholm
9,745
Divide Peak
10,033
Gallatin
Crest
Trail
Hyalite Lake
Hyalite Peak
10,296

BIKE Hyalite

BIKE Bozeman, Hyalite Area Trails

HYALITE ON WHEELS

72. History Rock/South Cottonwood

Point to Point: 11.2 miles
Elevation gain: 1,864 feet
Top Elevation 7,974 feet
Difficulty: Hard / Technical Descent
Land: Custer Gallatin National Forest

The History Rock area has meadows that offer moderate loops, plus a more challenging climb that connects to the South Cottonwood trail.

Pass the meadows and the climb goes through forest on a steep single track that passes by History Rock, an historical, graffiti-marked limestone boulder that is autographed by early pioneers who passed through the area in the 1800's.

The switchbacks get tighter and steeper, demanding balance and effort to keep up the momentum for the climbs. Views to the south open up before the steep, forested section that crests on an overlook of Blackmore Peak.

This is the connection point to South Cottonwood trail via a steep and rowdy (but ridable) descent.

From Langhor Divide, soak in views of Blackmore Peak and the wilderness beyond. The trail drops on a steep, loose track through an open meadow before entering steep switchbacks into the forest.

The trail then becomes rocky and rooty with a few more technical, but ridable, sections through steeper switchbacks. The trail then parallels South Cottonwood Creek back to the last forested section before connecting to the South Cottonwood trail junction.

To the left (east) South Cottonwood trail follows along the creek to connect with Wheeler Gulch, Wheeler Pass and the rugged terrain northwest of Mount Blackmore. Hang a right.

The trail then parallels South Cottonwood Creek all the way back to the last climb within a mile of the parking lot.

Look out for downed trees in the upper South Cotton trail, especially in early season.

Exit the South Cottonwood trail and head to the parking lot.

The lower South Cottonwood trail is one of the most popular South Bozeman trails for hiking and trail running year round.

Expect to see many people in the first few miles of the trail and yield with a smile.

Search History Rock #424
Custer Gallatin National Forest
Trailhead: (45.498465 -110.984403)

Riding by History Rock

Erik Walnum descending into South Cottonwood

HYALITE ON WHEELS

73. Emerald Lake Trail

Out and Back: 10 Miles
Elevation gain: 1,994
Top Elevation 8,923 feet
Difficulty: Hard
Land: Custer Gallatin National Forest

The Emerald Lake Trail #434 is a true gem of a single track ride to an alpine lake.

Emerald Lake is one of the best out and back forested mountain bike rides in the region.

Mostly shaded, the single track winds between boulders and contours above the East Fork of Hyalite Creek, running in a parallel drainage to the Hyalite Creek trailhead (also a great hiking trail).

The trail steepens after a few water crossings and begins arduous switchbacks before cresting to more open views and the last few rises into the lake basin.

The rough and rocky trail will challenge climbing skills (this is a tough one to ride up clean) but it rewards the effort with a fast and rough descent, ending with a serene flowing trail back to the parking lot.

Guaranteed you will work up a sweat climbing into the Emerald Lake basin.

The lake may compel you into taking a refreshing dip.

Heather Lake sits within a half a mile above the Emerald Lake basin. I have seen mountain bikers on the steep, rocky trail, but going up is a hike and bike for most people.

The descent from Emerald Lake is fast and fun with a flowy finish back to the trailhead.

Search Emerald Lake
Custer Gallatin National Forest
Trailhead: (45.458608 -110.920887)

Emerald Lake - worth the effort

SPANISH PEAKS TEASER

Road closure in the spring makes this four mile out and back paved mountain road a good option while waiting for mountain trails to dry out.

At the entrance to Gallatin Canyon from the north is the turn off (to the west) for the northern access to the Spanish Peaks, the northern Madison Range, and the Lee Metcalf Wilderness (where mountain biking isn't allowed).

The road passes through Ted Turner's flying "D" Ranch. It is gated through spring, but is open to foot and bike travel.

The four-mile stretch of paved road has the feel of being in the mountains and is a joy to ride in the spring with no cars on the road. Plus the ride is a great way to warm up for the spring biking season. Wildlife can often be seen - deer, elk, bear, and, maybe, a wolf, plus birds, like sandhill cranes, returning to the area in the spring. Bison are raised on the ranch and can be seen in the fields next to the road.

GARNET MOUNTAIN LOOKOUT

Extend the ride by biking up Storm Castle Road, past Rat lake and to the top of the peak for a 11.3 mile loop, climbing 2,300 feet

Near the north entrance to Gallatin Canyon - to the east and crossing Gallatin River - is the access to the Storm Castle and Garnet Mountain trails. Both trails are open to bikes, although Storm Castle is so steep that it isn't ridable for most people.

Garnet Mountain has a steep and strenuous black-level trail that climbs directly up the peak to the lookout. However, a loop option that spreads the elevation gain out across more miles starts on the road along Storm Creek, then turns right on gravel roads and converted ATV trails and past Rat Lake before continuing to the summit.

PORTAL CREEK

The Portal Creek trailhead on the east side of the Gallatin River provides access to trails that finish just southeast of Big Sky. However, these trails are in grizzly country and entail a long shuttle on a rough road and are not featured in this book. (See section about bears)

The deeper trail system to the east of the Gallatin River is a long bumpy shuttle to access the Portal Creek trailhead. Routes finish just south east of Big Sky. There are some good riding options in this area but aren't featured in this book due to long access drives and grizzly country. See bears section.

Other trails with access from Gallatin Canyon enter wilderness and are not open to mountain biking. They are described in the hiking section of this book.

BIG SKY

The south end of Gallatin Canyon opens up to views of Lone Mountain and the town of Big Sky to the west. Many trails in the Big Sky area are open to mountain biking.

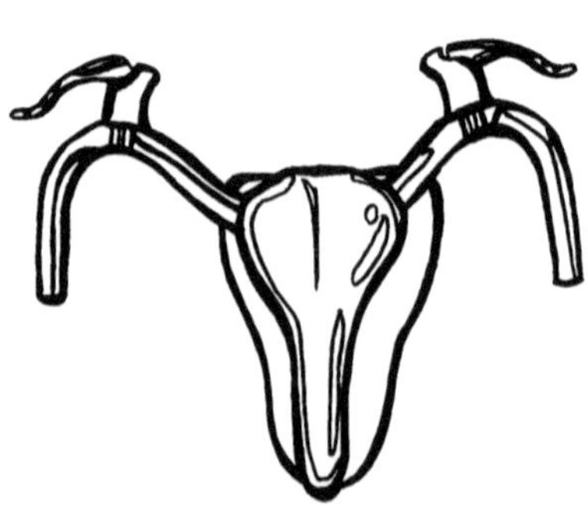

"Steer"sculpture by Gregg Chambers

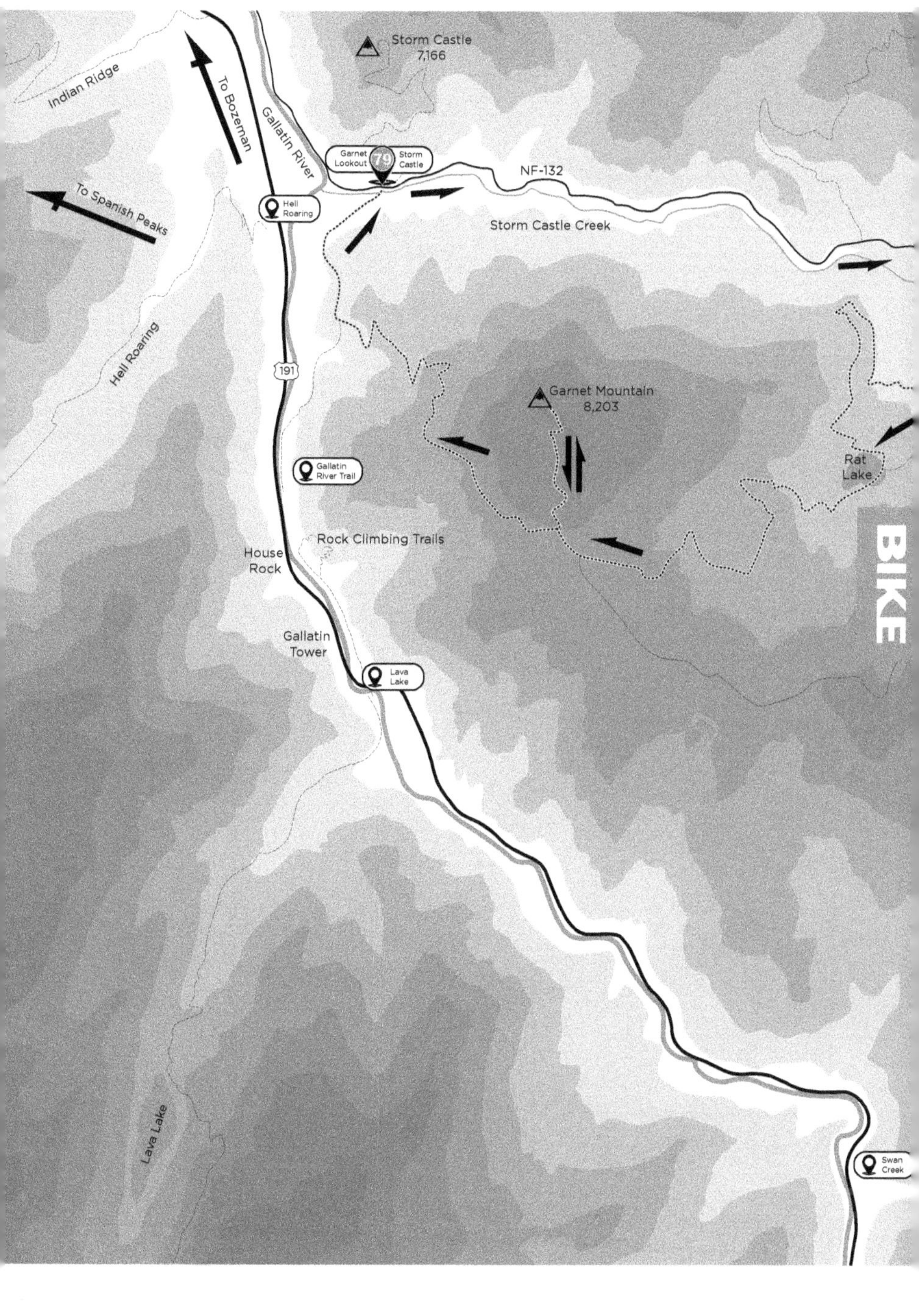

Storm Castle
7,166
Indian Ridge
To Bozeman
Gallatin River
Garnet Lookout
79
Storm Castle
NF-132
To Spanish Peaks
Hell Roaring
Storm Castle Creek
Hell Roaring
191
Garnet Mountain
8,203
Rat Lake
Gallatin River Trail
Rock Climbing Trails
House Rock
BIKE
Gallatin Tower
Lava Lake
Lava Lake
Swan Creek

GALLATIN CANYON ON WHEELS

74. Spanish Creek Road

Out and Back: 7.5 miles
Elevation gain: 673 feet
Top Elevation: 6,102 feet
Difficulty: Beginner/Paved
Land: Ted Turner's Flying "D" Ranch

While not technically a mountain bike ride, the asphalt road into the Spanish Creek trailhead is open to biking in the spring. It is a US Forest Service road that passes through the Turner Ranch. The four-mile bike ride winds through scenic country where buffalo graze in the fenced pastures and deer and elk can be seen, as well as an occasional bear or wolf and migrating birds like sandhill cranes.

The road ends at the trailhead to Spanish Creek which accesses the trail system open only to foot and horse travel.

This early season road ride is a four mile stretch to the Spanish Creek trailhead. The entrance point to the Lee Metcalf Wilderness is closed to vehicles through the winter, but is open to foot traffic and bicycles in the spring before the gate opens.

Keep an eye out for grazing bison on Ted Turner's ranch (the Forest Service road passes through private land on this stretch).

Hills winding through scenic country is a great place for wildlife watching. Bears and wolves can been seen in this area and it is common to see bison, elk, deer and migrating birds like sandhill cranes.

Check conditions before you go as portions of the road can hold snow well into spring.

The road ends at the trailhead at Spanish Creek which accesses the trail system that is open only to foot and horse travel.

Destinations include Pioneer Falls and Spanish Lakes, as well as "the Blaze" ski run that is skiable into late summer.

Search Spanish Peaks Road
Flying D Ranch Gate closed in winter - spring: (45.494704581478096, -111.36884068924886)

Molly Bowman and kids ready to ride

75. Garnet Mountain Lookout

Out and Back: 8 miles
Elevation gain: 2,898 feet
Top Elevation 8,203 feet
Difficulty: Advanced
Land: Custer Gallatin National Forest

With a fire lookout at the top, this peak is best ridden as a loop from the Stormcastle parking lot or an out and back from the Storm Castle trailhead. To loop, ride up the gravel Squaw Creek Road along Storm Castle Creek.

Take a right to climb on a steeper cobblestone road to the Rat Lake double track trail. This area is popular with ATVs, but the climb to the summit is foot traffic and non-motorized bike only. You may want to walk your bike the last half mile out and back to the fire lookout at the summit.

The challenging descent will demand your attention with its sharp corners and steep sidehill drop-offs connected by a flowing forest trail.

Hang a right at the junction to head down a rocky, steep sidehill that contours through a thick forest with dramatic overlooks into the Gallatin River valley.

This attention-grabbing descent is a challenging classic and will demand your attention with sharp corners, high consequence sidehill drop-offs connected with flowy forest trail.

Tapering steepness leads to flowy forested sections, then the trail crosses the bridge over Storm Castle Creek at the bottom and returns to the parking lot.

Search Garnet Mountain
Custer Gallatin National Forest
Trailhead: (45.441322 -111.222927)

Jason Yager & Laine McNeill, Garnet Mountain lookout

BRIDGERS ON WHEELS
BRIDGER RANGE TRAILS

From short out and back rides to long hike and bike peak bagging options, the Bridgers are packed full of mountain biking possibilities.

The most accessible point from Bozeman is the iconic college "M" trail at the southwestern point of this range. Climbing above the white painted "M" is the 20 mile Bridger Ridge trail that summits Mount Baldy, Saddle Peak, passes by Bridger Bowl and Ross Peak, then ascends Naya Nuki and Sacajawea Peaks and down to the popular trailhead access point at Fairy Lake on the northeast side of the range.

The lower foothills trail - a similar length as the ridge trail - traverses the Bridger Mountains on the lower western flank, rejoining the trail near the summit of Sacajawea Peak.

While the character of these trails is rough and rugged, there are sections that are ridable for bikes.

Multiple finger ridges extend perpendicularly from the ridge forming canyon drainages. These western Bridger trails have a similar character - entering forested canyons and switchbacking up ridges.

More moderate trails have smoother single track and, also, exposed sidehills, like in Johnson Canyon and Corbly Gulch.

All of these western Bridger trails are moderate to advanced in difficulty, offering out and back, loop options and bike to hike peak- bagging adventures.

In the Brackett Creek area on the east side of the Bridger Mountains, Middle, North and South Bracket Creeks flow under the highway, with parking lots on both sides. The west side of the road connects a loop trail of double track and great single track to the ridge and the base of Ross Peak. This Brackett Creek loop has single track flowing south and looping back along the South Brackett Creek loop to the parking lot or connecting to the Crosscut Mountain Sports Center's newly created mountain bike trails.

Extend your adventure with a bike and hike of Ross Peak. Stash your bike above the ridge trail before making the scramble to the summit.

Search Bracket Creek Middle Trailhead:
(45.858430 -110.881410)
Maps: Beartooth Publishing: Bozeman

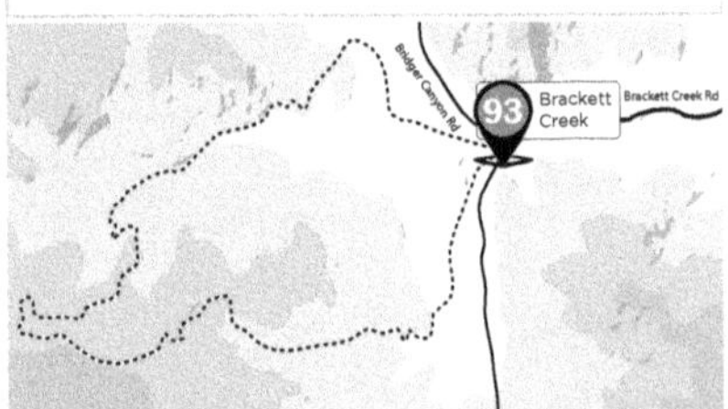

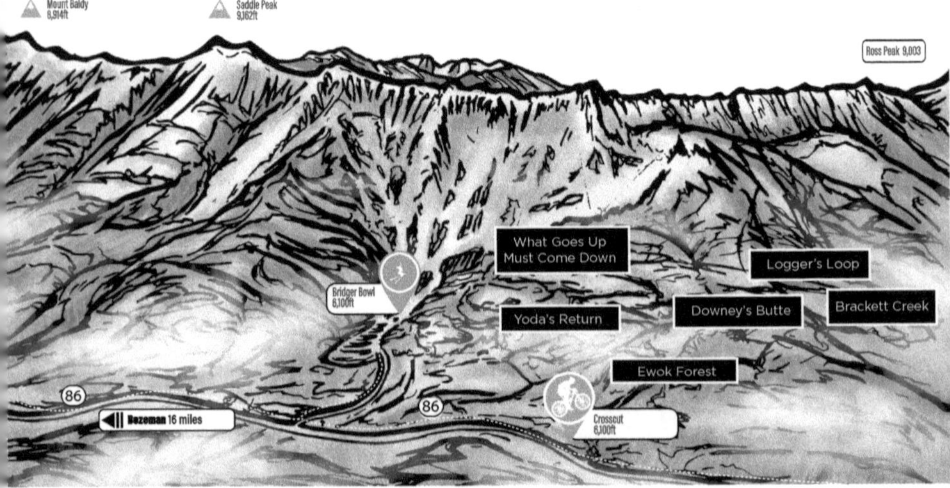

Bridger Bowl and Crosscut Mountain Sports Center trails on the east side of the Bridger Mountains

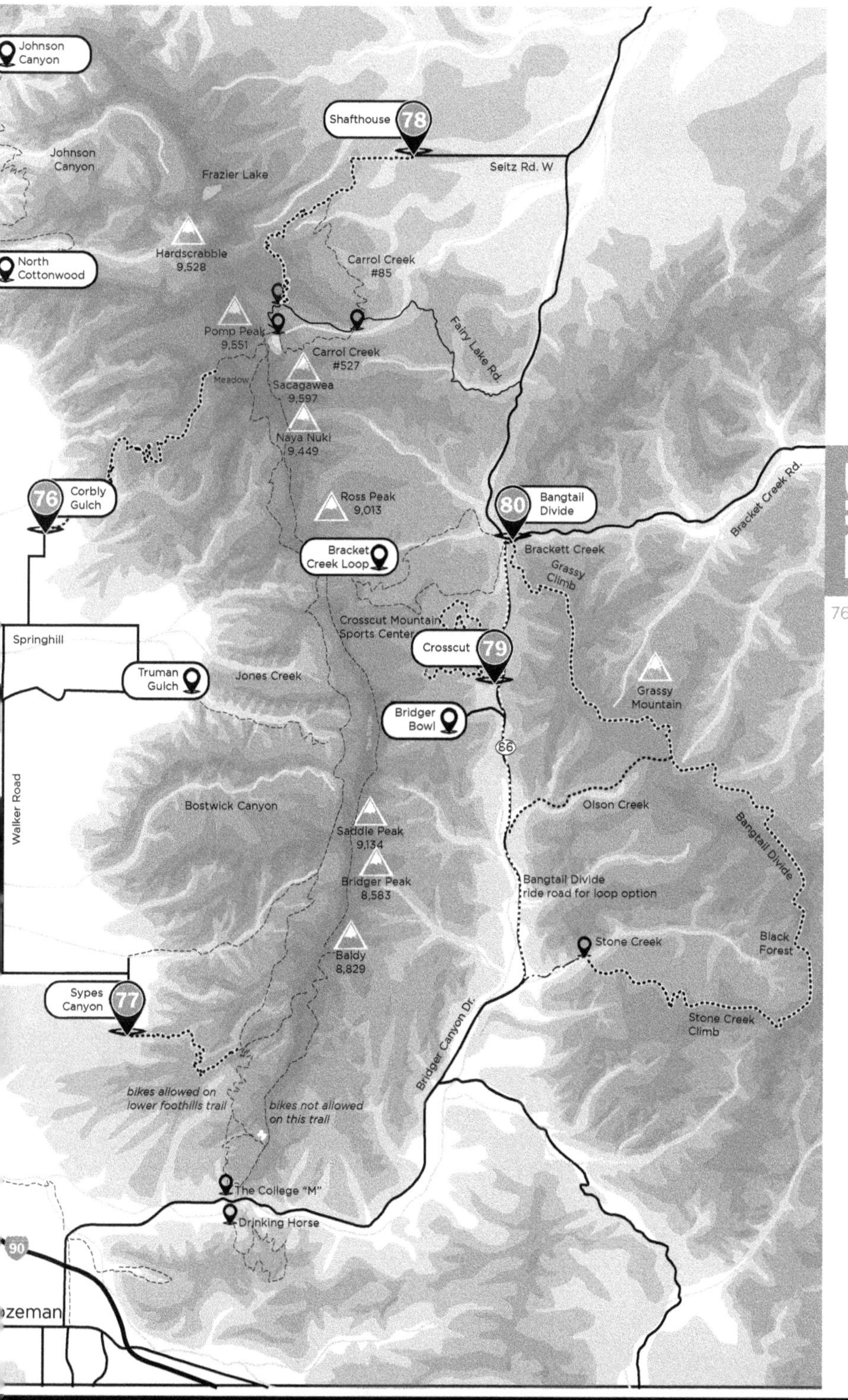
Johnson Canyon
Shafthouse 78
Johnson Canyon
Frazier Lake
Seitz Rd. W
Hardscrabble 9,528
North Cottonwood
Carrol Creek #85
Pomp Peak 9,551
Carrol Creek #527
Fairy Lake Rd.
Meadow
Sacagawea 9,597
Naya Nuki 9,449
76 Corbly Gulch
Ross Peak 9,013
80 Bangtail Divide
Bracket Creek Rd.
Brackett Creek
Bracket Creek Loop
Grassy Climb
Crosscut Mountain Sports Center
Springhill
Crosscut 79
Truman Gulch
Jones Creek
Grassy Mountain
Bridger Bowl
86
Walker Road
Bostwick Canyon
Olson Creek
Saddle Peak 9,134
Bangtail Divide
Bridger Peak 8,583
Bangtail Divide ride road for loop option
Stone Creek
Black Forest
Baldy 8,829
Sypes Canyon 77
Stone Creek Climb
Bridger Canyon Dr.
bikes allowed on lower foothills trail
bikes not allowed on this trail
The College "M"
Drinking Horse
90
ozeman

BIKE

76-81

BRIDGERS ON WHEELS

76. Corbly Gulch

Out and Back: 4.1 Miles
Elevation gain: 1,994
Top Elevation 7,090 feet
Difficulty: Moderate
Land: Custer Gallatin National Forest

If you are looking for an aspect similar to Sypes Canyon with a smoother flowy trail, check out Corbly Gulch farther to the west.

The standard ride is an out and back to an overlook and meadow.

Extend the outing as a hike and bike by stashing the bike near the meadow and hiking up the steep, rocky trail, which is seasonally used by dirt bikes. Alpine meadows emerge from the forest and lead up to the summit ridge trail to Sacajawea, Naya Nuki and beyond. The Corbly descent flows down the contours and is noticeably designed for mountain biking.

The last half mile of the Corbly road is very rutted and rough due to vehicles driving on the clay soil early in the season when wet. Huge ruts and rocks require a vehicle with high clearance and, ideally, four-wheel drive.

Johnson Creek at the far west side of the Bridgers is also built for bikes. This trail winds in and out of Mill Creek Canyon and sidehills to North Cottonwood Canyon where most riders return on the same route. This is a good moderate ride with exposed side-hilling on the northwest edge of the Bridger Mountains.

Search Corbly Gulch #544
Custer Gallatin National Forest
Trailhead (45.868820 -111.015787)

Bryan Schaeffer & Jeff Peterson, Corbly overlook

BRIDGERS ON WHEELS

77. Sypes Canyon

Out and Back: 6.2 Miles
Elevation gain: 1,620 feet
Top Elevation 6,824 feet
Difficulty: Hard
Land: Custer Gallatin National Forest

From the trailhead, bike along the fence into a shaded creek bed section. A few steep sections will get you primed for the long haul ahead. Emerge to an open area with a prominent prow in the trail where a tree hangs precariously on the side of the steep hill (see illustration on page 73). There are some short, very rocky sections that are difficult to ride.

Continue back into the forest where the switchbacks emerge in earnest. The climb is steep but mostly shaded with a few ridgeline sections that open up for valley views along the way. This prominent ridge extending perpendicularly from the main ridge follows interesting contours and increasingly exposed steep sections.

The final climb to the top of the trail junction and turn around point for the out and back ride is on exposed cobble stone with some very steep challenging sections to ride.

From the junction you can connect to the North Cottonwood trail or to the Foothills trail to the college "M" trailhead. Heading towards the "M" trail, there is a very steep section through a cliff band right off the junction that may have you carefully walking your bike down.

Sypes Canyon trail has a steep and rocky start from the top but also provides panoramic views across the valley. The rough start rolls into tree-covered forested flow sections and some more rough, rocky spots before the trail pops out at the parking lot.

The lower section can be very busy, so watch your speed.

Search Sypes Canyon Trailhead: (45.745070 -111.007824)
Maps: Beartooth Publishing: Bozeman

Trail Time Share: No mountain biking in Sypes Canyon on Saturdays June 16 through September 5

Bryan Schaeffer keeping the rubber side down on the Sypes Canyon descent

BRIDGERS ON WHEELS

78. Shafthouse

Out and Back: 10 miles
Elevation gain: 2,782 feet
Top Elevation 8,315 feet
Difficulty: Hard
Land: Custer Gallatin National Forest

On the east side of the Bridger Mountains below Sacajawea and Hardscrabble Peaks is the Shafthouse Trail #540.

This can be ridden as an out and back from the trailhead at the far north east plains up by Frazier Creek, but the climb is long steep and relentless.

The Shafthouse loop is connected by 527 ATV double track which can be accessed by the same trailhead or via parking on the Fairy Creek Road.

To avoid the rough upper section of the Fairy Lake road, park at the lower parking lot which leads directly to the ATV track 500 as a lower loop variation.

The ATV double track is steep and winds through dense forest to Fairy Lake. There is a bike rack at the trailhead it you want to add in a hike up Sacagawea or Naya Nuki. Ride down the road from the Fairy Lake trail head to the Shafthouse single track trailhead (540) in a cow pasture. The single track is very steep and sustained but worth the effort with dramatic views of Sacajawea, Naya Nuki, the "Great One" ski chute, the Frazier Lake basin and panoramic views of the Bangtails, the Crazy Mountains and rolling prairie to the east.

The Shafthouse descent is steep, but not too technical, and is a "rip-roaring" fun ride.

Continue straight to the northeast parking lot (Shafthouse?) or turn right on the Carrol Creek ATV trail and return to the Fairy Lake road and parking lots.

Search Shafthouse #540
Trailhead: (45.945423 -110.914028)
Maps: Beartooth Publishing: Bozeman

Loki and last light on Shafthouse, Sacagawea, Naya Nuki Peak and "The Great One" chute in the background

BRIDGERS ON WHEELS

79. Crosscut Mountain Sports Center

Dedicated Bike Trails: 14 Miles
Base Elevation: 6,100 feet
Top Elevation: 6,847
Difficulty: Moderate
Land: Custer Gallatin National Forest

Crosscut Mountain Sports Center's bike trails follow similar lines to their Nordic ski trails counterparts in the winter.

The outer Loggers Loop double track is a thoroughfare connecting single track trails that shoot off and weave through trees, berms and contours.

Numerous trails built with biking in mind have numerous flowing contours, berms, stump jumps and other obstacles designed for mountain biking.

Meander through the "Ewok Forest" past the skills area, where you can practice balance and drops, before starting the climb *What goes up* to a beautiful op-out and having *Good Clean Fun* and descending trails like *Crazy Woman* and the epic *Must Come Down* on your way to *Yoda's Return* and back to the base area.

Trails open for biking
in the beginning of July.
Visit Crosscutmt.org for info
Trailhead (45.82870,-110.88404)

NICA girls showing their GRIT on Yoda's Return

BANGTAILS ON WHEELS

80. Bangtail Divide

One Way: 24 Miles
Elevation gain: 3,500 feet
Top Elevation 8,000 feet
Difficulty: Hard/Strenuous
Land: Custer Gallatin National Forest

The Bangtail trail runs from the south, at Stone Creek, to the north, at Grassy Mountain and to the other Bracket Creek trailhead to form the classic Bangtail Divide trail. This 24-mile single track offers steep and rocky ascents, flowing forest trails and contours.

Shuttle cars from south to north - Stone Creek to the Bracket Creek trailhead.

To loop the route, park at the Bracket Creek trailhead and ride south on the road to the Stone Creek trailhead. Loop back up single track making a 30+ mile ride. Other variations include looping Olson to Crosscut trails or Skunk Creek on the east. Shorter loop options at Bracket Creek/ Grassy Mountain as well as Stone Creek. Check the Trail Forks for variation loops.

Out and back options include a single track towards Grassy Mountain or Stone Creek from the Olson Creek Junction.

Check the Trailforks app for variation loops. Many other options are possible in this popular mountain biking area.

Search Bangtail Divide Trail, Custer Gallatin National Forest Trailhead (45.856264 -110.880094)

SADDLE PEAK
9,159"

ROSS PEAK
9,004"

Bridger Mountain views on the Bangtail Divide trail

Pristine single track on Grassy Mountain, The Bangtails

BIG SKY ON WHEELS

BIG SKY AREA TRAILS

The Big Sky Community Organization (BSCO) is working on a master trails plan for Madison and Gallatin counties. The recreation plan will shape future trail development projects and serve as a guide for maintaining existing trail systems to connect Big Sky resort, Moonlight Basin, Spanish Peaks, The Yellowstone Club and the The Town Center.

BSCO serves as the parks and recreation facilitator for the unincorporated Big Sky, with a plan to build one trail a year for the next five years and maintain and improve existing connections between trailheads. The town of Big Sky has plans for a network trail system for commuting and recreation.

Mountains to Meadows trail is a favorite, with a moderate flow line and connecting the resort to the meadow. Shuttle cars or use the bus to ride this one-way trail.

Other trails veer off the popular Ousel Falls hiking trail and are designed for biking. Even though they are close to residential areas, Yellow Mule and other loops venture into grizzly country, so take precautions. (See the "bear country" section of this book)

During the Big Sky Biggie race, these are pre-ride routes that represent a good sampling of cross country riding in the area.

More trail information on these routes can be found on the Trailforks app or visit the Big Sky Resort web site.

Recommended Big Sky Trails

Search - Mountain to Meadow, Ralph's Pass, Hummocks & Uplands, The North Fork / Ridge Trail, Gambler Trail, Snakecharmer, Grizzly Loop, Porcupine, Buckridge to Yellowmule, Ousel Falls & Otter slide

BSCO village trails with Lone Mountain in the background

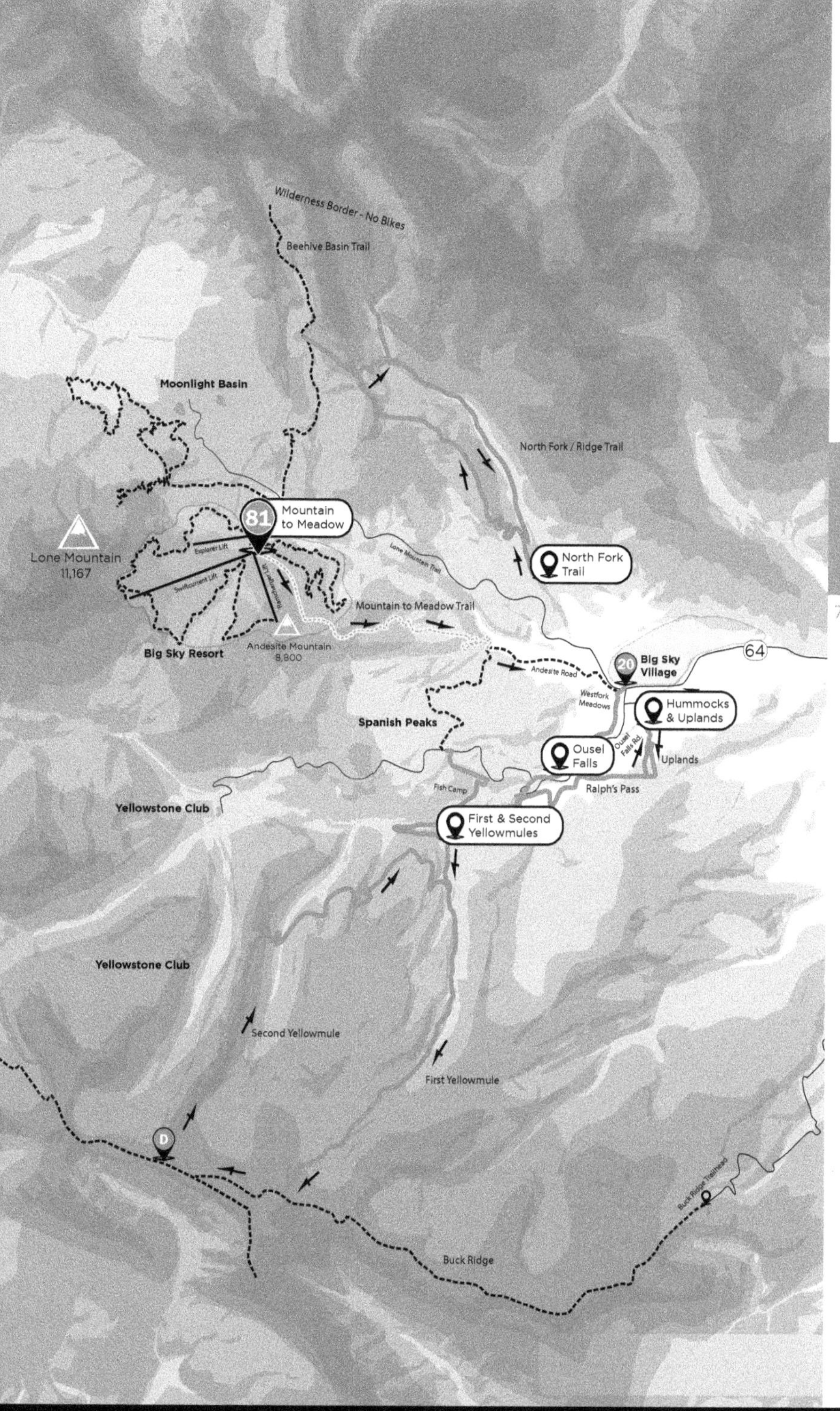

Big Sky Resort, Mountain To Meadow, Big Sky Village, Yellow Mules, Big Sky Area Trails

Big Sky Resort area has a rich history of mountain biking, beginning in 1996 with original downhill trails like Moose Tracks.

As the biking program evolved, the Big Sky Resort Bike Park has grown to three lifts, providing access to trails ranging from moderate flow trails to expert downhill and tech trails.

Big Sky Resort offers the only lift-accessed biking in southwest Montana. Other lift-accessed mountain biking areas are at Discovery near Anaconda and at Whitefish Mountain Resort.

Big Sky Resort hosts enduro events in the summer as well as challenging long-distance cross country races like the Big Sky Biggie.

Machine-built flow trails around the resort offer great riding options for the entire family. With a full fleet of downhill bikes, protective equipment, and instruction, the Big Sky Resort Bike Park is an ideal place to practice mountain biking skills.

Easier terrain is accessed from the Explorer lift, while more advanced riders can work their way from green to double black diamond runs off both Ramcharger and Swift Current lifts.

Finishing the day with a ride down Snake Charmer and connecting to the Mountains to Meadow trail down to Big Sky Town Center Village is an ideal way to way to finish the day.

Visit bigskyresort.com for more info
Day Parking (45.28879287944319, -111.40197426162379)

Christine Baker and Layne Hamblin riding up the lift at Big Sky

BIG SKY ON WHEELS

81. Mountain to Meadow Trail

One way: 7.5 miles
Elevation gain: +550 feet -1,720
Top Elevation: 8,034 feet
Difficulty: Moderate
Land: Big Sky Resort

The Mountain to Meadow trail is the sculpted single-track from Big Sky Resort to the Big Sky Meadow or town center.

Start from the Ramcharger lift (as seen in drawing) climb up the upper south fork trail in Big Sky resort on Andesite mountain to reach the top of Big Horn ski run.

A clear marker sign labels the start of the trail that flows down to the mountain to paved roads just outside of Big Sky Village in the Meadow.

It is possible to extend the route by climbing on paved roads through the Spanish Peaks development to connect with the Fish Camp trail to the Yellow Mules via Ralph's pass or finish on the Ousel Falls trail.

Search Mountain to Meadow Trail, Big Sky, MT
Day Pa Parking(45.28879287944319, -111.40197426162379)

Kiersten Schaeffer getting ready to ride the Mountain to Meadow trail, Big Sky Resort

WEST OF BOZEMAN ON WHEELS

WESTERN DESERT TRAILS

West of Bozeman away from the mountain ranges - Bridger, Hyalite, Gallatin and Madison - the weather tends to be warmer and drier throughout the year with less snow accumulation in the winter. Trails to the west of Bozeman make great shoulder season biking destinations. While the snow is still melting in the mountains, head for the trail systems at Copper City, Madison Buffalo Jump and Lewis and Clark Caverns for early season biking on dry single track.

With beginner trails and dedicated paved paths for bikes, the Missouri Headwaters State Park north of Three Forks is another great place to ride in the spring. Southwest Montana Mountain Biking Association (SWMMBA) posts trail conditions for early season riding. Some US Forest Service roads (ie in Gallatin Canyon and the road to Hyalite Reservoir) are available to bikers and hikers before the gates open to vehicles.

You can also find more trip reports on the TrailForks website or app.

Spring is great time to get out on your bike! Make sure everything is working well and dust off the cobwebs from the bike's winter storage before exploring these early season trails.

The summer months can be especially hot and dry in these areas. Bring more water than you think you will need. Avoid riding in the middle of the day and watch for rattlesnakes and prickly pear cacti.

Riding along the cliff edge of the Madison Buffalo Jump

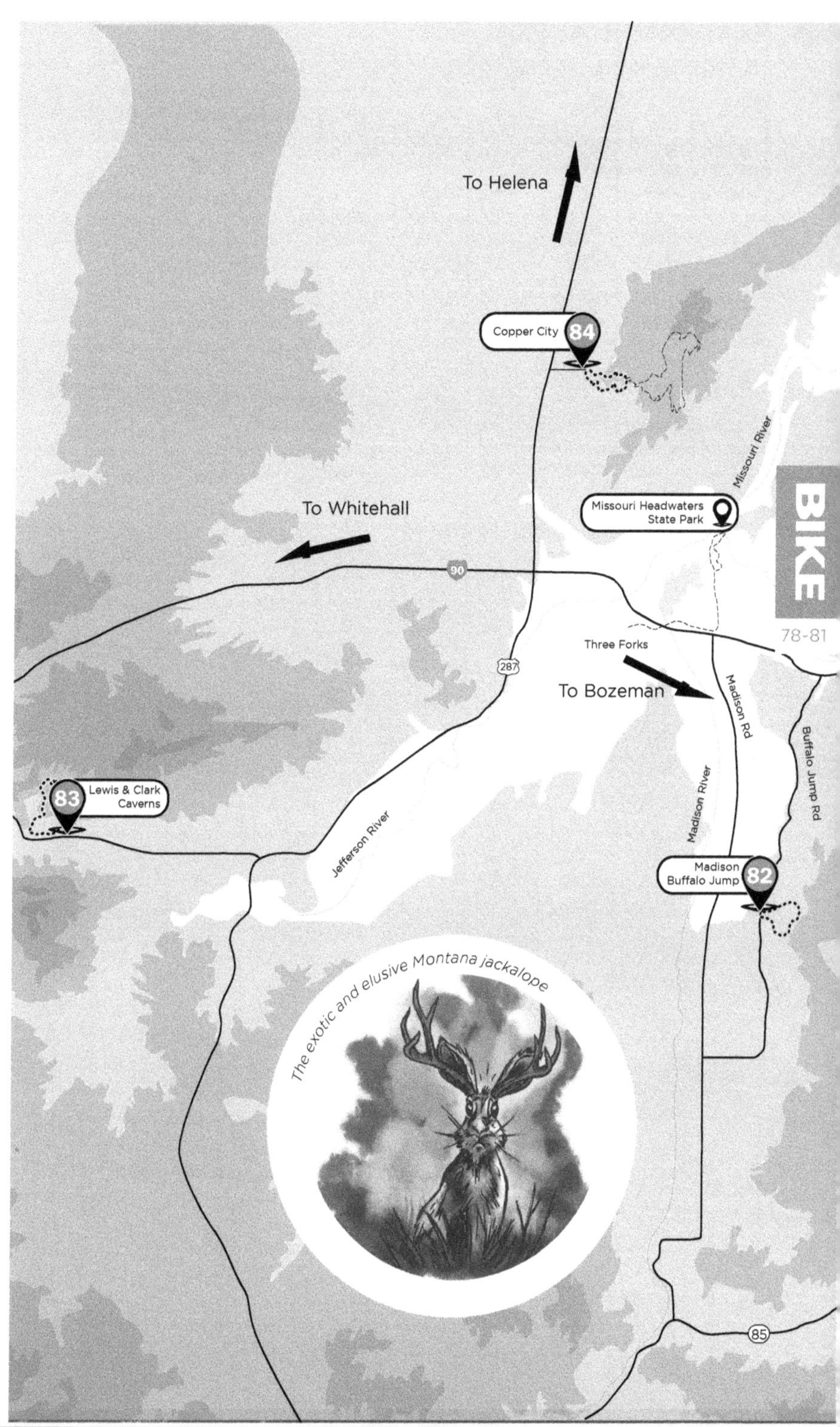

Missouri Headwaters State Park, Copper City, Madison Buffalo Jump, Bozeman Trails West

82. Madison Buffalo Jump

Total Miles: 10 miles
Elevation gain/loss + 2,048eet
Top Elevation: 4,554'
Difficulty: Moderate/Advanced
Land: Madison Buffalo Jump State Park

The Madison Buffalo Jump State Park is a good place to ride during the shoulder seasons.

The "pishkun", which translates to deep blood kettle, was used by native people for nearly 2,000 years to corral bison and make them stampede over the cliff where they were harvested.

The contours of the buffalo jump make for great mountain biking, with views of the surrounding landscapes and a connection to the past as you imagine the scenes that took place there.

This area is best for biking in the spring and fall as it can be hot there in the summer.

From the parking lot trails climb abruptly to the left and right. The center track along the creek bed is the flattest trail.

The left trail climbs to offer views of the buffalo jump from the tepee rings vantage point. Continue on the trail, dropping into a juniper- filled gully with tight washes and several rock obstacles before emerging out to the open creek bed to the north of the jump.

Climb the single tight switchback to gain the driving area and platform of the buffalo jump rim. In the spring a rocky wash may have water for a thirsty dog.

Ride the outer loop and the connecting inner loop to the driving area (bison were corralled here and pushed towards the cliff edge).

The southern connection dead ends at a fold in the cliff and isn't passable without some scrambling and carrying your bike. The state property extends to the barbwire fence where you can retrace your path or ride the outer section before returning to the base.

Search Madison Buffalo Jump State Park (free for MT residents) Trailhead (45.79476224975848, -111.47208898771902)

MADISON BUFFALO JUMP
4,554"

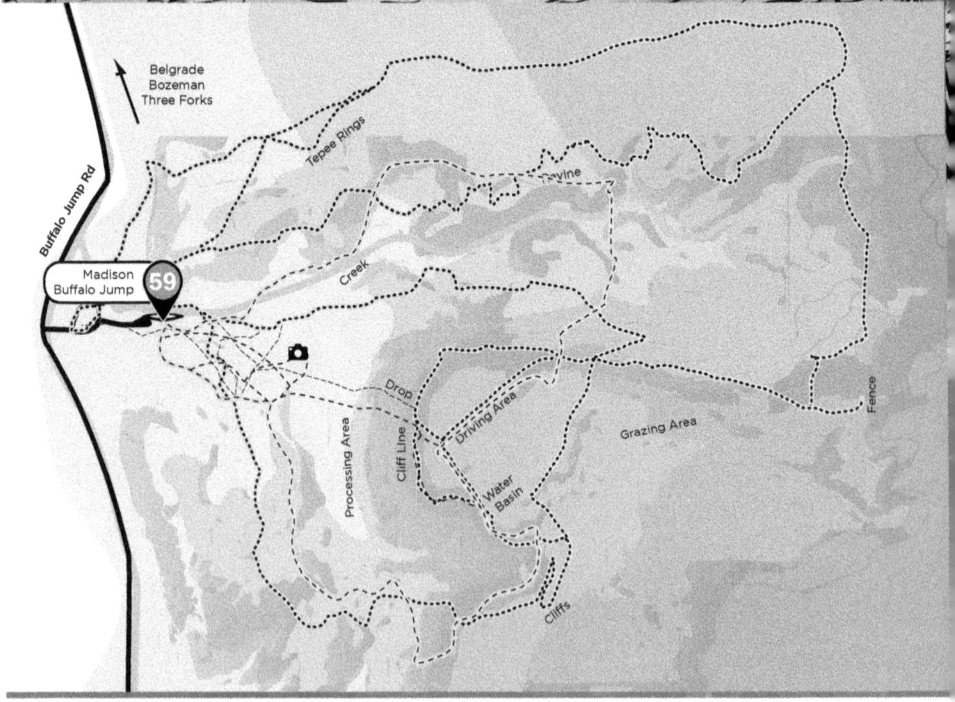

Madison Buffalo Jump trail system

MADISON ON WHEELS

83. Lewis & Clark Caverns

Total Miles: 13.66 miles
Elevation gain: 2,638 feet
Top Elevation: 5,438
Difficulty: Moderate/Hard
Land: Lewis & Cark State Park

The area west of Three Forks is snow free earlier in the season than the Bozeman area.

The areas around Three Forks are a micro-climate, often contrasting from snow-attracting Bozeman.

A centrally divided double loop trail climbs up the middle with the option of descending to the left or right. Or take a few laps and do both.

When the caverns are open to visitors, buy a ticket and take a guided tour of the caverns named after Lewis and Clark (who never actually explored them or knew about them).

Fishing access trails and the Cave Gulch trail to the west are easy warm-up rides.

Trails to the east climb steeply and have rock features to test your climbing skills. The Middle View trail has many switchbacks.

Hone your switchbacks on the Middle View Trail.

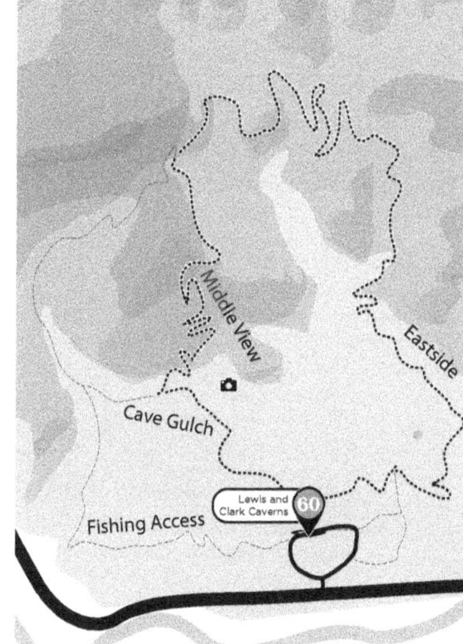

Search Danmore Gypsum Mine, Middle View and East Side Trail Loop Trailhead (45.82344703200818, -111.85069786955147)

Jason Yager putting the pedal to the metal

COPPER CITY ON WHEELS

84. Copper City Trails

Distance: 27 Miles total Trails
Elevation gain: 2,444 feet
Top Elevation 5,408 feet
Difficulty: Moderate
Land: Bureau of Land Management

The most recent mountain biking attraction located between Bozeman, Butte and Helena is the Copper City trail system built by the Southwest Montana Mountain Bike Association (SWMMBA). Copper City has approximately 23 miles of single track trails built for mountain biking and named after historic local mines.

The trails are also used by hikers and trail runners. The large parking lot is equipped with outhouses, a wind block, tool stations and an adjacent pump track skills park. The parking lot fills up early in the day and the area is hot, especially in the summer.

There is no water available at this area, so take more water than you think you will need. Watch for rattlesnakes. Copper City is a great place to take the family. It is dog-friendly and has trails to test the skills of all riders, from the entry level Green Eagle loop to the double black diamond one-way downhill courses like Merry Widow or Never Sweat. Trails increase in difficulty the farther you get from Green Eagle Loop.

Look for signage or use the TrailForks app. Climb High Ore, choose your technical descent lines to the west or continue up and over the top to access longer loops like Descending Angel and Boss Tweed. Save some energy for the steep switchback climb - Trident - that includes some technical rocky outcrops.

The downhills feature banked corners and flowy sections with some rocky outcrops and bluffs. Copper City is a fantastic riding destination, especially in the spring or fall when other trails are still wet or snow covered.

Search Copper City Trails, Three Forks Trailhead (45.99088816116167, -111.56841000988476)

Meghan Schaeffer & Rowan Clark carving down Upper Ore, Copper City Trails

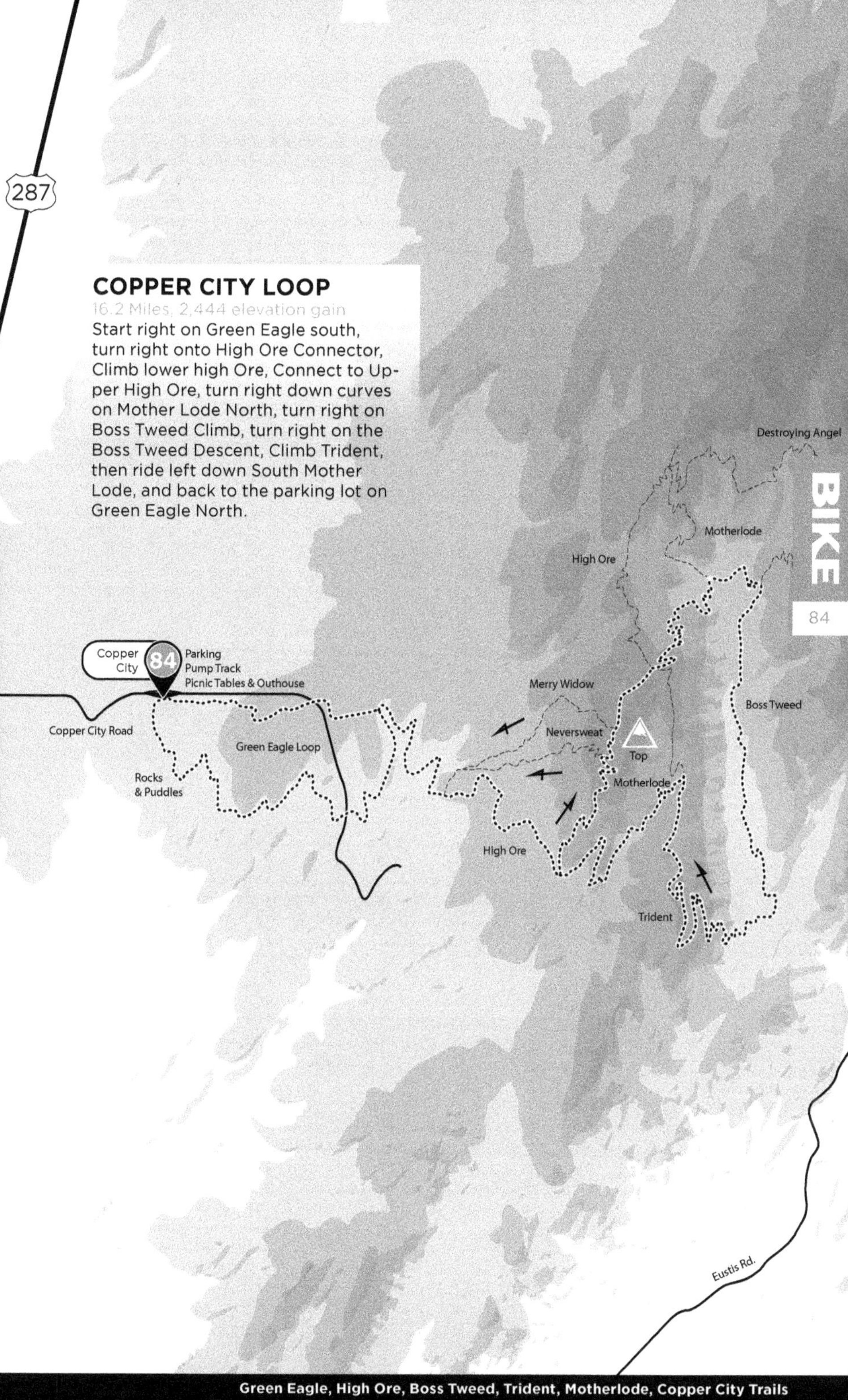
287
COPPER CITY LOOP
16.2 Miles, 2,444 elevation gain
Start right on Green Eagle south, turn right onto High Ore Connector, Climb lower high Ore, Connect to Upper High Ore, turn right down curves on Mother Lode North, turn right on Boss Tweed Climb, turn right on the Boss Tweed Descent, Climb Trident, then ride left down South Mother Lode, and back to the parking lot on Green Eagle North.
Destroying Angel
Motherlode
High Ore
Copper City
84
Parking
Pump Track
Picnic Tables & Outhouse
Merry Widow
Boss Tweed
Copper City Road
Neversweat
Green Eagle Loop
Top
Rocks & Puddles
Motherlode
High Ore
Trident
Eustis Rd.
BIKE
84
Green Eagle, High Ore, Boss Tweed, Trident, Motherlode, Copper City Trails

ADDITIONAL RESOURCES

OUTDOORS WITH BRYAN SCHAEFFER PODCAST

The simplest thing we can do to improve our physical & mental health for ourselves, our family and the planet is to exercise outdoors in nature every day.

This Podcast is getting outside and offline with accomplished skiers, hikers, runners and mountain bikers.

With expert tips on fitness, planning, gear and how to have the best experiences exploring year-round trails, this is your trailhead to adventure. Join us as we explore the thriving communities within these life-long sports.

Scan QR codes to listen.

Watch "The Last Best Bike"
- Single Track Mind
Short animated film by Bryan Schaeffer.
A bicycle is more than a series of tubes, cables, gears, pulleys and pistons - it is a time machine. Human powered by pedal strokes, whirring gears have the power to transport to a simpler time and place.

Jason Lunden
- Bike Fitting, Excel Physical Therapy
A proper bike fit will keep you riding with less pain and greater performance. Here are some tips on adjustments to get the most out of your ride.
https://excelptmt.com/services/professional-bike-fitting

Molly Bowman
- Executive Director, Bozeman Youth Cycling (BYC)
Bozeman Youth Cycling began with a few families riding together in Lindley Park and grew to be the thriving program that it is today.
https://bozemanyouthcycling.org

Heidi Makoutz
- Bozeman NICA Mountain Biking Head Coach
Bike into your best self with Bozeman's head NICA coach Heidi Makoutz.
https://bozemanyouthcycling.org/byc-programs/bozeman-nica

EJ Porth
- Associate Director, Gallatin Valley Land Trust (GVLT)
The Gallatin Valley Land Trust's Main street to Mountains trails connect Bozeman to local mountain biking adventures right from town.
https://www.crosscutmt.org

Christine Baker
- Vice President of Mountain Sports at Big Sky Resort
Learn about the progression of downhill riding in one of only three lift-accessed mountain biking centers in Montana.
https://www.crosscutmt.org

David Tucker
- SWMMBA Director of Outreach
David Tucker of the Southwest Montana Mountain Bike Association talks about the rapid growth of the organization and how the legacy of mountain biking advocacy stems from the efforts of biking promoters from the past.
https://www.southwestmontanamba.org

Scott Schmidt
- Director of Trails, Crosscut Mountain Sports Center
Schmitty talks about the origins of Bohart and the transition to Crosscut, plus current trail building and some daydream schemes to connect the east Bridger trails.
https://www.crosscutmt.org

Adam Johnson
- Big Sky Community Organization - Park and Trails Director
Big plans are in the works for connecting communities in the Big Sky area with biking trails.
https://bsco.org

Natalie Osborne
- Race Director, The Big Sky Biggie
Race director of Big Sky's epic cross-country mountain bike race (The Big Sky Biggie) Natalie Osborne talks about the creation of the event, the course details and how you can get involved with this classic event.
https://bigskybiggie.com/

Mel Cronin
- Director of Development, SWMMBA
Bozeman Pedal Project co-founder Mel Cronin loves Bozeman mountain biking communities. Her roles at Bozeman Pedal Project and SWMMBA help foster enjoyment of biking for riders in the region.
https://bozemanpedalproject.com/rides

Hailey Renner
- The Bike Kitchen
Bozeman's Bike Kitchen is the place to learn how to fix your bike or build a bike. Hailey Renner takes us through what the Bike Kitchen does and invites us to come in and check out this unique place.
https://www.bozemanbikekitchen.org

Jason Donald
- Mechanic, Owenhouse Cycles
Bike mechanic and former racer Jason Donald shares how to get your bike in the best operating shape for safety and performance and, also, tells us what he takes with him on long exploratory rides.
https://owenhousecycling.com

ADDITIONAL RESOURCES

OUTDOORS WITH BRYAN SCHAEFFER PODCAST

Watch "Somewhere in Montana" - Mountain Bike Ride

Short film by Bryan Schaeffer riding somewhere in Montana. Let's Ride!

Rob Funderburk - General Manager, Bangtail Bikes & Skis

Rob Funderburk of Bangtail Bikes has been in the business for many years. He talks about the cycling industry, past and present, and how Bozeman's growth can be a positive for building and supporting trails.
https://www.bangtailbikes.com

Tim Hawke - Architect, Copper City Trails

Tim describes how Punk Rock built the popular Copper City mountain bike trails by Three Forks.
https://www.southwestmontanamba.org/copper-city

The Montana way is with a smile and a nod: the two-finger steering wheel wave on remote dirt roads, the "Howdy" and "How's it going?" when passing on the trail. Montanans are proud and friendly people who value public lands for hiking, biking, fishing, hunting, and skiing. This is the way.

Get the scoop on mountain biking SW Montana. Visit TheLastBestBIKE.com for future interviews, videos, articles and more.

These shops are excellent resources to get you out and riding:

- Bangtail Bike & Skis
- Owenhouse Cycling
- Chalet Sports
- The Roundhouse
- Alter Cycles
- Second Wind Sports
- Summit
- Bozeman Bike Kitchen
- Bozeman REI
- The Gear Wizard
- Grizzly Outfitters - Big Sky
- Timber Trails - Livingston

Kiersten Schaeffer riding by Bangtail Bike Shop on Main Street, Bozeman, MT

For updates, more info and links go to: ***www.thelastbestski.com***

85. Sunset Hills
86. Bridger Creek Golf Course
87. Sacajewia Middle School
88. Sourdough
89. Mount Ellis Meadows
90. Bear Canyon/Goose Creek
91. Lick Creek Trailhead
92. Bridger Bowl
93. Bracket Creek Loop
94. Crosscut Mountain Sports Center
95. Lone Mountain Ranch
96. Beehive Basin
97. Porcupine Creek
98. Tepee Creek
99. Fawn Pass
100. Rendezvous Trail System

BEST GROOMING NORDIC TRAILS

Crosscut Mountain Sports Center, Lone Mountain Ranch, Rendezvous, Sunset Hills, Sourdough

COMMON BACKCOUNTRY SKIN TRACKS (ungroomed)

Bridger Bowl (off season) History Rock, Lick Creek, Goose Creek, Blackmore, Hyalite, Mount Ellis Meadows

MODERATE BACKCOUNTRY TOURING (ungroomed)

Fawn Pass, Tepee Creek, Porcupine Creek, Mount Ellis Meadows, Bracket Creek Loop

MODERATE TO ADVANCED BACKCOUNTRY (ungroomed)

Beehive Basin, Bridger Bowl sidecountry and The Ridge, Blackmore, Hyalite Peak, The Blaze

BEST BEGINNER SKIING IN BOZEMAN WINTER

Lindley Park, Sacajewia Middle School, Gallatin Regional Park

THE LAST BEST **SKI** MONTANA

ULLR THE NORSE GOD OF SKIING & HUNTING
THE BRINGER OF SNOW

FOREWORD

by Andy Newell

Head Coach at Nordic Team Solutions & four-time Olympic skier

CALLING ALL-AROUND WINTER ATHLETES

If you're looking for an explanation of how rugged, wild, and untamed the Montana mountains are, you've flipped to the wrong page.

If you're looking for someone to boast about how gnarly a thrill-seeking skier must be to tackle these mountains, you've got the wrong guy.

Yes, the mountains of Southwest Montana can be both rugged and wild, it's what lured me and countless other winter sports enthusiasts to this area in the first place. But you don't need to read this book to know that. Those of us lucky enough to experience their natural wonder know they need little hype.

Instead, this book is for those looking to explore the winter landscape of southwestern Montana in ways as versatile as the terrain they offer.

Within the pages of this book lies an invitation to daydream about the endless skiing possibilities and adventures layered within the mountains, like the series of snowstorms that create the playground. This guide is meant for my fellow skiers, young and old, advanced and new, steep chargers and backcountry gliders. Even the most experienced local can lose sight of Montana's winter potential, if we are not reminded where to look.

I first met Bryan because we seemed to cross paths often in the most uncommon places. He's the kind of person you might run into on dawn patrol ski touring the furthest most peaks of the Northern Bridgers, then encounter once again heading out with a headlamp to skate ski Sourdough in the late afternoon. We bonded because to us, there is not just one way enjoy a day of skiing. Sliding on snow can be enjoyed in so many ways, as limitless as the enormous ridge lines and vast public lands Montana provides.

When a passing winter storm dumps feet of snow we gravitate toward the powder boards. During a sparkling late spring freeze cycle there is nothing better than a backcountry crust cruise on skinny skis. When skiing is more than a weekend hobby, winter aficionados choose an adventure that best suits the day and conditions. In places like this the weather, snowpack, and terrain call the shots. You're either summoned or you're not, invited by the mountains themselves despite the most well-crafted plans.

While not all days on skis unfold the way we anticipate, every outing is an adventure to those who are willing.

Is an adventure anything more than an exciting and unusual experience? A true advocate of the outdoors welcomes others to experience their adventurous world; they don't exclude, and Bryan is a natural guide on paper and in person.

Whether you are skiing the Hollywood Headwall or touring up Mt. Ellis for the first time, your sense of adventure is one of the same, in my opinion. Your consciousness is heightened, your heart beats with intent, it's the same experience for us all. An adventure can only really be measured by those who lived it. It's a moment in time to be cherished by them and not judged by a bystander.

Every day on skis is a unique opportunity to awaken your senses to this feeling of exhilaration.

Go find your adventure.

Andy Newell classic skiing on Sourdough trail

Frozen Waves

Dropping weightlessly through the cold smoke, the snowboard lifts silently into the next floating turn, falling through the air through the lightest fluffy powder.

Cold smoke to corduroy—gliding over countless kilometers of untouched setup skate tracks, feeling the undulations across the contours of the land sliding forward.

The sun rises, casting shimmers through snow crystals and warming the frozen landscape.

Gloved fist bumps, pole taps, a "Wahoo" and "Let's do that again!"

Moments like these are why we ride in all its forms.

There is a winter athlete in every family member.

We have interviewed expert Nordic, backcountry and alpine skiers to help you get the most out of the long winters here.

This book is intended to desegregate skiing in the greater Bozeman area so your entire family can make the most of our long, beautiful winters here.

Let's go ride!

INTRODUCTION

Winters are long, cold and snowy in Bozeman, MT.

Constant storm cycles routinely dump cold smoke powder over the Bridger, Gallatin and Beartooth ranges.

The season lasts from November into April, and the snowpack grows. The abundance of snow the area provides opportunities for many types of skiing.

Some of the top winter athletes, instructors, avalanche experts and program directors in the area shared their expertise for this book.

This book is designed to give you expert advice on where to go, when to go and what to focus on, covering different techniques at different skill levels in the sport.

Information on gear, safety, technique and locations will help you make the most of your winter in Southwest Montana.

Gliding over snow is joyous, whether it is riding 8 inches of cold smoke at Bridger or gliding across a masterfully groomed skate track at Lone Mountain Ranch. These moments of pure joy bring us back again and again to explore the ever-changing canvas of snow.

Justin Bigart doing laps on Bacon Rind

A BRIEF HISTORY

Winter adventurers have been skiing in the Bozeman area for over a century. Pine Hills (Story Mill) and Bear Canyon were some of the first locations near town frequently skied in the early 1900s.

Like other western states, Montana imported its early ski culture from Scandinavian immigrants who established Nordic skiing.

In 1935, the first tow lift in Montana was built near the Karst Dude Ranch in the Gallatin Canyon. This was the start of organized skiing in the Bozeman area. The Karst Ranch slope was used for an annual ski jump competition.

Other venues such as Lionshead Resort in West Yellowstone made their debuts, opening up more alpine skiing terrain to larger group of skiing enthusiasts. The nonprofit Bridger Bowl opened in 1955 and added a chairlift in 1964.

Ski touring access up logging roads began developing into bigger plans. The dream of TV anchor Chet Huntley was realized in the forming of Big Sky Resort in the winter of 1973. The Bridger Ski Education Foundation originally chartered in 1975.

Driving off the hype from Bill Koch's silver medal in the 1976 Olympics, West Yellowstone Rendezvous trails were built specifically for Nordic Skiing. This area became the early winter training grounds for the US Ski Team in the early 80s.

Alpine, Nordic and freestyle ski clubs in the Bozeman area combined to become a unified Bridger Ski Foundation in 1991.

In 1995, Big Sky Resort opened the 11,253-foot rock/glacier summit of Lone Peak by completing a tram to the summit, opening access to over 300 degrees of skiing off the peak. Acquiring Moonlight Basin in 2013 made the new Big Sky Resort "the biggest skiing in America" with more than 4,500 skiable acres accessible under one pass.

Bohart Ranch and Crosscut Nordic combined in 2016 to form the new Crosscut Mountain Sports Center.

In 2019, Uphill Pursuits began hosting Skimo races on the old Bear Canyon slopes, bringing the evolution of skiing in Bozeman full circle.

Bozeman's ski future looks bright, thanks to the committed people who have invested in all the aspects of this vibrant ski community.

Reference:
https://www.outsidebozeman.com/magazine/archives/winter-2016-17/bozeman-historski
https://bigsky2025.com/timeline
https://www.bridgerskifoundation.org/about/history

Cold smoke to Corduroy

WINTER SAFETY

Skiing and snow sports can be dangerous.

You can fall, things can fall on you. You could get hypothermia or frostbite or get sunburned. You could get lost or run into on an overcrowded run.

Using the right technique, wearing the correct gear and properly evaluating terrain and conditions are all important to having fun and being safe in the winter.

This book is designed to help, but remember that conditions are always subject to change. Variables are what make skiing interesting, but also can be dangerous.

Do your research, get proper avalanche training and keep up your fitness and safety chops. That will make the experience more fun and rewarding.

A major concern for backcountry skiing is avalanche risk assessment. Take a course from friends of Gallatin Valley Avalanche Center.

Make sure you check the forecast and the avalanche danger website. Perhaps most important, know what is and is not avalanche terrain.

RISKS

Winter driving is its own sport. With a few of these tips, you will be safely on your way to the ski area or trailhead.

Tip No. 1 is to go slow. Everyone thinks that Montana used to have no speed limit. This isn't actually true. The law advised drivers to proceed at a "reasonable and prudent" speed. Seasoned Montanans know the road you can easily drive over 80 mph in the summer isn't the same road during or after a snowstorm. Icy, snowy conditions make a "reasonable and prudent" speed much slower than the summer, but many drivers don't heed this warning and drive summer speed on hazardous winter roads.

Four-wheel drive can help you accelerate and keep traction, but it won't do a thing to slow you down in an emergency stop. Remember, go slow. Even acceleration and deceleration are the goal. If you start to slide, turn into the slide and pump the brakes (hopefully your anti-lock brakes are already doing it for you). These winter-handling skills are a good thing to practice in a safe setting, in the vehicle you drive to go skiing. Watch the soft shoulder in the winter. I have pushed out many a car that's only a foot or two off the plowed road.

If you do go off the road, point your front tires in the direction back to the plowed surface. Bring a small snow shovel as well as a door mat or towel to put under slipping tires for traction (it works wonders). If that doesn't work, a tow cable is typically the next step. Many folks carry these to help travelers stuck in the snowbank.

Rule No. 2 is that you are going to spend a lot on tires! Snow tires that are chemically designed for colder temperatures with specially designed tread for snow and ice are a must-have for winter travel. Many now come siped to help push water out and gain traction on wet roads. Studded tires can be good in regions that are completely snow covered during the winter.

Practice pre-stopping ahead of the stoplight so you don't accidentally slide through it. Give yourself plenty of time and drive safely!

Driving isn't the only risk when you're participating in winter sports. Here are some others.

Doug Chabot, director of the Gallatin National Forest Avalanche Center, making safe turns through the cold smok

Frostbite/Hypothermia:

Be sure to know the signs of these dangerous winter maladies.

Injuries from trauma: Know basic first aid, and learn where the nearest medical centers are. Cold: Wear clothes in layers. Pack warmer insulation for stopping or in case of equipment failures.

AVALANCHE SAFETY

The number one skill the avalanche experts I interviewed gave for avalanche safety is to understand what is avalanche terrain. The top piece of gear for this is an inclinometer, which will help you to determine the slope angle.

Slope angles between 30 and 45 degrees are prime for avalanches. Slopes lower than that generally don't have the gravity and force to create a slide. Although, like many things in avalanche safety awareness, there are hidden dangers such as steeper slopes above that can be triggered by skiing below. Ron Gregg, the founder of Outdoor Research, and his party died in an avalanche like this.

The mellow skiing we refer to in this guide as backcountry touring is generally out of avalanche terrain. Steeper terrain, similar to what you might ski on at a ski area, often falls into the 30-45 degrees area. Venturing into this avalanche terrain requires training (find local courses at mtavalanche.com), all of the avalanche safety equipment and constant monitoring of the conditions through a local service like the Gallatin National Forest Avalanche Center. Sign up for the free email list.

Like fanatic surfers chasing storms, changing snow conditions are what make this sport adventurous, exciting and potentially dangerous. There are top-notch resources available locally. To be safe in mountain terrain in the winter, take advantage of the excellent resources available locally.

TRAIL ETIQUETTE

- Yield to skiers coming up the hill.
- Don't walk in groomed ski tracks.
- Bring dogs only to dog-allowed ski trails and pick up and remove their poop.
- Make room for passing. Don't walk or ski abreast on high-traffic trails.
- Follow directional signs for loops.
- Use restroom facilities where available or pee off trail and cover with snow (leave no trace).
  - Ski in control at all times.
  - Give 15 feet of space when passing downhill skiers.

For suggestions about safety gear to wear while downhill skiing, listen to the interview with ski photographer Bob Allen on page 259.

For alpine and backcountry skiing, wear a helmet. Wearing Knee pads, elbow pads and hip pads provide warmth, as well as protection against rock, trees and other obstacles.

AVALANCHE SAFETY GEAR

For backcountry skiing in avalanche terrain, here are some must-have items:

Inclinometer (to determine angle of slope—30-45 degrees is prime avalanche)

Beacon (be sure to test the battery)

Extendable probe

Snow shovel

Helmet

GET THE GEAR

Unlike barefoot nude water skiing, you will need some accessories for this sport.

Each technique has different equipment requirements to make skiing more fun.

We recommend supporting local businesses for the best service. These shops are excellent resources to get you equipped to make the most of the long winters in the Bozeman area.

- Bangtail Bikes for Nordic and backcountry touring
- Uphill Pursuits for Nordic and Ski Mountaineering (skimo)
- Round House for alpine equipment and rentals
- Big Sky Resort Rentals
- Bridger Rentals

OUTFIT EARLY

It can be a real challenge getting outfitted for a ski season, especially with a family.

The Bridger Ski Foundation ski swap is a good place to start. Held annually in October at the Gallatin County fairgrounds, the swap provides great deals for skiers. Plus, a percentage goes back to BSF to support the ski organization programs.

If you are just starting in a specific type of skiing, renting your equipment might be a good option. Higher-end rentals allow for testing more performance gear and can be the only way to get a real idea of how the ski will perform in action.

The Round House offers annual rentals for younger kids. Downhill boots, poles and skis are rented in the fall and returned in the spring. There is even an option to change sizes during the season if your little skier has outgrown the gear.

Every fall, go through your ski fleet and inspect it to make sure bindings are working, skis are waxed, and edges are sharpened. Check out your goggles and helmets, try on base layers, shells, hats and gloves. Don't spoil your first day out with equipment that doesn't fit or work any more.

BIATHLON

Originating in Norway for military training, biathlon is the activity inspired by Norse god Ullr (the god of skiing and hunting).

Early international biathlon competitions in the late 1950s used high-caliber ammunition and courses through a variety of terrain more similar to a modern-day orienteering course. Various targets were spread out over a variety of terrain.

In 1978, the format became a single target range of five round targets distanced at 50 meters, with ski loops of varying length and difficulty depending on the race. Firearms were standardized to a 5-shell cartridge of .22 ammunition, open sights and a minimum weight limit.

Biathlon clubs utilize this specific terrain and training for safety and learning the nuances of this technically complex sport.

West Yellowstone and Crosscut offer demo days and publicly accessible races at certain times in the winter.

In the late 1950s, early international competitions used high-caliber ammunition on snow courses with targets spread out in a variety of terrain. It was a lot like a modern-day orienteering course.

In 1978, the format became a single target range consisting of five round targets distanced at 50 meters, with ski loops of varying length and difficulty. Firearms were standardized to a five-shell cartridge of .22 ammunition, open sights, and a minimum weight limit.

Modern-day biathlon is on fixed courses with single shooting ranges. Upon skiing into the shooting stadium, athletes take a shooting stance' either standing (4.5 inch target or prone (1.8-inch target). The biathlete has a .22 rifle with double slings worn like a backpack.

The rifle must be pointing to the sky or at the target. When skiing into the shooting stadium, athletes remove their poles while steadying their breathing. The rifle is quickly rotated from carry into shooting position in a well-rehearsed movement. The biathlete loads the bolt-action rifle with the first round and shoots at one of the five targets. If a target is hit, a satisfying "tink" sound resonates and the target flips from black to white.

As mentioned, the biathlete has five shots to hit five targets on a 50-meter range. If a target is missed, a 150-meter penalty lap must be skied, or a time penalty is added for each missed target. When shooting is finished, the biathlete re-slings the rifle into carry position and exits the shooting area. All skiers utilize the freestyle technique, otherwise known as skating.

Courses have a standard percentage of flat terrain and hills. There is typically at least one steep section. Standings are based on time.

Seth Hubard at the scope, coaching Crosscut Mountain Sports Center - Anna Sellers photo reference

Swix wax thermometer in the snow with quick reference on glide wax for the temperature

WAXING ABOUT WAXES

Snow is an ever-changing medium. The nature of frozen water is in constant flux. Snow falling as stellar dendrites accumulates on the ground and forms a snowpack. The space between the ground and the surface air's temperature gradient (if warming) will sinter the snow, compacting the snowpack. Cooling can facet layers in the snowpack, making weaker layers. Read more about this in the avalanche safety section.

Applying the right ski wax for the snow temperature is crucial with Nordic skiing. Ski wax performance is temperature-dependent. Warmer conditions have a wetter snow that requires warmer waxes such as red to yellow. These temperatures are generally better for skate skiing. Skis with more base structure are faster in warmer, wetter snow. This is like siping a tire with small cuts that allow water to escape. In colder conditions, this same structure will catch faceted snow and increase friction, resulting in slower skis.

Colder temperatures cause the snow to crystallize or facet, creating harder, sharper snow. A smooth base that doesn't grab these facets will be faster. The structure of the ski should be flatter. Hard waxes are more durable and hold up longer by breaking the crystals and forming a thin, smooth layer with less friction.

A snow thermometer will give a more accurate reading than the air temperature.

Picking the right ski wax is more crucial with Nordic skiing, where you have to put your own effort into gliding.

One additional note about waxes: with safety and climate considerations, fluorocarbons are being phased out of the industry. Youth racing doesn't allow them at all, and Master's Racing and the World Cup circuit will follow suit. Replacement waxes are more environmentally friendly.

GROOMING

Before you go out on the groomed trails, take a peek at the grooming report. The local Bozeman Trails are groomed by the Bridger Ski Foundation. This nonprofit organization relies on non-mandatory trail passes and donations from the community.

The quality of the Nordic skiing depends greatly on the grooming skill and frequency.

BSF operates at great expense to maintain the quality of the winter trail systems. They offer completion youth programs and training programs for masters as well.

Colder temperatures - 20 degrees or colder - are often better for classic skiing. Warmer temperatures—20s and 30s—are generally better for skating.

Early and late season conditions may be less optimal with a softer snowpack and dirtier snow with rocks and pine needles on the track.

Hot waxing ski bench in a Bozeman garage

Oksana Masters Training for more Paralympic Medals
Photo reference - courtesy Crosscut Mountain Sports Center

SKIING IS FOR EVERYONE

HOW TO APPROACH
THIS LIFETIME SPORT

We all start somewhere. Regardless of our God-given abilities, we don't reach our full potential without the help of others. Consider what opportunities you have for improving your skiing. Find a good coach and ask lots of questions to learn about your specific strengths and weaknesses. Skiing is a lifetime sport that is available to all, regardless of age or physical abilities. Both the very young and older adults can experience the joy of gliding across snow.

The ski community here in SW Montana is made of many different groups with far-reaching impacts. These groups are all passionate about skiing and the incredible power of working together to provide skiing opportunities for everyone.

Cliff Montagne explained how the Bridger Ski Foundation started from grassroots to the current thriving multi-faceted organization that it is today. Big Sky Resort's Christine Baker described how the Montana Ski Area Association partners work together to develop policies to improve the skiing experience and, in this time of the pandemic, to develop policies to improve the skiing experience and to implement safe practices at ski areas.

ADAPTIVE SKIING

Eagle Mount Bozeman has a ski/snowboard and cross-country ski/snowshoe program for adaptive athletes, taking riders of all ages to Big Sky, Bridger, Moonlight Basin and The Yellowstone Club. Crosscut holds cross-country skiing and sit skiing sessions.

Skiing makes us happier, not just as individuals, but within entire communities.

That is why we are building this book experience. We encourage you to explore the QR code links to interviews, videos, GPS maps and more. This resource is designed to help you start learning about a new aspect of the sport, if you desire to do that, by providing information on who to talk to about getting started, coaching, avalanche safety, and where to go to have the best day on skis.

I hope this book encourages you to explore boundaries and introduces you to some new friends through skiing.

Nordic Center Director Fay Johnson & friends dog hours at Crosscut Mountain Sports Center

FAMILY SKIING

It can be challenging to get the entire family out in the winter. You have to get skis and poles that fit growing kids. You have to track down boots, hats, gloves, coats, long underwear, sunglasses for the entire crew, and you need spares in case gear is lost.

Sled attachments for strollers like the chariot handle well, collapse for storage and enable the entire family to get out together. Pack a warm down jacket or blanket in the enclosure and you might be able to get in a nice ski while junior takes a nap.

In the drawing below, the family takes an out-and-back ski trip up Mill Creek in the Paradise Valley on a cold, crisp morning.

We follow a lively and noisy dog sled team that gets quieter as it quickly moves off into the distance. The only sounds we hear are the gliding of skis on snow, our quiet breathing, and our own beating hearts as we glide into the stillness of winter.

WINTER WONDERS

Where ice climbers scale icy walls, the chipping sounds of ice picks and the clanging of metal carabiners and screws, resonate from the canyon walls. In contrast to these sounds, the murmuring of water flowing under the ice on a nearby creek breaks the silence in a more natural way.

Winter uninterrupted is silent, disturbed only by heart beats and the swooshing of skis across snow. These quiet places are a refuge in this season, forming frozen cathedrals for our private thoughts.

The next time you are out in the snow, pay attention to the crunch underfoot as you walk on snow shoes, the "swoosh" of skis gliding on silky snow or the "poof" of dropping into a powder stash. Savor these sounds - the sparseness of winter is a gift to the spirit.

Schaeffer family skiing Mill Creek on a cold clear morning - Photo Reference Seth Neilson

CARVING TIME

To spend a day of skiing at a downhill ski resort may require some planning ahead. Just as with purchasing airline tickets or booking a hotel, look into the practices and rules of your destination before you go. Book tickets in advance and make early preparations for Montana's downhill ski areas.

For spur-of-the-moment excursions, Nordic or backcountry trips offer more flexibility. Some of the local Nordic centers have online purchasing of a trail pass that can be printed and carried with you.

Town trails are free to access with a suggested donation to the Bridger Ski Foundation to fund grooming.

We have listed some great options for local backcountry touring near Bozeman. Many other trails to explore are shown on the regional GPS map, accessible on page 225.

The author carving at Big Sky

SKIJOR

Getting Towed (or towing) Your Dog

Skijoring is a winter sport in which a person on skis is pulled by an animal, typically a horse or a dog. Horse skijoring races can be seen at the 320 Ranch located between Big Sky and West Yellowstone. The ranch allows access to the cross country ski trail heading east from the ranch.

It takes some training to get your pooch to behave on a skijor line. Skijor lines are easy to find online. They consist of a waist belt (or climbing harness) attached to elastic-enforced webbing that provides some give. Many of these are the right length for trail running but require an additional runner and carabiner to give more length for skiing. Otherwise, you may run over the back of the dog's legs on skis. Your dog will need a chest harness as a neck harness puts too much force on the neck.

Another option is a dog hiking pack, which can act as a harness with some storage space for musher's cream, treats and poop bags.

Remember, pick up the dog poop and make the dog pack it out.

Not all dogs have a towing aptitude. To find out if your dog does, train beforehand. Practice on flat, straight or slightly uphill trails first. Less crowded open trails are a good place to practice, and try not to get tangled up in the lines.

Sourdough and Mill Creek are good dog spots for skijoring.

Dogs can wreck groomed trails and aren't allowed at most Nordic centers during normal operating hours. You can take your dog to Sourdough groomed trails, but please be sure to use the poop bag trash can. The first couple miles of the Sourdough trail can be very crowded, but it is less crowded past the bridge.

Crosscut will have open hours for dog skiing on all trails; check the website for updated info.

There are a few Big Sky community trails that allow dogs. Mill Creek in the Paradise Valley is a popular spot for dog sledding and skijoring.

Dog Foot Strategies

Many backcountry skiers enjoy being able to ski with their dogs. Whether it is skijoring or seeing your four-legged friend run blissfully through the snow, getting out with your dog can be an awesome form of exercise for both of you.

Dog paws have an amazing circulation system that keeps them warm in cold temperatures. This feature, however, melts snow, which can then form into uncomfortable ice blocks that get wedged between the pads.

Treatment for these ice blocks includes occasionally pulling them off by hand when you notice the dog stopping and biting at their paws. Ointments and booties can be used as prevention, if necessary. Apply Vaseline or a more expensive musher's cream liberally to the space between the pads. Trimming excess fur will reduce the amount of snow that can ball up in these problem areas. Booties are less messy, but some dogs just won't wear them. Make sure to get a size that doesn't bind and that allows for the foot pads to expand. If the booties keep falling off, apply athletic tape around the collars of the booties.

Kiersten and Loki Skijouring along Bozeman Creek

MONTANA'S ROOF

The rugged Absaroka-Beartooth mountain ranges lie north of Yellowstone National Park. This is one of the wildest alpine areas in North America.

The west side of the range rises from the Yellowstone River in the Paradise Valley. The pronounced Emigrant Peak to the south has some dramatic ski lines.

Mill Creek, the northern drainage of Emigrant Peak, is one of the most popular spots for cross-country touring and dog sledding in Paradise Valley. Pine Creek accesses the steep and challenging Black Peak. Elephant Head on the north end of the western Beartooths is relatively close to Livingston.

Deep in the Absaroka-Beartooth wilderness is the 12,808' Granite Peak, the highest point in Montana.

On the east side of the range is the Beartooth Highway, a National Scenic Byways All American Road. It is closed most of the year due to extreme weather.

he Crazy Mountains - Skier Simon Peterson

Andy Newell making turns on Helmet, Sphyx in the background

Notable mountain ranges in the SW Montana Greater Yellowstone region include:

Bridgers, Gallatins, Hyalites, Tobacco Roots, Crazy Mountains, Absaroka-Beartooths, Madisons, and Lionhead Mountains.

Find ultimate adventure in scaling big Montana peaks on skis.

Gallatin Peak - Spanish Peaks
Mount Blackmore - Hyalites
Saddle Peak - Bridgers
Banana Chute - Ross Peak
The Great One - Naya Nuki
Sacagawea Peak - Bridgers
Emigrant Peak - Paradise Valley
The Sphinx - Madison Range

Consider hiring one of the local reputable guiding services in the area. Day trips, overnight, and hut tours led by experts with local knowledge is a safe and fun way to get a big mountain adventure and improve your backcountry skiing skills. Find links to guiding services at

thelastbestski.com

Explore further with Backcountry Skiing Peaks and Couloirs of Southwest Montana - A guide to skiing notable peaks and couloirs in the Gallatin, Madison, Bridger, Tobacco Root, Crazy and Montana Absaroka Mountain Ranges www.skiingmontana.org

Bridger Ski Foundation Coach - Heidi Makoutz

GEAR

"

Man, I'll tell you what - walking in boots, you can tell something about somebody right away.

-Cory Birkenbuel, Ski Instructor

"

Hard-shell backcountry ski boot

Q: How many pairs of skis do you need to make the most out of ski season in SW Montana?

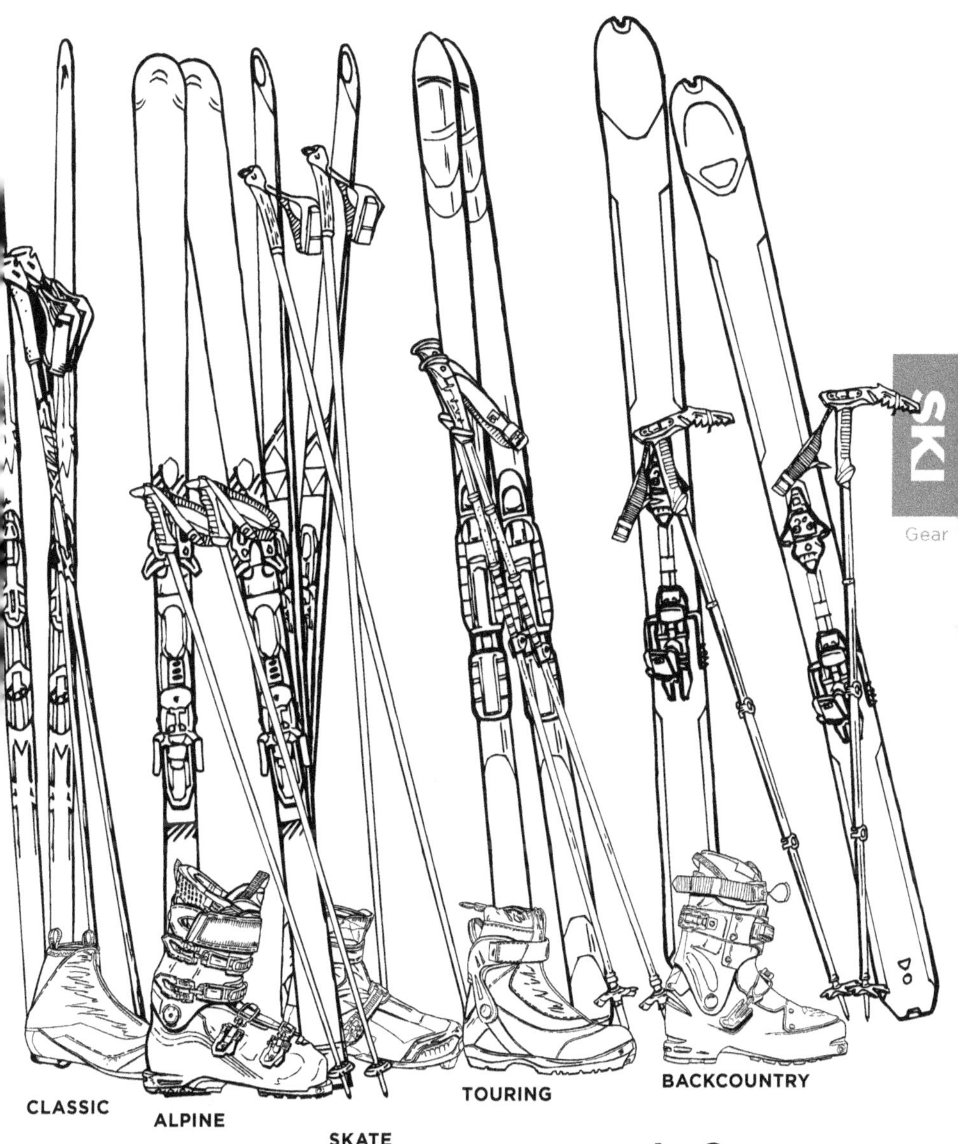

A: One more.

SKI
Gear

TECHNIQUE

CLASSIC - CROSS COUNTRY

Diagonal Stride
Double Pole
Kick Double Pole
Herringbone
Klaebo Run

Classic skiing, using a diagonal stride technique, is built upon a basic walking motion.

Shifting your full body weight onto the ski compresses the wax pocket on the kick zone and provides grip to squirt the other ski gliding down the track.

Beginners will employ a shuffling movement while getting the feel of skis underfoot.

As balance and skill improves, a skier's kick becomes more pronounced, facilitated with extra power from pole plants.

More advanced techniques apply more power to the poles, like double poling and kick double poling.

Classic skis vary in width and base finishes. Higher-performance skis are lighter weight, have wax and waxless options, and more modern twin skin applications or "zeros" for warmer conditions.

Talk to a ski shop expert to find the right ski(s) for you.

All the Bozeman town trails and Sourdough (Bozeman Creek) are groomed by the Bridger Ski Foundation for skate with classic tracks. Hyalite is groomed occasionally by the Forest Service. These narrow trails through forests around Hyalite Reservoir lend themselves to the classic technique, as it is a bit narrow for skating.

SKATE - CROSS COUNTRY

V1
V2
V1 Offset (Paddle Stroke)
Flying V1
V2 Alternate

First-time skate skiers should practice getting the feel of shifting body weight from side to side like the weight-driven pendulum on a grandfather clock.

The skis are typically slightly shorter than a classic performance ski. Skate boots have a high-ankle collar for stability. Skate poles are also longer than classic, sizing up to your lower lip. The extra height gives more power on the double-pole motion.

As balance and coordination improve, skate skiers can focus on shortening their power phase and lengthening their glide phase.

Skate skiing's multiple gears are technique types or strokes: V1 is for long steady climbs and V1 offset, or paddle stroke, is for steep climbs; V2 and V2 alternate are for higher-speed and varied terrain.

With the many kilometers to practice on in the Bozeman area, skate skiing challenges all ages and abilities as a life-long pursuit that combines fitness, technique and the right gear.

For Nordic skiing instruction contact:

- The Bridger Ski Foundation
- Crosscut Mountain Sports Center
- Montana Endurance Academy
- Lone Mountain Ranch Nordic
- Nordic Team Solutions

Andy Newell kicking and gliding, Sourdough

Erika Flowers V1 Offset, Sunset Hills

BACKCOUNTRY - TOURING

Classic Striding
Herringbone
Snow Plow
Telemark Turn
Kick Step Corners

Touring skis span the gap between performance cross-country race skis and heavier backcountry mountaineering skis. These tend to be wider, while still fitting in a classic track.

A common setup for a versatile touring ski has a wood core with metal edges and a fish-scale kick zone. Some models will have a bit more side camber to make tele turning easier, while others have a partial removable skin for the kick zone.

Touring skis are more forgiving and can be a great choice for skiing under questionable conditions or where there is no grooming.

They are more forgiving on trails are part boot-packed and part ski trail.

Lower level meadows are a fun place to explore and get in a few telemark turns while removing the avalanche risk associated with steeped slopes.

Use the same setup you would use for backcountry skiing. The term "side country" refers to the spaces on the edge of established ski resorts. These areas are often accessed by lifts and are either hiked to or "skinned" to in order to reach the ridges and bowls outside of the ski area, allowing the explorer to gain easier access to more remote terrain.

Be aware that these areas are not monitored by ski patrol, so you need to bring a transceiver, probe and shovel, and know the avalanche conditions and weather forecast, etc. the same as skiing in the backcountry.

Jim & Claudia Schaeffer Ski Touring, Tepee Creek

BACKCOUNTRY - Off-piste

Skinning Up
Herringbone
Kick Step Corners
Wedge Turns
Parallel Turns

Ungroomed backcountry skiing requires heavier boots and skis than does backcountry touring.

These skis are more similar to what you might ski on at an alpine resort, but they have a skinning mode for climbing. For instance, telemark skis with wire gate bindings, or a backcountry setup like Dynafit, allows the heel to lift from the ski while skinning uphill. The toe is bound by pins to allow articulation. There is a downhill mode, where the heel can be locked in position to allow for alpine turns while descending.

Full-length skins—formerly animal skins, but now a synthetic hair with straps and adhesive—cover the base of the skis to give grip while climbing. These are removed and stowed for the descent. This set-up works great for skiing in steeper terrain and in remote backcountry - for climbing in bowls and up peaks.

The gear for backcountry skiing ranges from a lighter ski for climbing straight uphill (skimo racing) to a wider, full mountain and powder ski for more float. With heavier equipment, you have to modify your skinning technique. Focus on sliding, not over lifting. Slide and apply pressure to gain traction. Switchbacks can be tricky to learn initially. Side-hilling takes some balance. The advantage of a full backcountry set-up over a touring set-up is that on steeper, more rugged terrain, the skis provide more float and the ability to power through choppier snow.

Ben Werner Making First Tracks, The Bridgers

Dan Lakatos skiing Yellowstone Club

TECHNIQUE

ALPINE - DOWNHILL

Groomers
Park
Slalom
Freestyle
Big Mountain

A downhill ski package has the heaviest and most performance-driven build, maximizing edge control. These skis use hard-shell boots. The more expensive downhill boots have removable liners that can be custom-sized for optimum comfort and performance. Poles should come to slightly above the hip.

Skis vary from thin racing skis to wide powder skis. Skis suitable for all around skiing on the ski hill have wide tips and tails and a thinner midsection.

Visit a local ski shop to find the best pair(s) for you. Equipment plays a large role in your skiing enjoyment. If you aren't sure what is best for you, try out some demo skis before committing to a purchase.

Other standard safety gear includes goggles, a helmet, knee pads and padded long underwear.

Terrain will dictate your technique. Rolling groomed runs are a carver's paradise for making sweeping s-turns and powering edge to edge.

Skiing powder means putting more weight on the back of the skis to gain float over deeper snow. Moguls are short, choppy, knee-intensive turns.

Varied terrain in resort alpine downhill skiing is a fun, fast way to explore wintry mountain landscapes.

SAWTOOTH PEAK
11,488"

Cory Birkenbuel, Upper Ridge, Maverick Mountain

Karl Birkeland skiing the Beartooths

Shannon Griffin skiing the "cold smoke" at Bridger Bowl

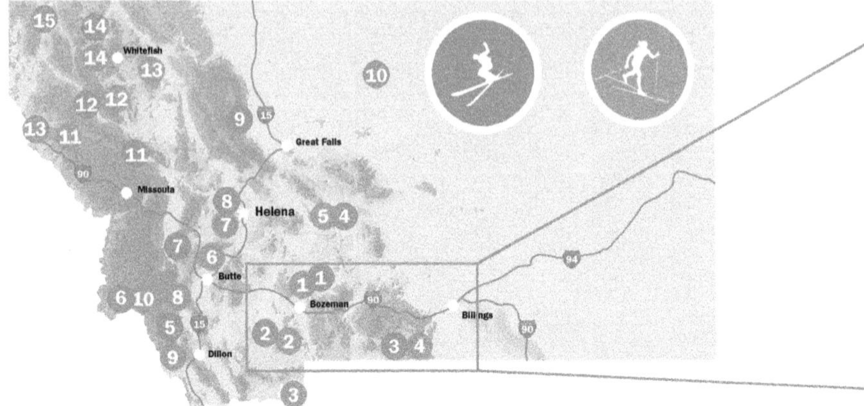

THE LAY OF THE LAND

Montana's Downhill Ski Areas

1. Bridger Bowl Ski Area
2. Big Sky Resort
3. Red Lodge Mountain
4. Showdown Montana
5. Maverick Mountain
6. Lost Trail Ski Area
7. Discovery Ski Area
8. Great Divide
9. Teton Pass
10. Bear Paw Ski Bowl
11. Montana Snowbowl
12. Blacktail Mountain
13. Lookout Pass Ski & Recreation Area
14. Whitefish Mountain Resort
15. Turner Mountain

Groomed Cross-country Ski Trails

1. Crosscut Mountain Sports Center, Bozeman Town Trails
2. Lone Mountain Ranch
3. Rendezvous Ski Trails
4. Red Lodge Nordic Center
5. Silver Crest Winter Recreation Area
6. Homestake Lodge Cross-country Ski Center
7. MacDonald Pass Trails, Bill Roberts Golf Course Ski Tracks
8. Mount Haggin Nordic Ski Area
9. Elkhorn Hotsprings Ski Trail
10. Chief Joseph Cross-country Ski Trail
11. Blacktail Nordic Trails
12. Bigfork Community Nordic Center
13. Izaak Walton Inn Cross-country Ski Trails
14. Glacier Nordic Center

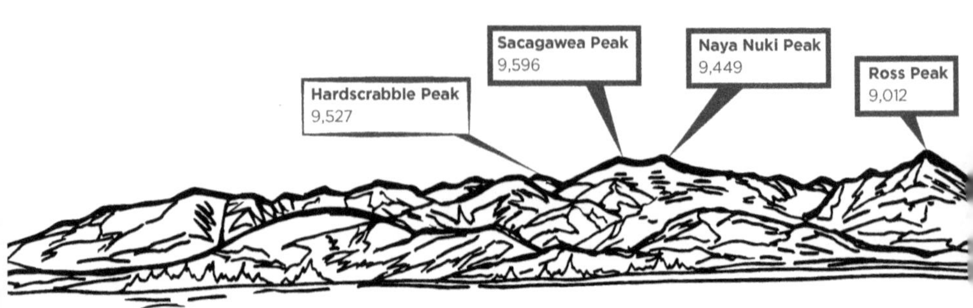

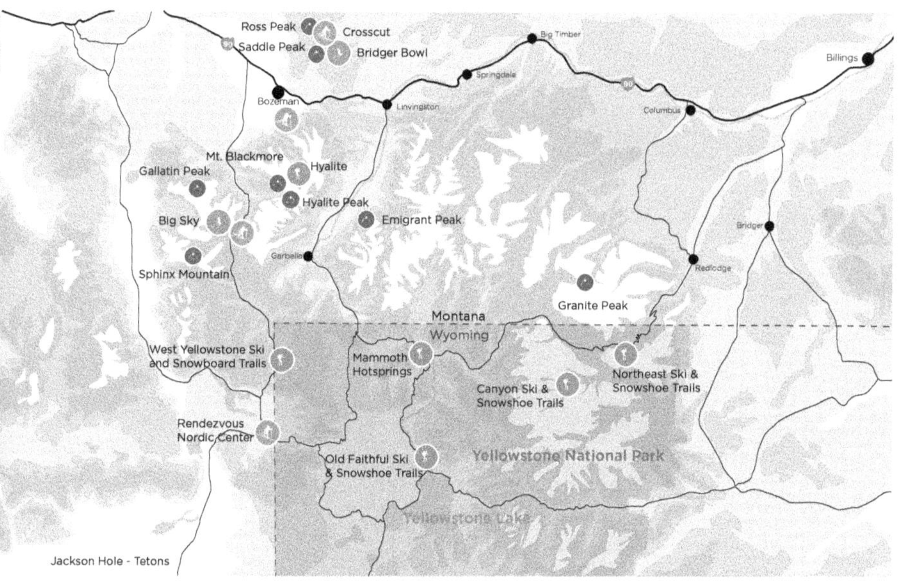

This book focuses on the greater Bozeman Big Sky area (Bozone), including the Bridgers, Bozeman Town Trails, Hyalite and the Gallatin Range, Big Sky and the Madison Range, the Gallatin corridor to West Yellowstone, Yellowstone National Park and Paradise Valley.

This book is by no means a definitive guide to all the skiing accessible in this area. It is a source of information, as it describes recommended trails for the different types of skiing, as shown on the regional GPS map above: groomed Nordic, Nordic touring, resort alpine and backcountry mountaineering).

Visit the GPS map on the website for trailhead pins, GPS routes and locations of mountain objectives. This overview map should help give the lay of the land and some pointers for finding more information for your next ski adventure in the region.

On the web-site's GPS map, note that groomed Nordic trails are marked by yellow dotted lines, backcountry routes that are boot packed or that are boot-packed or ski-packed are in gray lines, and meadows, bowls or open-ski backcountry spots are blue lines.

There are many touring routes for exploration in Yellowstone National Park. The web-site has links for more information about these trails, as well as information about winter access, as all roads in the park are closed except the road to Cook City. In Montana winter access to Yellowstone is from West Yellowstone and Gardiner. Snow coaches and motorized transit provide transportation to some of the interior locations where you can ski along Yellowstone's renowned geothermal features.

We focus on a variety of skiing destinations to explore, beginning with the Bozeman area, then south to the Big Sky area and to Yellowstone.

The Bridger Range looking north from Bozeman

Kiersten, Meghan and Loki enjoying the gradual Mount Ellis meadows descent

BOZEMAN ON SKIS

Bozeman Area Trails

Sunset Hills: BSF Grooming & Snow Making
Highland Glen: BSF Grooming
Sacajewia Middle School: BSF Grooming
Regional Park: MEA Grooming
Kirk Hill: MEA Grooming

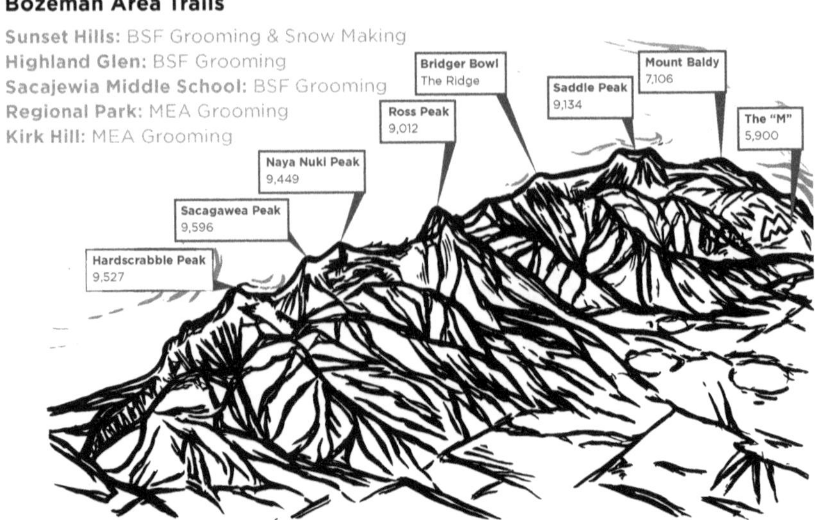

With inspiring panoramic views of the Bridger Mountains right at the front porch of "The Valley of Flowers," Bozeman's vibrant Nordic ski community has flourished over the past half-century.

At nearly a mile high and the apex of many storm cycles, Bozeman benefits from long, snowy winters. When other parts of the state are clear of snow and with grasses sticking out, Bozeman holds onto the snowpack longer and gets more frequent dustings of the famous "cold smoke." The area's proximity to the Bridger Mountains means the "Bridger cloud" drops loads of feathery light powder.

With access to ski trails at four locations right in town, it is easy to reach a trailhead for a lunch time or after-work daily ski.

The Gallatin Valley Land Trust town trails, many of which are used in the summer for hiking, trail running and mountain biking, are groomed by the Bridger Ski Foundation. Lindley Pavilion is the staging grounds for beginning BSF and Montana Endurance Academy Nordic programs.

The author training by towing his daughter in the chariot at the Golf Course Trails

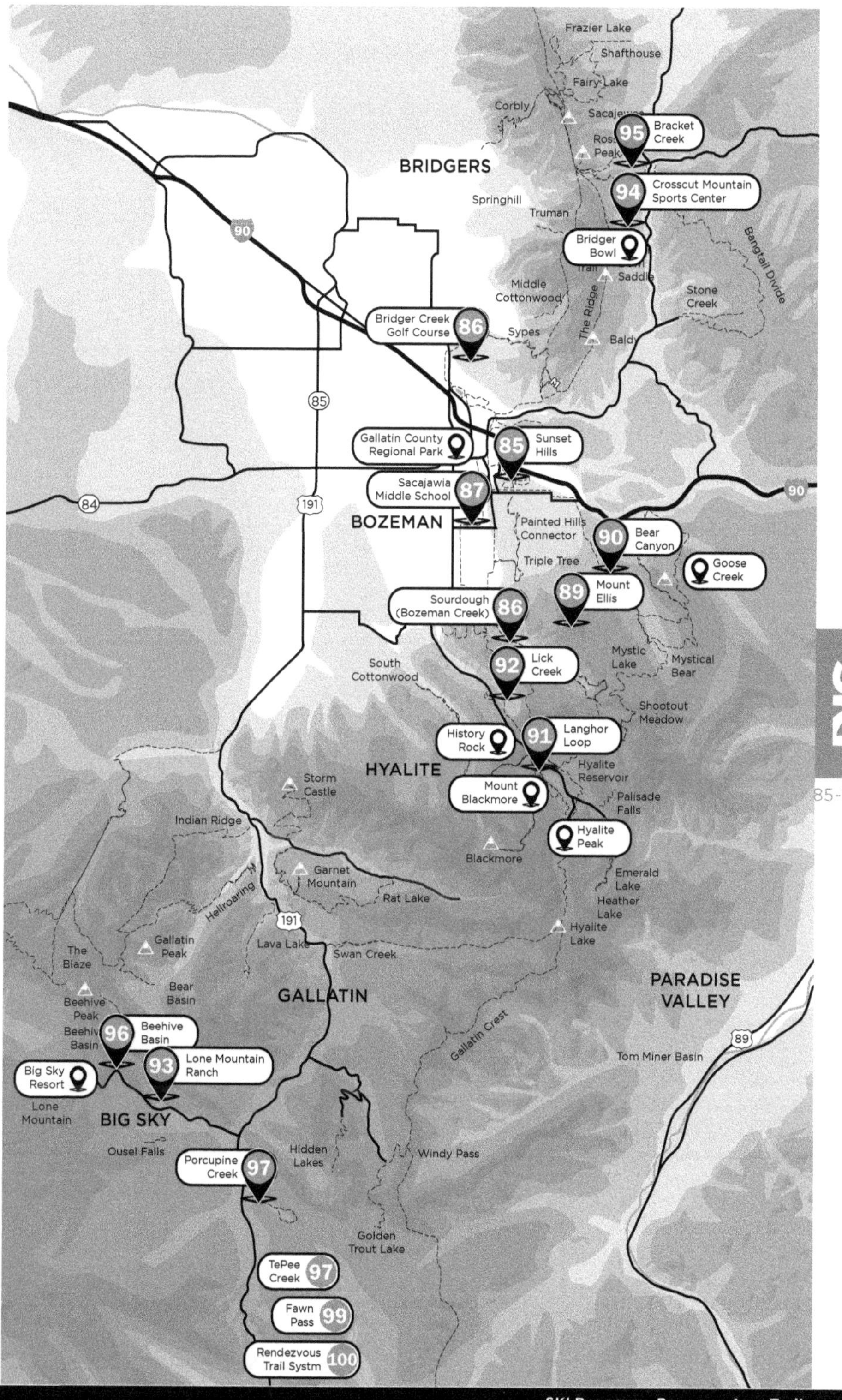
Frazier Lake
Shafthouse
Fairy Lake
Corbly
Sacajawea
Ross Peak
95 Bracket Creek
BRIDGERS
94 Crosscut Mountain Sports Center
Springhill
Truman
Bridger Bowl
Bangtail Divide
Middle Cottonwood
The Ridge Trail
Saddle
Stone Creek
Bridger Creek Golf Course 86
Sypes
Baldy
90
85
Gallatin County Regional Park
85 Sunset Hills
90
84
191
Sacajawia Middle School 87
BOZEMAN
Painted Hills Connector
90 Bear Canyon
Goose Creek
Triple Tree
89 Mount Ellis
Sourdough (Bozeman Creek) 86
South Cottonwood
92 Lick Creek
Mystic Lake
Mystical Bear
Shootout Meadow
History Rock
91 Langhor Loop
HYALITE
Storm Castle
Hyalite Reservoir
Mount Blackmore
Palisade Falls
Indian Ridge
Hyalite Peak
Blackmore
Garnet Mountain
Rat Lake
Emerald Lake
Heather Lake
Hellroaring
191
Hyalite Lake
Gallatin Peak
The Blaze
Lava Lake
Swan Creek
Bear Basin
PARADISE VALLEY
GALLATIN
Beehive Peak
Beehive Basin
96 Beehive Basin
Gallatin Crest
89
Tom Miner Basin
93 Lone Mountain Ranch
Big Sky Resort
Lone Mountain
BIG SKY
Ousel Falls
Hidden Lakes
Windy Pass
Porcupine Creek 97
Golden Trout Lake
TePee Creek 97
Fawn Pass 99
Rendezvous Trail Systm 100

SKI

85-100

85. Sunset Hills / Highland Glen

Distance: Sunset Hills Loop 2.12 miles
Difficulty: Easy to Advanced
Top Elevation: 4,922 feet
Grooming: Bridger Ski Foundation
Land: Bozeman Deaconess Hospital

The new snow-making system ensures a long season of groomed trails right in town. Local groups organize fun community races annually.

Park at Highland Glen to ski the winding training loops at Sunset Hills, Lindley, the short loop by the haystacks or meandering Highland Glenn loops. This area is heavily used by the Bridger Ski Program for training and lessons.

Search Sunset hills, Lindley park Visit BridgerSkiFoundation.com for trail maps and more information

86. Bridger Creek Golf Course

Distance: 8 kilometers Loops
Difficulty: Easy
Top Elevation: 4,790 feet 367 gain
Grooming: Bridger Ski Foundation
Land: Bridger Creek Golf Course

The Bridger Golf Course is groomed by the Bridger Ski Foundation and is a great place to ski some mellow laps along aspen groves and open, softly rolling contours. It's a hiking loop and dog park at snowfill recreation center in the summer.

87. Sacajawea Middle School

Distance: 1 kilometer Loop
Difficulty: Easy
Top Elevation: 5,308 feet
Grooming: Bridger Ski Foundation
Land: City of Bozeman

A one kilometer (more-or-less) loop behind Sacajawea Middle School is groomed when there is ample snow.

All Bozeman town trails are family-friendly and open to the public. Before you go out on the groomed trails, peek at the grooming report.

The local trails are groomed by the Bridger Ski Foundation. This nonprofit organization relies on non-mandatory trail passes and donations from the community.

Donations for a trail pass to cover the costs of grooming can be made to the foundation online.

The Gallatin County Regional Park groomed trails provide another easy access option for Nordic skiing on the west side of town. You can find a tight labyrinth of winding loop trails on a section of land in the Southwest corner next to the sledding hill.

Some years local ski clubs groom additional town loops.

Check the Bridger Ski Foundation website and the Montana Endurance Academy website for updated grooming conditions.

Search Bozeman Golf Course,
Bridger Ski Foundation
Trailhead (45.72135,-111.03649)

Search Sacajawea Middle School
Bozeman, MT
Trailhead (45.64390, -111.04858)

Groomed skate track with snow making at the Sunset Hills

BOZEMAN ON SKIS

88. Sourdough

Distance: 30 Kilometers Out and Back
Difficulty: Easy - Moderate
Top Elevation: 6,526 feet 1,893
Grooming: Bridger Ski Foundation
Land: Custer Gallatin National Forest

Groomed by BSF, these trails steadily climb along Bozeman Creek, dropping down to a crossing at almost five miles in with the option to ski another five miles up to Moser or Mystic Lake. The first couple miles can be crowded with walkers, runners, skiers and dogs. Above the bridge, crowds disperse and the conditions generally hold up well for a good part of the season.

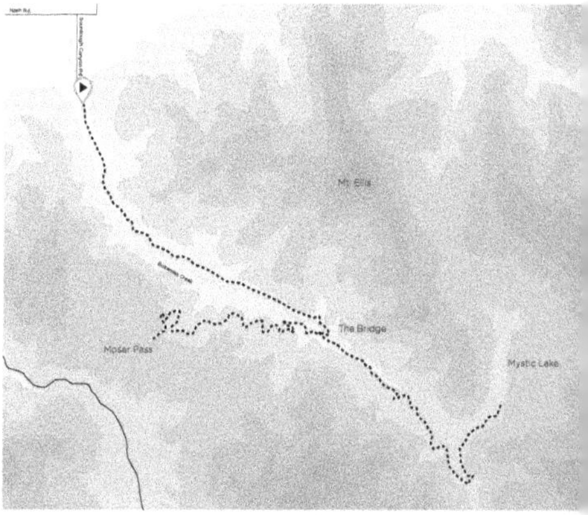

Mystic Lake | Moser Pass

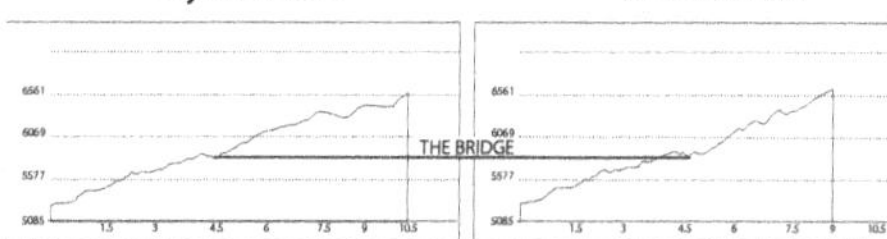

Search Sourdough Canyon
Bozeman, MT
Trailhead: (45.592258,-111.026241)

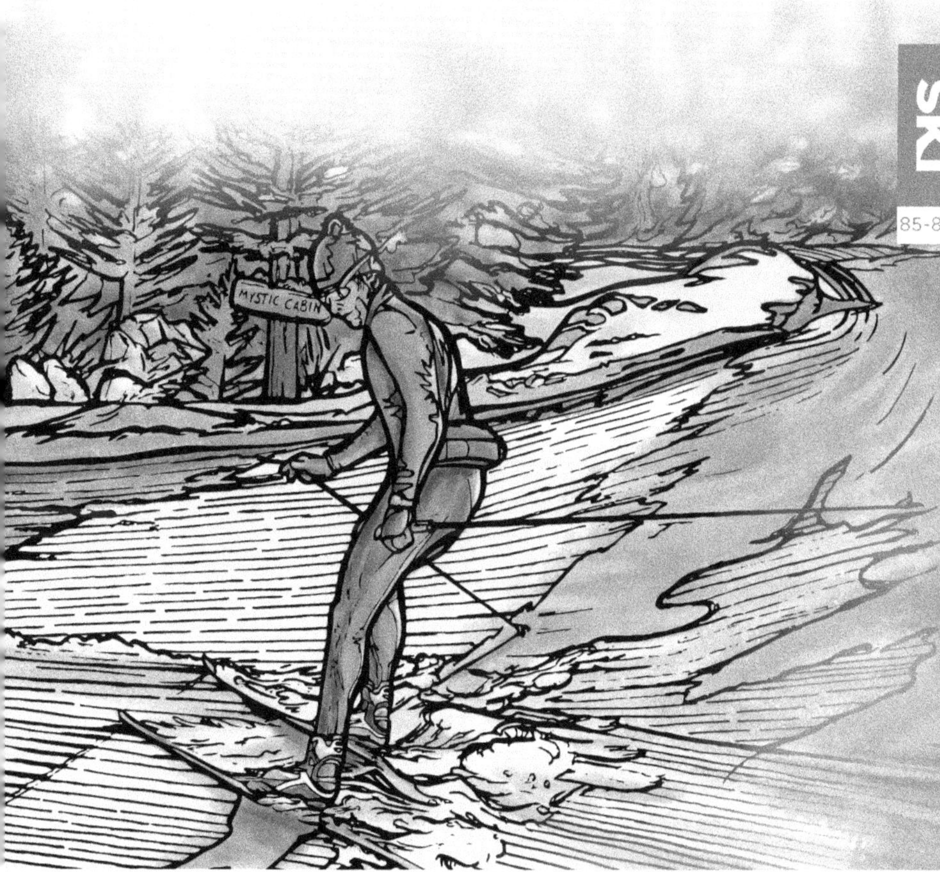

SKI

85-88

Drew Laskowski performing a hockey stop after a brisk return from Mystic Lake

89. Mount Ellis Meadows - Little Ellis

Distance: 6.2 Miles Out and Back
Difficulty: Moderate
Top Elevation: 7,726 feet 2,428 Gain
Grooming: No - boot/ski pack
Land: State School Trust Lands

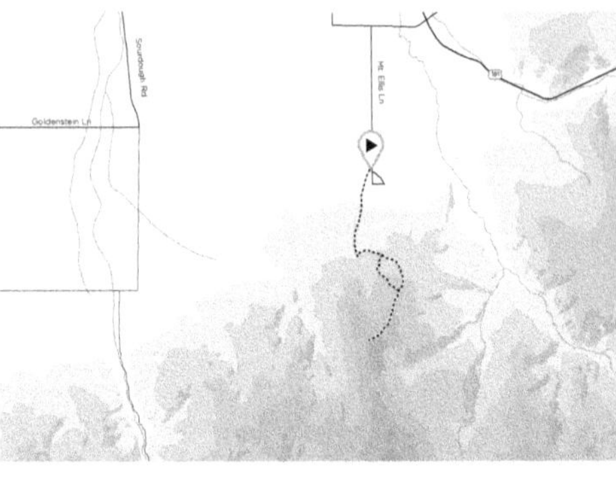

The north-facing Mount Ellis and Little Ellis trails keep the snowpack well into later spring. The wide one-mile apron opens to sage and grasses before tapering to evergreens with Nordic and skin tracks on the road-grade climb, which weaves up and around the peak to open to glades and great close-to-town late-season backcountry skiing.

At a mile up, the wide, one-mile apron road/trail enters the trees and starts winding up Little Ellis. The main road can be used out and back for cross-country skiing. Skin tracks will lead up to the ridge for some backcountry turns. Continue along a ridge to the summit of Little Ellis and on further to Mount Ellis for a longer backcountry ski adventure.

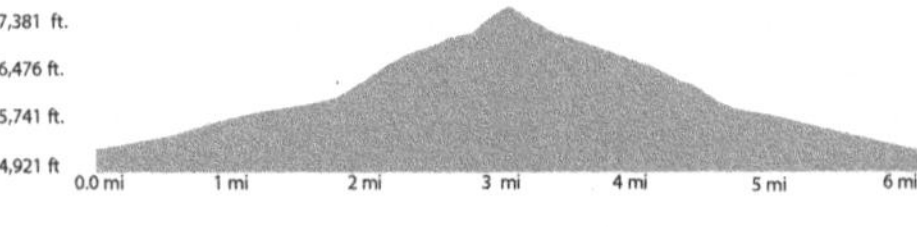

Search Mount Ellis Trailhead
Bozeman, MT
Trailhead (45.62975,-110.96032)

MOUNT ELLIS
8.331"

LITTLE ELLIS
7,726"

Loki scoping out his descent line from the summit of Little Ellis Mountain

BOZEMAN ON SKIS

90. Bear Canyon

Distance: 5.2 Out and Back
Difficulty: Easy
Top Elevation: 6,033 feet 1,243 gain
Grooming: No - boot/ski pack
Land: GVLT - Custer Gallatin NF

The oldest ski hill in the area was in Bear Canyon (1940s). Now it has been revitalized as home for the informal skimo (skin up and ski down) Wednesday night races.

Dogs aren't allowed on the groomed town trails with the exception of Sourdough. The Bear Canyon winter trail is another option for getting dogs out on the trails.

Search Bear Canyon 440
Bear Lakes Loop Bozeman, MT
Trailhead (45.608768,-110.924000)

Nearby Goose Creek Meadow on the back side of Chestnut Mountain climbs a road to some south-facing mellow meadows for low-risk tele turns. Drive up the fire road past Trail Creek road. Be prepared for winter driving and variable conditions on the road. Pick a line that stays out of private property, returning to your vehicle.

Search Goose Creek Trailhead
Bozeman, MT
Trailhead (45.60934, -110.85635)

Anne cleaning snow from Loki's pads, See dog foot care section

HYALITE ON SKIS

91. Langohr Loop

Distance: 8.32 Loop
Difficulty: Moderate.
Top Elevation: 7,005feet 902 gain
Grooming: USFS / BSF
Land: Custer Gallatin National Forest

Loop the lake on tight, old-school - sometimes groomed, sometimes not - classic tracks. (As these trails are only occasionally groomed by the Forest Service, tracks are often set by other skiers.)

Search Nordic skiing in Hyalite Canyon Trailhead (45.489286791531285, -110.97830985290099)

There is a popular snowshoe route from the Hyalite Reservoir parking lot, as well as access to backcountry skiing on Mount Blackmore. History Rock is also a popular skin track to backcountry ski bowls. See white arrows in map to the right to indicate popular backcountry skiing skin and descent routes.

92. Lick Creek Ski

Distance: 5 kilometers Loops
Difficulty: Moderate
Top Elevation: 7746 feet
Grooming: None - skin track
Land: Custer Gallatin National Forest

This area features out-and-back climbing out of the forest into a nice bowl at the top and the other side of the ridge.

Other backcountry routes to Hyalite include Lick Creek Backcountry, with a meadow at the top and other side facing the Sourdough drainage. Climb back out for a run down the other meadow and back along the skin track through the trees. History Rock has three levels of meadows, the snow often improving the higher you go. Climb Mount Blackmore and Hyalite Peak for bigger mountain adventures.

Keep an eye out for ice climbers dangling off canyon walls. Hyalite is home to the December Ice Fest where climbers from all over the world come to celebrate mountain culture and challenge themselves on the hundreds of routes in Hyalite Canyon.

Find more detailed route info for these areas on the GPS map.

Search Lick Creek trailhead ski Trailhead (45.44742,-110.96229)

Anne Schaeffer skiing the scenic viewpoint by Window Rock cabin

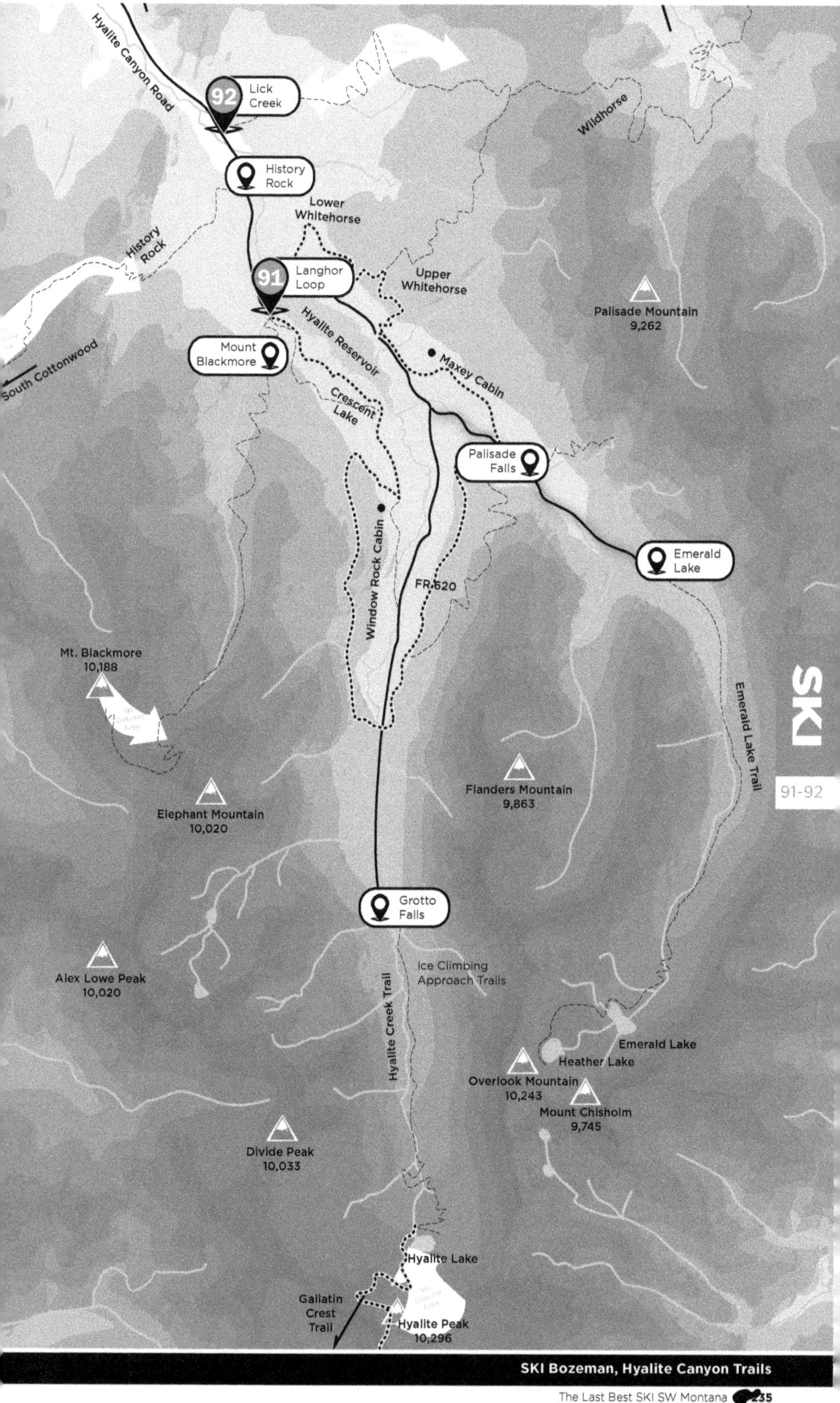
Hyalite Canyon Road
92
Lick Creek
Wildhorse
History Rock
Lower Whitehorse
History Rock
91
Langhor Loop
Upper Whitehorse
Palisade Mountain
9,262
Mount Blackmore
Hyalite Reservoir
Maxey Cabin
South Cottonwood
Crescent Lake
Palisade Falls
Window Rock Cabin
Emerald Lake
FR 620
Mt. Blackmore
10,188
Emerald Lake Trail
Flanders Mountain
9,863
Elephant Mountain
10,020
Grotto Falls
Ice Climbing
Approach Trails
Alex Lowe Peak
10,020
Hyalite Creek Trail
Emerald Lake
Heather Lake
Overlook Mountain
10,243
Mount Chisholm
9,745
Divide Peak
10,033
Hyalite Lake
Gallatin
Crest
Trail
Hyalite Peak
10,296
SKI
91-92

SKI Bozeman, Hyalite Canyon Trails

BRIDGER BOWL

ALPINE SKI AREA

Founded: 1955
Top Elevation: 8,800 / 2,500 vertical
Number of Runs: 75
Lifts: 8
Skiable Acres: 2,000
Average Annual Snowfall: 300'
Land: Custer Gallatin National Forest

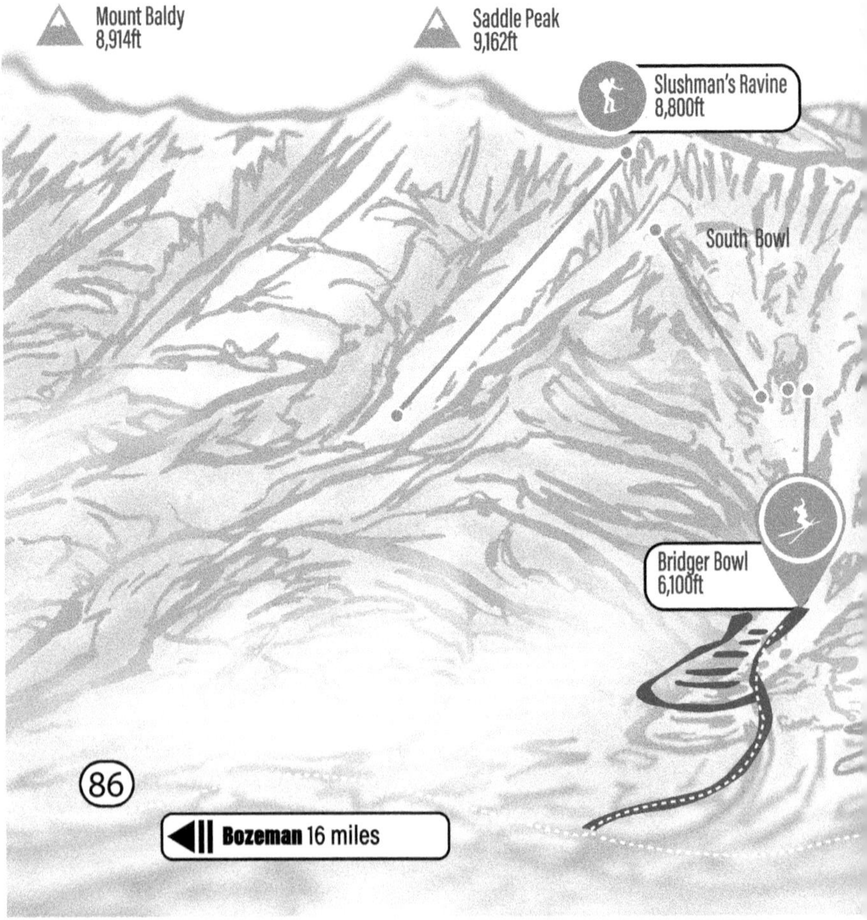

Mount Baldy
8,914ft

Saddle Peak
9,162ft

Slushman's Ravine
8,800ft

South Bowl

Bridger Bowl
6,100ft

86

Bozeman 16 miles

CROSSCUT MOUNTAIN SPORTS CENTER

NORDIC SKI TRAIL SYSTEM

Founded: 1987 (Bohart Ranch)
Base Elevation: 6,100
Groomed Trails: 35 Kilometers
Acres: 256 Crosscut / 276 Bohart
Land: Custer Gallatin National Forest

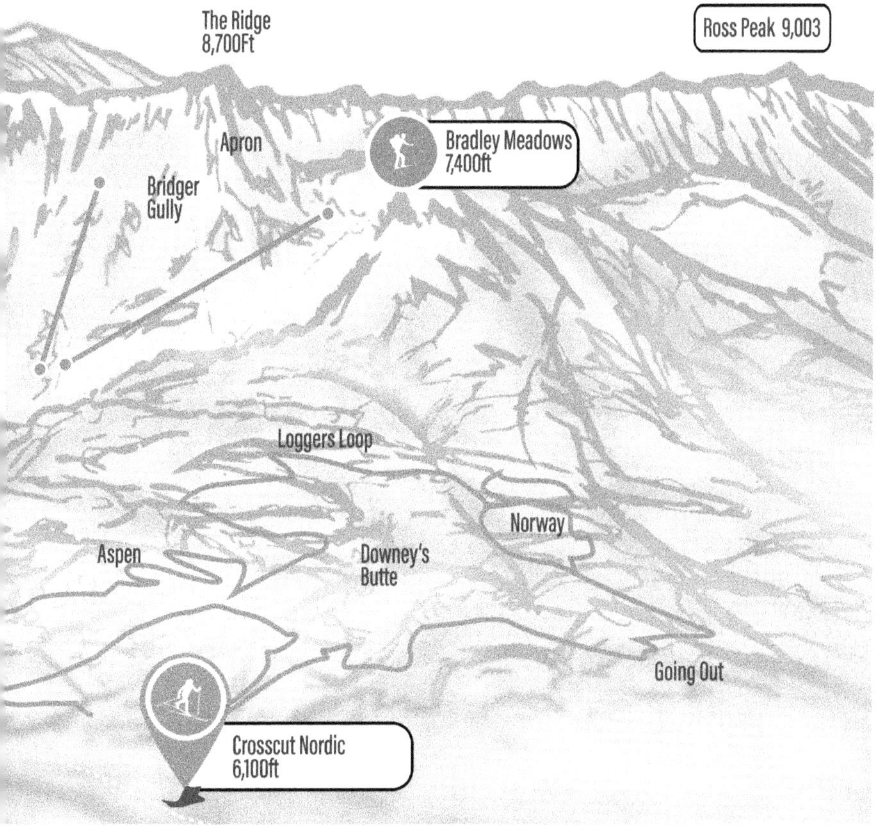

Justin Bigart leading the way on King & Queen of the Ridge Laps

The Bridger Mountain Range runs north to south and its primary winds move west to east.

The Bridgers catch the air masses, forming a long cloud that hangs over the range known as the (BBC) Bridger Bowl Cloud. Snow storms dump straight down, leaving Bridger's famous "cold smoke" powder.

Bridger Bowl Ski Area has grown exceedingly popular in recent years. A 16- mile drive from Bozeman make the area popular.

The massive parking lot fills quickly with skiers' vehicles, even during the shoulder seasons (with back country skiers).

Even pre-season or post-season backcountry tailgaters make quite a scene during the shoulder seasons.

New kid-friendly lifts from the lodge give easy access from the rental shops for new skiers. Virginia City and Powder Park lifts access the wide mellow cruiser "slow skiing" runs. A bit more off the beaten path, the Alpine lift accesses moderate terrain of groomed and tree skiing as well as the backcountry access point for Bradley Meadows.

The family-friendly appeal of the lower terrain at Bridger Bowl and the half-hour drive from Bozeman make it extremely popular and often crowded.

Step up the steepness and terrain from bowls off the centrally located Bridger lift or expert terrain on "The Ridge," where you can access bowls and chutes above the lift-accessed resort. Other gates open to give access to side country.

The higher-terrain ridge and side country have an almost cult-like following of loyal shredders looking for the freshest stash of the cold smoke.

Visit bridgerbowl.com for more info
Parking Lot (45.817459271713716, -110.89636782140761)

Jason Lunden & dog Buddy taking a skinning break in late season by the Bridger lift, Bridger Bowl

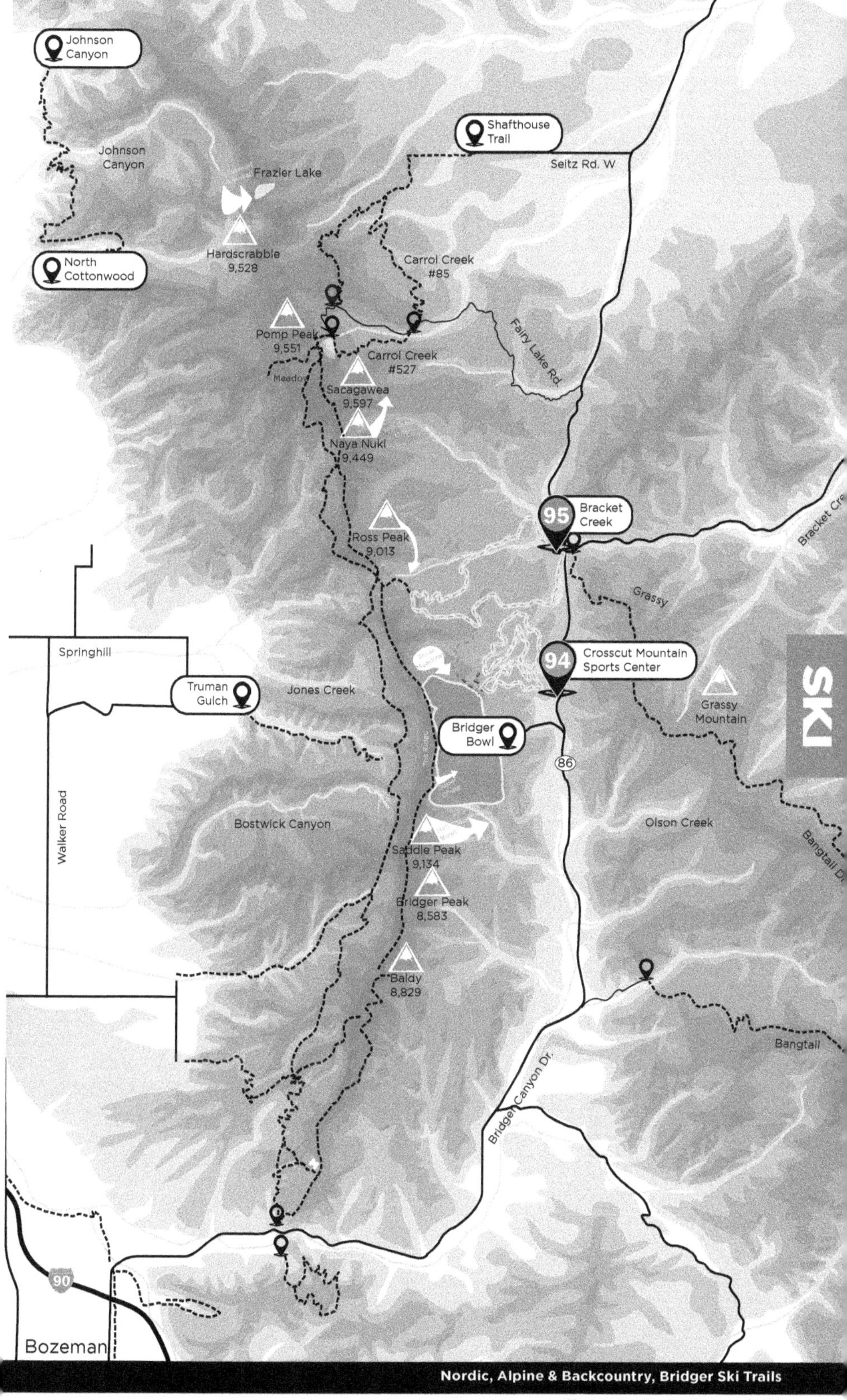
Johnson Canyon
Johnson Canyon
Frazier Lake
Hardscrabble 9,528
North Cottonwood
Shafthouse Trail
Seitz Rd. W
Carrol Creek #85
Pomp Peak 9,551
Carrol Creek #527
Fairy Lake Rd.
Sacagawea 9,597
Naya Nuki 9,449
Ross Peak 9,013
95
Bracket Creek
Bracket Cr
Grassy
94
Crosscut Mountain Sports Center
Springhill
Truman Gulch
Jones Creek
Bridger Bowl
86
Grassy Mountain
SKI
Walker Road
Bostwick Canyon
Saddle Peak 9,134
Olson Creek
Bangtail D
Bridger Peak 8,583
Baldy 8,829
Bangtail
Bridger Canyon Dr.
90
Bozeman

Nordic, Alpine & Backcountry, Bridger Ski Trails

BRIDGERS ON SKIS

93. Brackett Creek Loop

Distance: 7.8 Mile Loop
Difficulty: Moderate
Top Elevation: 7,645 feet
Grooming: No - boot/ski pack
Land: Custer Gallatin National Forest

Just north of Bridger Bowl past Crosscut Nordic area is Brackett Creek. The South and Middle Forks of Brackett Creek connect to create a nice touring loop. Ross Peak emerges in the background and offers steeper terrain for some bowl laps or a challenging run down the Banana Chute (shown in the background).

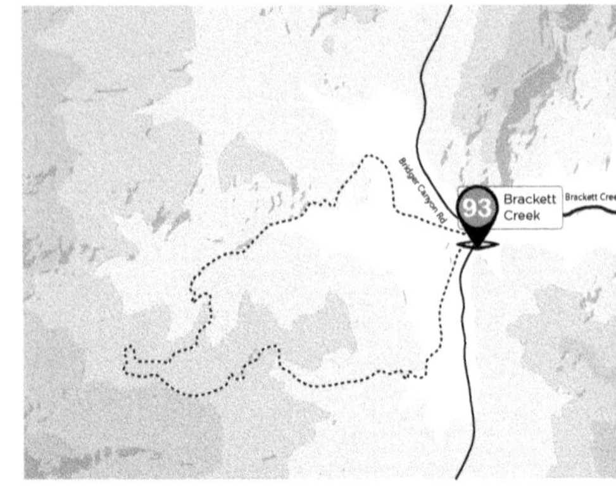

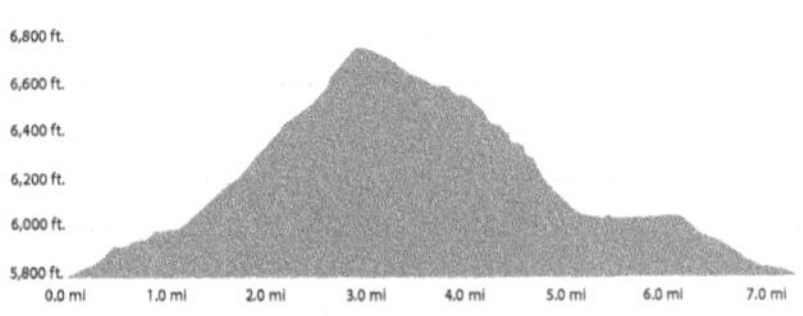

Search Brackett Creek Trailhead
Bridger Mountains
Trailhead (45.85853, -110.87967)

Anne liberally applying paraffin to ski bases on a sticky-snow spring day, Brackett Creek

BRIDGERS ON SKIS

94. Crosscut Outer Loop

Distance: 45 Kilometers of Trails
Difficulty: Beginner to Advanced
Top Elevation: 6,471 feet 1,504 gain
Grooming: Crosscut
Land: Custer Gallatin National Forest

Try this 18K loop to get the lay of the land: from the trailhead go right to climb to steeper trails, or left to rolling trails through aspen groves.

A recommended outer loop makes a counter-clockwise circumnavigation around all of the Crosscut Nordic Trails. From stadium go right to, North Bangtail, Meadow, Lookout, Going Out, Logger's, Norway, Logger's Return, Five Rings, South to Sweden, Aspen, Crosscut Loop, and returning to the ticketing area on the Bridger Creek trail.

Visit Crosscutmt.org for trail maps & grooming information
Trailhead (45.82870,-110.88404)

Dani Aravich training for the Beijing Paralympics at Crosscut Mountain Sports Center

Bryan heading out on a loop around Loggers - Crosscut Mountain Sports Center

BIG SKY RESORT

ALPINE SKI AREA

Founded: 1973
Top Elevation: 11,166' / 4,350' vertical
Number of Runs: 300
Lifts: 22
Skiable Acres: 5,700
Average Annual Snowfall: 400+"
Land: Custer Gallatin National Forest

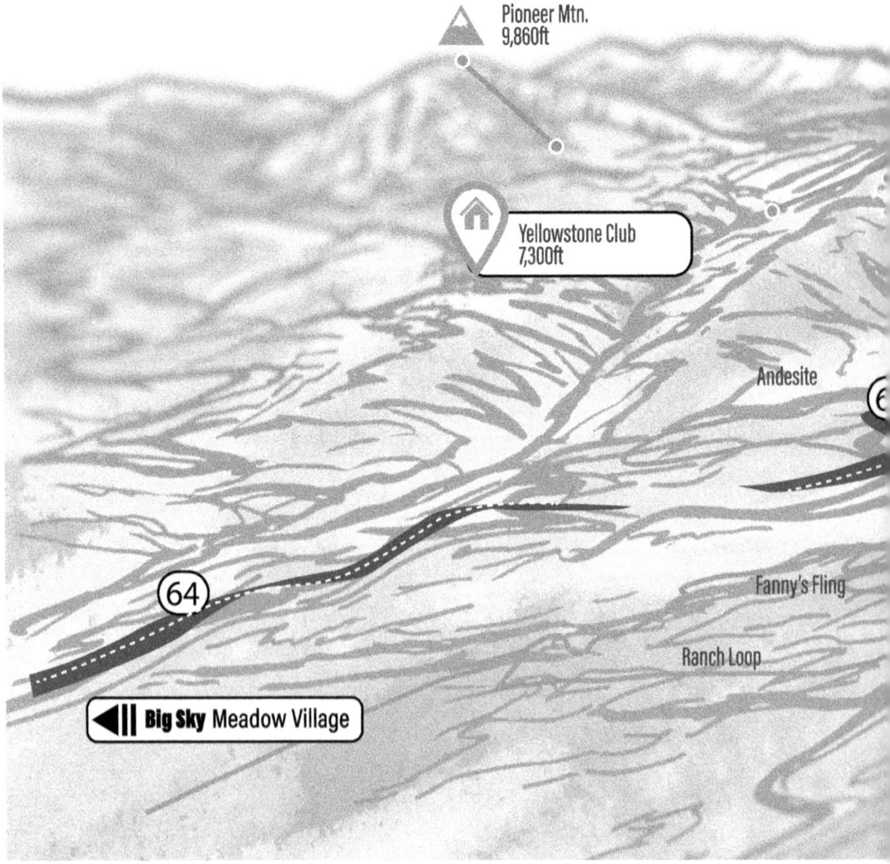

LONE MOUNTAIN RANCH

NORDIC SKI TRAIL SYSTEM

Founded: 1915 Homestead
Base Elevation: 6,200'
Groomed Trails: 85 Kilometers
Acres: 148
Land: Custer Gallatin National Forest

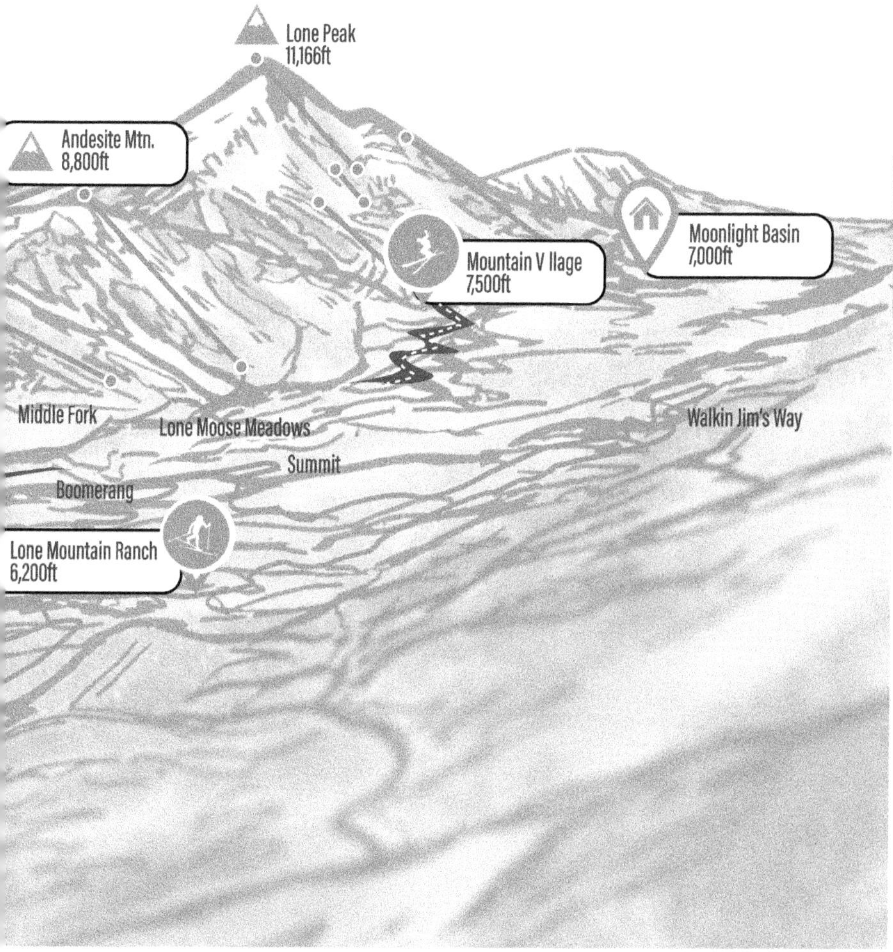

Lone Peak
11,166ft

Andesite Mtn.
8,800ft

Moonlight Basin
7,000ft

Mountain V llage
7,500ft

Middle Fork

Lone Moose Meadows

Walkin Jim's Way

Summit

Boomerang

Lone Mountain Ranch
6,200ft

BIG SKY ON SKIS

BIG SKY RESORT

Before the Lone Peak Tram was built, in 1995, standing on the summit of the peak was gained by rock hopping in the summer or by risking avalanche dangers in the winter.

The combination of the Lone Peak Tram opening up expert terrain on this perfect triangle-shaped peak and the merging of Big Sky with Moonlight Basin has provided the resort with the most skiable terrain of any resort in America.

With ski passes equipped with RFID scanners and heated high-speed and capacity lifts, Big Sky is investing in its future as a world-class resort. From double black extreme chutes and routes from the summit of Lone Mountain to seemingly endless miles of perfectly groomed corduroy, this peak has terrain for everyone.

Even if you don't plan on skiing down, taking a ride up to the summit on the tram is worth it.

From the Lone Peak Tram you look down into the Big Couloir and can certainly appreciate the expert skills of the skiers you observe there.

An advantage of having so much terrain is that if conditions are icy in one spot or wind-blown, another part of the mountain (or another mountain) can have more ideal conditions on the same day.

Christine Baker, Vice President of Mountain Sports at Big Sky Resort carving a turn

Kiersten Schaeffer skiing The Hanging Gardens, Big Sky

BIG SKY ON SKIS

95. Lone Mountain Ranch Loop

Distance: 85 Kilometers of Trails
Difficulty: Beginner to Advanced
Top Elevation: 7,923 feet 2,081 gain
Grooming: Lone Mountain Ranch
Land: Custer Gallatin National Forest

Long climbs on old logging roads transformed into pristinely groomed loops define Lone Mountain Ranch Nordic skiing. Lone Mountain Ranch has over 85 kilometers of groomed track from Big Sky Meadows to the base of the ski track to explore.

Pick up your day passes at the historic cabin/pro shop that offers coffee and hot chocolate, along with fireside chic and western ambiance. Lone Mountain Ranch also offers overnight accommodations to stay and ski.

Visit lonemountainranch.com
for trail maps & grooming info
Trailhead (45.27483,-111.32104)

A 20 kilometer loop climbs to the heights of the area with great views of Lone Mountain then zips downhill back to the ranch. From the cabin another route goes uphill on North Fork Trail, Walkin' Jim's Way, Siberia Loop.

Lone Mountain Ranch alternates grooming upper or lower trails. Be sure to check grooming conditions before you head out for a ski.

Wooden trail sign at LMR, Lone Mountain and Big Sky Resort in the background

BIG SKY ON SKIS

96. Beehive Basin

Distance: 7.2 Out and Back
Difficulty: Moderate to Advanced
Top Elevation: 10,154 feet 2,306 gain
Grooming: No - boot/ski pack
Land: Lee Metcalf Wilderness

Beehive Basin is a majestic glacial cirque at the foot of the Spanish Peaks. A skin track develops that parallels the creek up the basin, providing access to steeper chutes and glades on both sides. You can climb and side-hill into upper Beehive Basin with lots of ski options, tree skiing or climbing chutes and peaks, as well as crust skiing if conditions are right.

To check out the Beehive Basin trail, follow the follow the route of the summer trail, climbing steadily along Beehive Creek. You can climb to the upper basin or continue up benches into Beehive Basin proper and a higher connection point into Bear Basin. Beehive Basin is a gentle meadow, while the edges climb steeply in places to chutes and more challenging objectives, including the couloir up Beehive Peak.

Search Beehive Basin Trail 40
Big Sky Montana
Trailhead (45.30666,-111.38516)

Erika Flowers having "The best day ever" crust skiing with her husband Andy Newell at Beehive Basin

Erika Flowers crust skiing in Beehive Basin - Andy Newell photo reference

97. Porcupine Creek

Distance: 5.5 Mile Loop
Difficulty: Easy
Top Elevation: 6,398 feet
Grooming: No - boot/ski pack
Land: Custer Gallatin National Forest

At the creek, cut in through the trees to a slight climb and traverse .5 miles to an open amphitheater. This is a fantastic spot for a picnic with Lone Mountain in the backdrop. Follow the lollipop loop up through sagebrush-dotted hillside or ski some laps between the creek and the hills above. The snow sets up nicely in the springtime for crust skiing crust skiing, making the meadows in the first mile a great place to ski some speedy laps.

Search Porcupine Creek Road Trailhead (45.22328, -111.24214)

98. Tepee Creek

Distance: 7.5 Miles Out and Back
Difficulty: Moderate
Top Elevation: 7,775 feet 1,246 gain
Grooming: No - boot/ski pack
Land: USFS / Yellowstone NP

Tepee Creek drainage ascends above and to the right of Tepee Creek through sage brush and open bowls edged by lodgepole pines. Turn around at mile three, at the pass, where the grade starts to steepen, or follow the ridge to Daly Pass at 8,300 feet, make a loop back to the trailhead within Yellowstone National Park. Dogs aren't allowed in the park on the Daly Creek side.

Search Tepee Creek Trailhead Trailhead (45.06300, -111.16851)

Jim & Claudia Schaeffer skiing up Tepee Creek just like they did in the 1970's

The Schaeffers picnicking at Porcupine Creek

BIG SKY ON SKIS

99. Fawn Pass

Distance: 10.4 Mile Loop
Difficulty: Moderate
Top Elevation: 9,134 feet
Grooming: No - boot/ski pack
Land: Yellowstone National Park

The open spaces, beautiful views and lofty mountains in the distance make this edge of the park tour a spectacular ski playground. Cross snow and wooden bridges over Fawn Creek across from the Gallatin River. Gently ascend to the Bighorn Pass junction at 5.2 miles, where you can backtrack or make the loop back on the Bighorn Pass trail which ends on highway 191 a few miles south of the Fawn Pass trailhead.

Search Fawn Pass Trail head.
Trailhead (44.95075, -111.05882)

Raven

(Corvus corax)
Ravens are indeed intelligent; they are one of the world's smartest birds with intelligence similar to dolphins or chimpanzees.

My seven-year old daughter was surprised to hear that ravens are said to be as good at reasoning as a seven-year old human. She said, "They are like in first grade?!"

Anne Schaeffer skiing towards Fawn Pass Yellowstone National Park

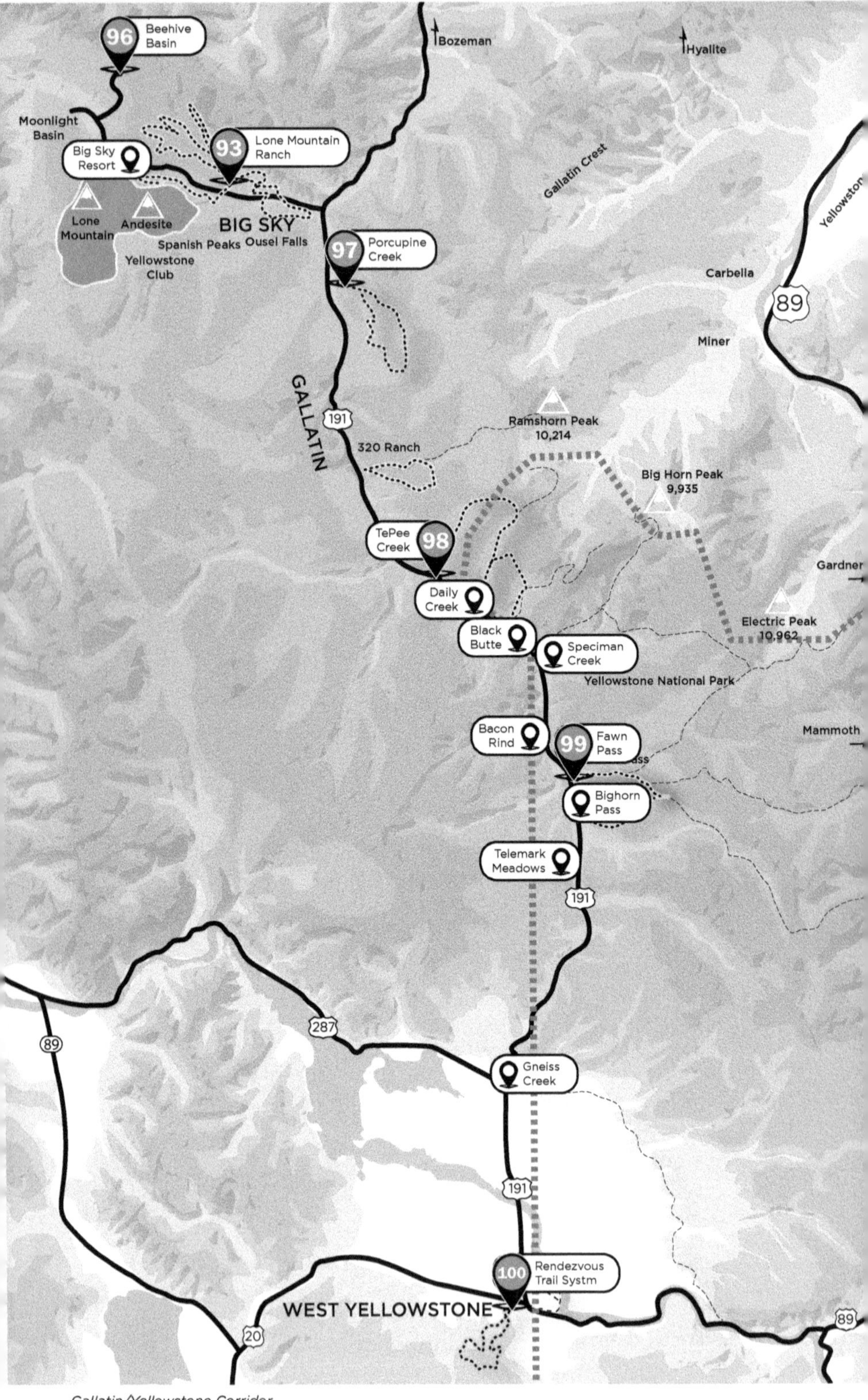

Gallatin/Yellowstone Corridor

WEST YELLOWSTONE ON SKIS

100. Rendezvous 15K Loop

Distance: 50k Total Trails
Difficulty: Beginner to Advanced
Top Elevation: 6,800 ft 1,663 gain
Grooming: W Yellowstone Foundation
Land: Custer Gallatin National Forest

West Yellowstone's high elevation, plus its snowpack, make it a Nordic skiing destination.

The site is the home of the end of the season Yellowstone Rendezvous race in March and the beginning of the season Yellowstone Ski Festival in November.

The Rendezvous trail system includes between 35 and 50 kilometers of professionally groomed cross-country ski trails. Winding through the Gallatin National Forest, this premier trail system is groomed from early November through late March and often into April.

Try this zippy fun 15k Loop. Point to point trails for this recommended loop - Junction 2 Junction, Jerry's Journey, Old Cabin downhill, skis running fast? Deja View West, Post-Tele Downhill, Hooty Hoo, In & Out to ffinish.

Search Rendezvous Trails
West Yellowstone Montana
Trailhead (44.65795644782188,
-111.10853608773901)

The author trying to figure out this ski skating thing, West Yellowstone, 1984

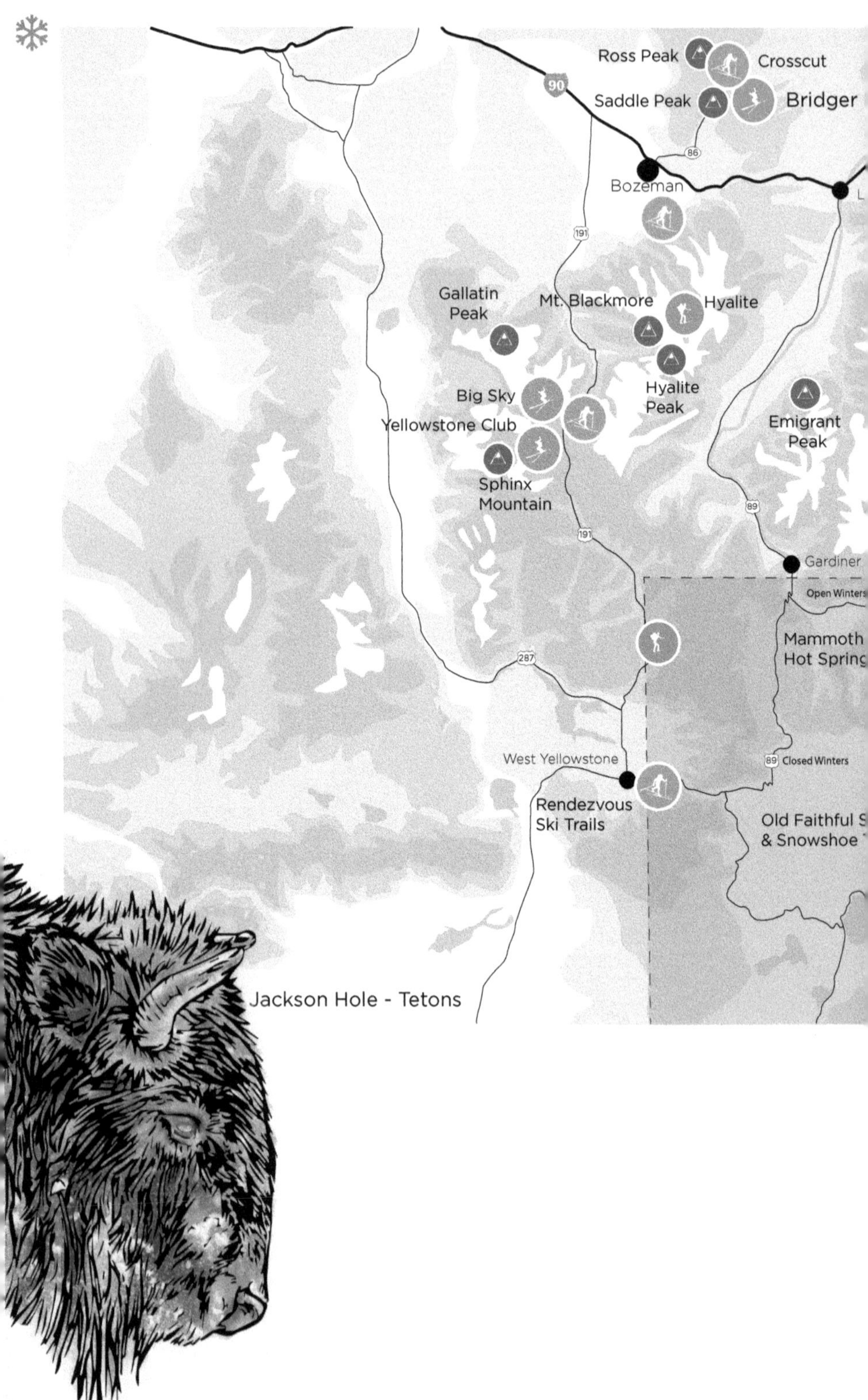
Ross Peak
Crosscut
90
Saddle Peak
Bridger
86
Bozeman
191
Gallatin Peak
Mt. Blackmore
Hyalite
Hyalite Peak
Big Sky
Yellowstone Club
Emigrant Peak
Sphinx Mountain
89
191
Gardiner
Open Winters
Mammoth Hot Spring
287
West Yellowstone
89 Closed Winters
Rendezvous Ski Trails
Old Faithful S & Snowshoe
Jackson Hole - Tetons

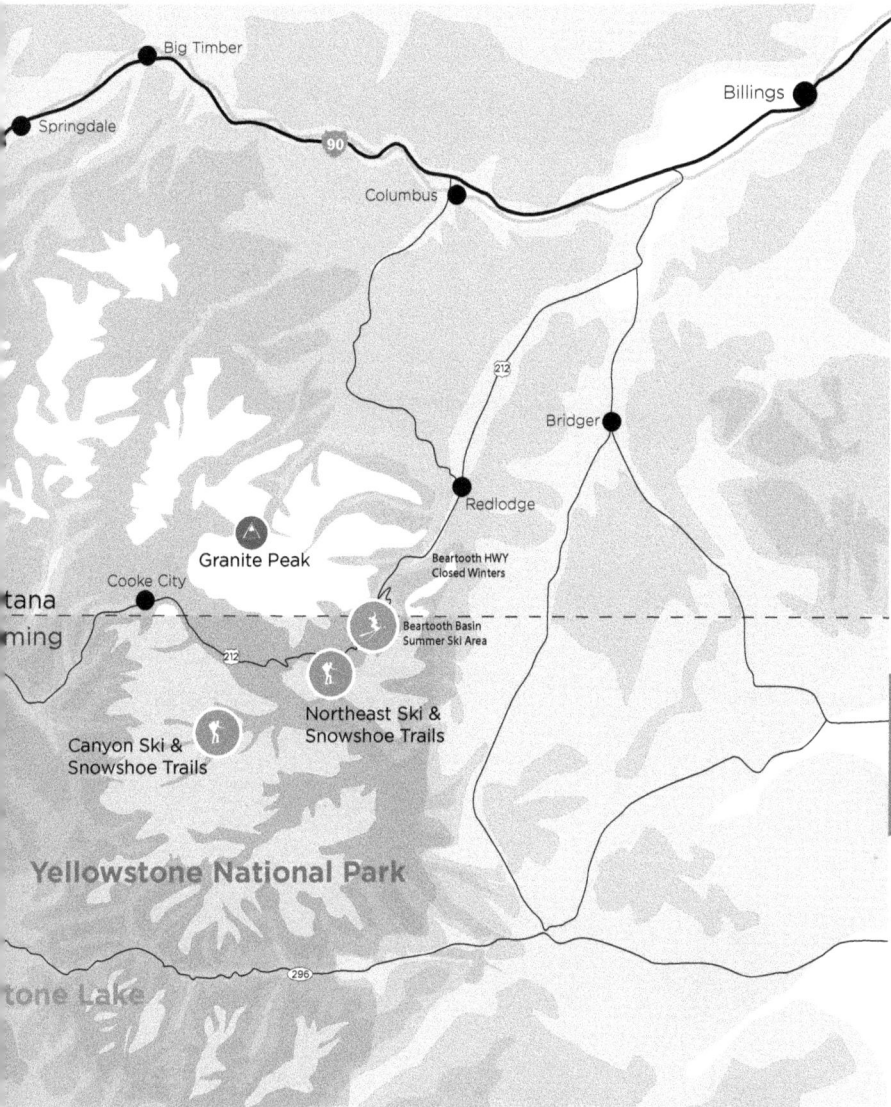

Big Timber
Billings
Springdale
90
Columbus
212
Bridger
Redlodge
Granite Peak
Beartooth HWY
Closed Winters
Cooke City
tana
ming
Beartooth Basin
Summer Ski Area
212
Northeast Ski &
Snowshoe Trails
Canyon Ski &
Snowshoe Trails
Yellowstone National Park
296
tone Lake

SKI

MAP

Kiersten and Meghan Schaeffer skate train, West Yellowstone Rendezvous Trails

The park receives millions of visitors in the summer. In the winter, the park mostly goes dormant. Most of the roads are closed, some of the animals are hibernating and it gets cold - real cold.

Access points to famous areas such as Old Faithful and south of Mammoth access are found via motorized shuttle service, coaches and sleds. These must be reserved in advance and some require group reservations.

So it takes some planning to expedition deeper into the park. Day trips and ski tours off the road without coach access are along the road from Mammoth to Cooke City.

Ski Trails in the West Yellowstone & Gallatin Corridor

Teepee Creek to Dailey Creek
Black Butte Ski Trail
Specimen Creek Ski Trail
Bacon Rind Ski Trail
Fawn Pass to Bighorn Pass
Telemark Meadows Ski Trail
Gneiss Creek Ski Trail
Riverside Ski Trail
Rendezvous Ski Trails (Groomed)

Old Faithful Ski & Snowshoe Trails

Lone Star Geyser Trail (Groomed)
Fairy Falls Ski Trail
Mallard Creek Ski Trail
Mallard Lake Ski Trail
Kepler Cascades Ski Trail
Spring Creek Ski Trail
Howard Eaton Ski Trail
Divide Ski Trail

Canyon

Canyon Rim Ski Trail
Cascade Lake Ski Trail
North Rim Ski Trail
Old Canyon Bridge Ski Trail
Roller Coaster Ski Trail

Northeast

Bannock Ski Trail
Barronet Ski Trail
Pebble Creek Ski Trail

Mammoth Hotsprings

Bighorn Loop Ski Trail
Bunsen Peak Ski Trail
Indian Creek Loop Ski Trail
Sheepeater Ski Trail
Snow Pass Ski Trail
Upper Terrace Ski Trail

Torrey skiing on her birthday

The Grand Prismatic Spring in winter, Yellowstone National Park

ADDITIONAL RESOURCES

OUTDOORS WITH BRYAN SCHAEFFER PODCAST

Perhaps the simplest thing we can do to improve our physical & mental health for ourselves, our family and the planet is to exercise outdoors in nature every day. This podcast focuses on getting outside and offline with interviews with accomplished skiers, hikers, runners and mountain bikers.

With expert tips on fitness, planning, gear and how to have the best experiences when exploring year round trails, this podcast is your trailhead to adventure. Join us as we explore the thriving communities within these life-long sports.

Scan QR codes to listen.

DJ Zepp
- The Eagle105.7FM

"This is my favorite type of book because it gets to the point." It's really the best of both worlds: a beautifully illustrated book and you get the digital world if you want it. It's always great to have a reference guide to get you started."

Andy Newell
- Coach Nordic Team Solutions and Four Time Olympian
Learn about how Andy approaches the ski season, developing mental/physical resiliency as an all round winter athlete and what to look forward to in the future of Nordic skiing in the Bozeman area.
https://nordicteamsolutions.com

Erika Flowers
- Nordic Ski Racer & North Face Athlete
"The access here is probably some of the best cross-country skiing access in the world. Just the fact that there is so much access here makes it a really ideal spot for a skier growing up."
https://skiingmontana.org

Heidi Makoutz
- Adult Nordic coach, Bridger Ski Foundation
As the lead instructor for the adult or "masters" programs, Heidi gives some pointers about getting out on the ski trails and continuing to develop skills and fitness, regardless of experience. "Ski into your best self" with coach Heidi.
https://nordicteamsolutions.com

Seth Hubbard
- Biathlon Program Director, Crosscut Mountain Sports Center
"This year when we were starting an official program, we decided to keep all these channels so we would have biathlon, cross country and US Paranordic as well. This is a great spot for it. Travel is easy, the community is great, the scenery is wonderful."
https://www.crosscutmt.org

Fay Johnson
- Nordic Center Director, Crosscut Mountain Sports Center
"Our enthusiasm and optimism is the community's response and interest in Crosscut. They recognize the fact that cross country skiing is a great alternative in these troubled times because you can distance so easily."
https://www.crosscutmt.org

Cliff Montagne
- Board of Directors, Crosscut Mountain Sports Cente
It isn't always how hard and fast one can go but how respectfully one can move and enjoy the activities of breathing, seeing, smelling and tasting, and talking and communicating with other people as well as with nature, it becomes a practice."
https://www.crosscutmt.org

Laurie Spence
- Nordic Center Director, Lone Mountain Ranch
You can get about ten minutes away from the Nordic center on the ski trails and not see anyone. It can be secluded."
https://skiingmontana.org

Dani Aravich
- US Paralympian
Paralympic Nordic skier and track athlete Dani Aravich talks about training, why exercising in nature is so important and what makes her home base between travel for competitions - Bozeman - so special.
https://www.daniaravich.com

Listen

Nick Michaud
- US Paralympic coach, Crosscut Mountain Sports Center
After missing the Olympics by one spot, Nick Michaud turned his focus to coaching a diverse population of Nordic skiers, including the US Paralympic Team that partnered with Crosscut.
https://www.crosscutmt.org

Dragan Danevski
- Co-founder of the Montana Endurance Academy
"In the beginning I had a very small group of people who were supportive. We tried little by little to convince the community that what we were doing was beneficial, not just for a small Nordic team, but for the community."
https://www.montanaenduranceacademy.org

Ben Werner
- Author of "The Bozeman and Big Sky Backcountry Ski Guide"
Ben Werner shares how he got into skiing, some of his favorite repeat locations and why he loves backcountry skiing in SW Montana.
www.bozemanskiguide.com

Watch "Cold smoke to Corduroy"
- The Last Best SKI animated short film
At the edge of America's last great wilderness of fire and ice there is a place - where winter is coming. A deep freeze fills the land and the snowpack sets up, transforming it into a different place altogether. Montana. Big Sky Country – the last best pla

Justin Bigart
- Ski Mountaineering Racing (Skimo)
It was something to do in the winter that felt like trail running. A lot of it had to do with gear and wanting to move quick in the mountains. Being able to move fast in the mountains is the best part. It is the fountain of youth.
www.usaskimo.org

Jason Lunden
- Split Boarder, Excel Physical Therapy
Splitboarder and Doctor of Physical Therapy, Jason Lunden, shares how to be physically ready for the ski season and safely find powder stashes.
https://excelptmt.com

Jim Schaeffer
- Former USFS Forester and Big Sky Liftee
Jim and Claudia Schaeffer (my folks) spent the winter of 1974-75 working at the new Big Sky Resort and cross country skiing in the area, including Yellowstone National Park.
https://www.nps.gov/yell/planyourvisit/skiing-and-snowshoeing.htm

Simon Peterson
- Photo editor of Outside Bozeman Magazine
Simon shares why he's not good about keeping secrets about great ski lines in the mountains around Bozeman.
"There shouldn't be any secrets. We need the user days to progress the sport, to keep the accesses open."
https://outsidebozeman.com

Karl Birkeland
- National Avalanche Center Founder
Bozeman has played a prominent role in avalanche safety in the United States. Before working for the National Avalanche Center Karl Birkeland founded the Gallatin National Forest Avalanche Center in 1990.
https://avalanche.org/national-avalanche-center

Doug Chabot
- Director, Gallatin National Forest Avalanche Center
Doug Chabot talks about adventuring with the late great Alex Lowe and his ongoing work with the Gallatin National Forest Avalanche Center. "It's not minutia; it's the basics. It's the foundational things that we can never forget about."
https://www.mtavalanche.com/gnfac

Chris Kussmaul
- Author Peaks & Couloirs of SW MT
A guide to Backcountry Skiing in the Gallatin, Madison, Bridger, Tobacco Root, and Montana Absaroka Mountains.
https://skiingmontana.org

Bob Allen
- Outdoor Sports Photo Journalist

Bob spends a lot of time skiing and perfecting the skills of the sport. He shares how using appropriate protective gear for the different styles of downhill skiing helps to ensure safe enjoyment of the sport.
http://boballenimages.com

Cory Birkenbuel
- Ski Instructor, Filmmaker

Yellowstone Club Ski instructor Cory Birkenbuel grew up shredding the slopes at Maverick Mountain. His school project, dubbed "Montana's Sweet 16," made him the first Montanan to ski all of Montana's ski areas in 16 consecutive days.
https://youtu.be/WHIkX9hFB0k

Dan Lakatos-Former BSF Freestyle Coach,
Vice President of Outdoor Pursuits at Yellowstone Club

Dan schools us on the progression of freestyle skiing and talks about why the Yellowstone corridor is such a special place in Montana: "From the outside looking in, you can't understand it; from the inside looking out, you can't explain it."
https://yellowstoneclub.com/experiences/ski

Christine Baker
- Vice President of Mountain Sports at Big Sky Resort

"We have 5,800 acres; that is a lot of space! It creates good skiing - if there isn't good snow on one side of the mountain, you know there is good snow on the other side of the mountain."
https://bigskyresort.com

Shannon Griffin
- Bridger Bowl Snowsports School Director

"Easy beginner terrain to steep technical chutes, trees and cliffs. Everything you could want is accessible and it's right there only 30 minutes away from town. The spirit at Bridger has really stayed as being a community area. It's where we get to go play."
https://bridgerbowl.com

Cory Birkenbuel
- If God Had a Voice - working with Warren Miller

Through a series of fortuitous events, Cory and Kevin Hilton were paired with the great Warren Miller to produce several short films in the tradition of the filmmaker's original works.
https://warrenmiller.com

Rob Funderburk
- Manager of Bangtail Bikes and Skis

Rob talks about the supply chain issues for the skiing and cycling industry and how the growth in Bozeman can be a positive for building and supporting trails.
https://www.bangtailbikes.com

Blaze Your Own Trails

If you are lucky enough to find yourself in SW Montana when the snow stops and the sun comes out, the winter is a blank canvas for ski touring. With the ground covered in cold smoke powder before the snowshovels and plows appear, the explorer's skis make first tracks.

In winter, especially after a fresh snow, many of the summer trails can be skied. Breaking trail through an undeveloped field field, whether it is in the Yellowstone backcountry or your backyard, can feel like adventuring into a winter wonderland. When the world is white and quiet, check the access, and go explore!

Anne Schaeffer touring undeveloped fields in South Bozeman as a Mourning Dove looks on, Spanish Peaks in the Background

Where to Eat

Hiking, trail running, peak bagging and backpacking , mountain biking and skiing burn a lot of calories. Fortunately there are no shortages of great food and beverage options in Bozeman. Here are some good choices:

> **You french fried when you should have pizzad; you are going to have a bad time.**
>
> **-Thumper, the cool ski instructor**
>
> **South Park**

Bozeman

These are some good choices for hearty comfort food to replace burnt calories from biking, hiking or skiing. See links to more choice restaurant and brewery locations on the website.

For takeout, go to Mountains Walking Brewery, with pizza, truffle fries and beer canned on-site to go.

MAP Brewing Company located across the lake from Bozeman Beach is the go-to spot for post-ride burgers and beer.

Backcountry Burger Bar carries fantastic beer and fried cheese curds that can't be beat. As a bonus, they package all carryout in compostable packaging.

The Pickle Barrel has been the go-to sandwich shop next to the MSU campus since 1974. The sandwiches are huge!

A local favorite hole-in-the-wall Granny's Doughnuts sometimes even lets you add sprinkles to your own custom doughnut.

Granny's Doughnuts and mountain biking

Livingston

Drive in for burgers, fries & real ice cream shakes at Mark's In & Out Burger is open in summer months.

Four Corners

Best Burger is right on the way to or from Gallatin Canyon. Drive through for classic burgers, fries and shakes.

See links to more choice restaurant and brewery locations on the website. **https://botnw.com/thelastbesttrails**

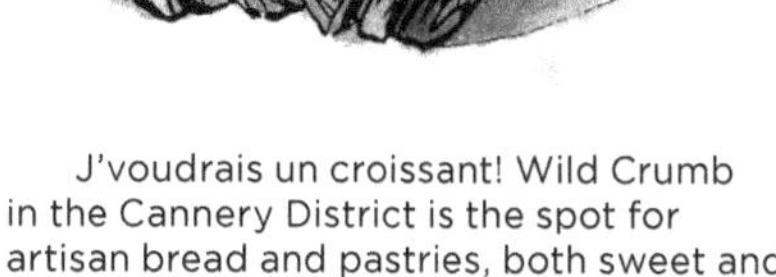

J'voudrais un croissant! Wild Crumb in the Cannery District is the spot for artisan bread and pastries, both sweet and savory.

Big Sky

Shedhorn Grill in Big Sky is in a mountain yurt off the Shedhorn lift that serves burgers and brats is a slopeside joy on sunny afternoons.

The Blue Moon Cafe is the spot for baked goods and pizza slice specials in Big Sky Village. A funky fun interior, with porch seats and a bit of the beaten path from the resort make this a great pit stop after a day on the slopes.

Crossection of the author's favorite "Bobcat" Pickle Barrel sandwich - not to scale

Bridger Bowl

Tucked away on a run on the side of Bridger, Alpine Hut is the perfect spot to stop in, warm up and grab a panini

Kiersten thinking about lunch at Big Sky Resort

Après TRAILS

Where to Soak

Western Montana is rife with geothermal activity, resulting in these local "hot spots."

Many trail systems in the state also have a great hot springs nearby.

Soak in Yellowstone-fed thermals in the Gardner River. The access road to the 1.3 mile out-and-back trail was washed out in the 2022 floods. Natural pools at the edge of the river, mix waters alternating from frigid to near scalding hot.

Check at the visitor center at Mammoth Hot Springs to find out if the Boiling River hot springs is open to the public.

Norris Hot Springs is near the Beartrap Canyon hike. The highly developed Bozeman Hot Springs is in Four Corners just off the highway between Big Sky and Belgrade.

Visit for more information on Montana Hot Springs.

bozemanhotsprings.com

norrishotsprings.com

yellowstonehotspringsmt.com

fairmontmontana.com

elkhornhotsprings.com

jacksonhotspringslodge.com

lolohotsprings.com

broadwatermt.com

quinnshotsprings.com

Enjoying the Boiling River, Yellowstone National Park

LODGING
Where to Stay

Located close to Yellowstone National Park, Big Sky, Bridger Bowl and all of the trails featured in this book, Bozeman is a recreation hub. Lodging rates in peak seasons will reflect that demand.

Many or most accommodations will vary depending on peak times of year, if there are sporting events, festivals or other activities happening in town. If you want to get the best deal best deal, it pays to plan ahead.

Some of the lodging options in Bozeman, Belgrade, Big Sky, Livingston, and Three Forks Include:

- Camping
- Air B&B
- VRBO
- Hotels
- Hostels

The Custer-Gallatin National Forest has a variety of campgrounds, both first come first serve and by reservation. Rustic cabins and fire lookouts are also available for rent.

Check the website for locations and avaiability.

- Dispersed Camping
- Campground Camping
- Group Camping
- RV Camping
- FIre Lookouts
- Cabin Rentals

TRANSPORTATION
How to get here

Bozeman -Yellowstone International Airport (BZN) is located near Belgrade and is the most frequently used airport in the state. It is ten miles from downtown Bozeman. Other nearby airports are in Butte, Helena, and Billings.

New airlines and new flight options connect to more cities directly. The airport continues to expand to keep up with the influx of out-of-state visitors.

Shuttle buses run to Big Sky from the airport. West Yellowstone offers snow coaches and snowmobiles for access to certain destinations in Yellowstone Park when most roads are closed.

Bozeman has a hub of trails and bike paths. The Gallatin Valley Trust (GVLT) has nearly 80 miles of trails connecting main street to the mountains.

The Big Sky Community Organization (BSCO) also has plans to continue connecting town trails to popular local hiking trails.

There is a bus system in Bozeman called the Streamline https://streamlinebus.com/ Main street Bozeman and the MSU campus are the major areas of bus use.

Uber also opperates in Bozeman.

Every trail in this book has a GPS coordinate that you can type in your map app on your phone to get directions to the trailhead.

Beartooth Publishing sells high-quality printed maps of the outdoor recreation areas mentioned in this book. These can be purchased at many outdoor shops in Bozeman.

Todd Bushman looking to shreading some fun lines in the Bridgers, Photo refrence Erik Bonnett

THE LIVING WATERS

Dr. Shane Doyle - Apsáalooke

The Apsáalooke (Crow) people have a saying that we each have three mothers - our birth mothers, our community aunts, uncles and others who look out for us, and Mother Earth. The First Nations people continue to practice a ceremonial way of life, honoring life and creation through prayer, humility, generosity and respect.

Water has been and continues to be the lifeblood of indigenous communities. Knowledge about sources of water and waterways was a part of the shared knowledge of indigenous people just as the distances between river forks and trail junctures were well known, as well as who inhabited each area. Rivers, streams and lakes were named after specific attributes (ie. the Yellowstone River was known as the Elk River), and these waterways were shared by all. Seasonal travels were dictated by the changing seasons, which also meant following the water (ie. snow melt and water flows moving across the land, leading to the growth of plants in the spring and following the bison as they migrated to greener pastures).

The Lewis and Clark Expedition and other explorers who mapped the West recognized the value of the area's waterways, and subsequent settlement of the state followed the Missouri and the Yellowstone Rivers, as well as their tributaries.

We all share in the health of our rivers, forests, and plains. We all belong to what the Crow call "Ashmmalixxiia," or extended family, as we all share this extraordinary place whose natural beauty is our collective wealth.

Trail Organizations & Human Powered Trail Recreation Communities

Gallatin Valley Land Trust (GVLT)

gvlt.org

United States Forest Service (USFS)

Bozeman Ranger District

Southwest Montana Mountain

Biking Association (SWMMBA)

southwestmontanamba.org

Montana Wilderness Society

Wildmontana.org

Anne Schaeffer filtering "The Living Water" while backpacking in the Pintler Range

ABOUT THE AUTHOR

Bryan Schaeffer was born in Bozeman and graduated from high school in Dillon.

Son of a Forester and an English teacher, he was always curious about what may be lurking around the next switchback, mountain pass or pitch, and is eager to share those experiences with others.

He graduated from Pacific Lutheran University in Washington with a Bachelor of Fine Arts Degree in Graphic Design.

Twenty years of his life were spent in the Seattle area working on his multimedia skills and exploring the rugged Cascade Mountain Ranges.

Bryan owns the award-winning creative studio SINTR®, based in Bozeman, where he lives with his wife Anne and three daughters. Along with his family and an-eager-to-explore golden doodle, he enjoys recreating on Montana's public lands.

He is the creator of Best of the Northwest, a video and GPS resource for hiking, biking and skiing trails in western Washington which includes over 227 trail videos with affiliated GPS tracks and helpful details about the trails.

The Schaeffer family after a high school NICA Mountain Bike Race. Photo Reference Stacie Lunden

INDEX

The Last Best Trails
Hike, Bike & Ski 100 Classic Bozeman/Big Sky Trails on Foot, Wheel, and Ski

A

B

C

D

E

F

G

H

I

J

K

L

M

THE LAST BEST
TRAILS
100 TRAILHEADS
GO
BOTNW.COM/THELASTBESTTRAILS

THE LAST BEST TRAILS MONTANA

The Montana way is with a smile and a nod: the two-finger steering wheel wave on remote dirt roads, the "Howdy" and "How's it going?" when passing on the trail. Montanans are proud and friendly people who value public lands for hiking, biking, fishing, hunting, and skiing.

This is the way.
The Montana way.

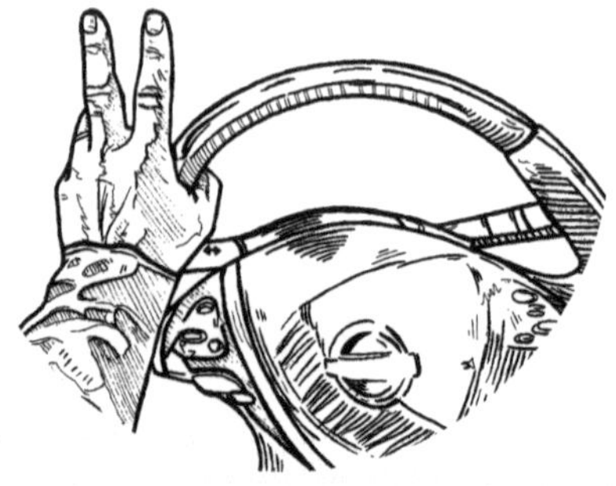

Visit:
TheLastBestTrails.com
thelastbesthike.com
thelastbestski.com
thelastbestbike.com
discovermontanatreasures.com
for interviews, videos, articles and more.

Happy Trails!

www.ingramcontent.com/pod-product-compliance
Lightning Source LLC
Chambersburg PA
CBHW041039050426
42337CB00059B/5061

* 9 7 8 1 7 3 4 7 0 6 6 6 6 *